SIR RICHARD STEELE, M.P.

Richard Steele

A portrait by Jonathan Richardson (1712). In 1720 Steele reported that he was ordering "new Editions" of this portrait, it being the one "that most Ladies chuse." (*The Theatre*, No. 11). From the original in the National Portrait Gallery, with permission.

SIR
RICHARD
STEELE,
M.P.

The Later Career

Calhoun Winton

THE JOHNS HOPKINS PRESS
BALTIMORE AND LONDON

for E.J.M.W.

Contents

Preface

THIS BOOK is intended to present the principal events in the later career of Richard Steele, between the death of Queen Anne in 1714 and his own death, in 1729, and to interpret, if perhaps in summary fashion, the significance of Steele's response to those events. As in the preceding volume, *Captain Steele,* the emphasis is on Steele's biography and there is only brief critical discussion of his literary works. The focus here, in fact, is somewhat further removed from the literary world than it was in *Captain Steele* because Steele himself devoted a greater proportion of his time and energies to politics in his later career than in his earlier life : the title indicates that in some respects this is a parliamentary biography.

Like all biographies, this one represents an interpretation. It is based on evidence from contemporary sources and I have exercised my best judgment in using material about Steele or leaving it out. This has resulted in omitting several of the best-loved anecdotes about Steele. They were left out, however, not because I felt they were unworthy of Steele or a discredit to his reputation but because the evidence persuaded me that they were not true.

It seemed to me, when I was thinking about this subject a number of years ago, that a straightforward biographical account of Steele's career would be useful to those who were interested in the eighteenth century. He was not a great figure but he was an important figure in his time, and his writings exercised a considerable influence not only in Great Britain but on the Continent and in the English-speaking colonies as well. He had not, I thought, received due acknowledgment in his own person, as distinguished from that shadowy figure known through Thackeray whose works are often ascribed to Addison in library catalogues. The task turned out to be more difficult than I had anticipated and, it must be admitted, there are still gaps in the account—when did his son Richard die and where is he buried? for example—which research and study have not closed.

More remains to be done, to fill in the portrait. A bibliography of Steele's works would be useful, as would formal studies of his religious and political thought. New biographical facts will come to light as the years pass. The basic story is here, however, from birth to death, in these volumes. How well it is presented the reader must judge.

Acknowledgments

It is a pleasure to record my indebtedness to institutions and individuals who have assisted this study in various ways. A fellowship from the John Simon Guggenheim Memorial Foundation, awarded soon after the publication of *Captain Steele,* enabled me to undertake research and writing of this volume. The University of Delaware also provided fellowship funds and time off from teaching for research. In the latter stages of writing, the University of South Carolina awarded me a travel grant for final research in England, a summer research assignment, and funds for typing and clerical assistance. The American Council of Learned Societies, through a grant-in-aid, assisted an earlier research trip to England. To each of these institutions I am most grateful.

A number of scholars have provided advice and assistance in various ways and I should like to record my thanks here. In this country, Professors Ronald Paulson of The Johns Hopkins University; Richmond P. Bond, University of North Carolina; Fredson Bowers, University of Virginia; George Kahrl, Elmira College; Bertrand Goldgar, Lawrence College; Shirley Strum Kenny, Catholic University of America; G. Ross Roy, University of South Carolina; and Louis Landa, Princeton University, have all helped me at some point. In England, I am indebted to Mr. A. E. Barker of the Society for Promoting Christian Knowledge, London; Dr. David Fleeman, Pembroke College, Oxford; Mr. D. Barlow, Public Record Office of Great Britain; Mr. Irving Gray and his successor Mr. Brian Smith, Records Officers, Gloucester Records Office; Miss Enid Dance, Muniment Room, Guildford Museum; Mr. R. H. Potts, County of Leicester Records Office; Mr. P. A. Bezodis, the Survey of London; Mr. C. F. H. Evans, F.S.A., the Charterhouse, Godalming, Surrey; Mr. Norman Long-Brown, Sutton's Hospital in Charterhouse, London; the Reverend G. C. Taylor, Rector of St. Giles-in-the-Fields; and the Reverend J. S. Brewis, Rector of St. James's, Piccadilly. In Scotland, Dr. Alexander Law offered both expert guidance and warm hospitality. I should like also to thank Mr. C. P. Finlayson, the Library, University of Edinburgh, and Dr. A. F. Buchan, the Grand Lodge, Freemasons' Hall, Edinburgh. In Wales I am particularly indebted for assistance to Mr. B. G. Owens, Keeper of Manuscripts, National Library of Wales, Aberystwyth; and Major Francis Jones, F.S.A., County Archivist, Carmarthenshire.

The staffs of many libraries and record offices have helped during the course of research for this book. I should like to single out for special thanks the staff of the Scottish Record Office, the Library Company of Philadelphia, and the Folger Shakespeare Library.

To Professor James Clifford of Columbia University I owe a special debt of gratitude for assistance and advice during the research for the book and for most helpful comments on the manuscript itself. Dr. James Osborn of Yale University offered several helpful suggestions for research, which I have attempted to explore. I am grateful also for his generosity in making available an unpublished letter of Steele's for this volume. The Earl of Harrowby, for the trustees of the Harrowby Manuscripts, kindly permitted use of materials at Sandon Hall, Stafford. I am indebted to the Duke of Marlborough for permission to work in the archives at Blenheim.

In the final stages of preparing the manuscript Peter Shillingsburg and Noel Polk gave me valuable assistance in research. Mrs. Betty Trueblood typed a difficult manuscript with skill and unvarying cheerfulness. Jefferys H. Winton was a valuable helper in proofreading. My indebtedness to my wife for encouragement, advice, criticism, and sympathy is imperfectly indicated by the dedication.

NOTE ON REFERENCES AND DATES

References to Steele's life and quotations from letters to and by him, unless otherwise noted, are derived from *The Correspondence of Richard Steele,* ed. Rae Blanchard (Oxford, 1941). Since this work is chronologically arranged, I have not ordinarily given page references. When cited, *The Correspondence* is abbreviated *Corr.* References to other volumes in Miss Blanchard's edition are as follows:

Engl. *The Englishman* (Oxford, 1955)
Per. Jour. Richard Steele's Periodical Journalism, 1714–16 (Oxford, 1959)
Tracts Tracts and Pamphlets by Richard Steele (Baltimore, 1944)
Verse The Occasional Verse of Richard Steele (Oxford, 1952)

Titles of scholarly journals, after the first reference, are abbreviated in accordance with the *Style Sheet* of the Modern Language Association of America. Other abbreviations used frequently are:

Add. MSS.	Additional Manuscripts
Aitken	George A. Aitken, *The Life of Richard Steele* (London, 1889)
BM	British Museum
CS	C. Winton, *Captain Steele: The Early Career of Richard Steele* (Baltimore, 1964)
DNB	*Dictionary of National Biography*
HMC	Historical Manuscripts Commission
Loftis	John Loftis, *Steele at Drury Lane* (Berkeley and Los Angeles, 1952)
London Stage	*The London Stage 1660–1800,* Part Two: 1700–1729, ed. Emmett L. Avery (Carbondale, Ill., 1960)
PRO	Public Record Office [of Great Britain]
Smithers	Peter Smithers, *The Life of Joseph Addison* (Oxford, 1954)
Theatre	*Richard Steele's The Theatre, 1720,* ed. John Loftis (Oxford, 1962)

Because a substantial amount of the primary source material used here has not been printed before, I have altered the practice of *Captain Steele* and quoted *verbatim* and *literatim* throughout, with the following exceptions: I have uniformly and silently substituted s for f and consonantal u has been changed to v. I have not attempted to reproduce the conventional signs for abbreviation and contraction in some of the manuscript sources. In the latter case, if the sense is severely obscured, I have expanded the contraction within square brackets thus: [when] for wñ.

Unless otherwise stated, all dates in this book are Old Style, except that 1 January, not 25 March, is taken as the beginning of the new year.

PERMISSIONS

Transcripts of Crown-copyright records in the Public Record Office of Great Britain appear by permission of the Controller of Her Majesty's Stationery Office. Transcripts of the Forfeited Estates Papers in the Scottish Record Office are printed with the approval of the Keeper of the Records of Scotland. The Marchmont Papers and the Scottish Society for Promoting Christian Knowledge Papers are in the custody of the Scottish Record Office. Quotations from manuscripts in the Department of Western Manuscripts, Bodleian Library, are made with the permission of the Keeper.

The Delegates of the Clarendon Press have kindly consented to quotation from the following works published by that press:

Peter Smithers, *The Life of Joseph Addison* (1954)
Richard Steele, *The Englishman,* ed. Rae Blanchard (1955)
The Occasional Verse of Richard Steele, ed. Rae Blanchard (1952)
Richard Steele's Periodical Journalism 1714–16, ed. Rae Blanchard (1959)
Richard Steele's The Theatre, 1720, ed. John Loftis (1962)
The Correspondence of Richard Steele, ed. Rae Blanchard (1941)
The Poems of Jonathan Swift, ed. Harold Williams, 2d ed. (1958)
The Correspondence of Jonathan Swift, ed. Harold Williams (1963–1965)
The Spectator, ed. Donald F. Bond (1965)

The quotations from *The Diary of Dudley Ryder, 1715–1716* are used with the kind permission of the editor, Professor William Matthews, and the publisher, Methuen and Co.

Quotations from manuscripts in the British Museum are by permission of the Trustees of the British Museum.

SIR RICHARD STEELE, M.P.

CHAPTER I

Le Roi le Veult

1 AUGUST 1714, seven o'clock on a Sunday morning. Queen Anne was dead. The Regents, bishops and peers all, styled the Lords Justices, proclaimed the accession of George, Elector of Brunswick-Lüneburg, and directed that the Duchess of Somerset, Groom of the Stole, deliver the Queen's corpse to the Lord Chamberlain "to be Open'd and Embalm'd." [1] Their major official function performed, the Lords Justices took their ease until the German prince should choose the date to arrive for a proper coronation. At their bidding, of course, thousands sped to keep the processes of government moving. The Queen's physicians, Doctors Arbuthnot, Laurence, Sloan, Shadwell, and Sir David Hamilton, met with surgeons Dickins and Blundel and apothecary Malthus at eight o'clock the following morning to supervise the autopsy and embalming of her ravaged corpse, and to issue such reports on her final illness as would agree with their prior diagnoses, however the reports might conflict.[2] On Wednesday night, with that macabre punctiliousness which surrounds royalty, the Queen's viscera, placed in an urn, were carried in a state coach to the Henry VII Chapel at Westmin-

[1] PRO, LC 5/202/229–31: "An Account of the Funerall of her Majesty Queen Anne."

[2] *Ibid.* See also Sir David Hamilton's comments in his MS. journal, p. 69 (Hertfordshire Record Office, Panshanger MSS.) : "How many have mention'd to me a Monstrous description of Dropsycal Swelling, of Her M[ajesty']s limbs & Elsewhere; w[he]n I have been Vindicating Her Constitution, as without any Tendency to it, & Tho' Her Royal Body, w[he]n Dissected declar'd [the] truth thereof. . . ."

ster and buried privately there. The Lord Chamberlain and Vice Chamberlain supervised the opening of the tomb. This much could be done, but no more, without the new King's permission.

Joseph Addison, who had been elected to the post of secretary to the Lords Justices on the nomination of Lord Halifax, was for a few weeks perhaps the busiest man in British public life. At the center of preparations for King George's arrival, he also held in his hands the threads of national strategy and diplomacy which ran to every capital in the Western world: reading envoys' reports, scrutinizing a list of army officers for political reliability, preparing an address of thanks to the sovereign he had never seen.[3] Although Addison was busy, most other men of substance had time to reflect on the uncertainties of the situation. Some had reason to believe little good would come their way upon the new King's accession. Swift, resting at the home of his friend John Geree in Berkshire, was at work on a poem that reviewed the failures of his efforts on behalf of Oxford and Bolingbroke. Bolingbroke's assurances in a letter that the Tories' "misfortunes may perhaps to some degree unite us" elicited the response from Swift that we "have certainly more heads and hands than our adversaries; but, it must be confessed, they have stronger shoulders and better hearts."[4] Swift knew that what was perhaps possible for a peer of the realm was quite impossible for an Irish dean who had the sin of wit and who had, furthermore, backed the wrong horse. Some, on the other hand, expected to be rewarded. Not least hopeful was Richard Steele, who reported to his wife Prue on the fourth of August that he had been assured "of something immediately" by the Regents. He found it necessary, it is true, to borrow fifty pounds on the sixth from Edward Minshull to pay off another creditor (and Minshull would prove to be a

[3] Smithers, pp. 285–93.
[4] *The Correspondence of Jonathan Swift,* ed. Harold Williams, Vol. II: 1714–1723 (Oxford, 1963), pp. 101, 112.

most persistent creditor himself), but this was nothing unusual. "I . . . stay at S^{nt} James's because they talk of Great news, which I will bring You," he wrote Prue two days later. The following week he was invited by his old friend Cadogan to dine with Baron Bothmer, the King's envoy, to discuss a project Steele had in mind for coining farthings. Here was an enterprise to begin the new reign with in Steele's best manner: like the lotteries he had proposed in 1712, but closer to the source of wealth, money-making in two senses of the word. Bothmer's function was to provide recommendations to King George about preferment; a favorable report from Bothmer would presumably produce an instance of the King's favor. Or would it? No one could be sure until the first of the Hanoverian kings of England arrived in his other realm and made his wishes known, in French or German.[5]

It appeared to some that he was taking an unconscionable time in doing so. Addison and the regents could not get Queen Anne's body below ground for almost four weeks, while they awaited direction from Hanover. Everyone of note wished to be present when King George stepped ashore at Greenwich, to read the earliest indications of displeasure or favor in the sovereign countenance. Predictions without number about the date and place of his coming were retailed in newspapers. "I shall need," one place-seeker wrote to his brother, "to go down and waite on him when ever He comes ther, tho ther will be crowd enough, one would not be out of their duty." [6] One could not

[5] BM, MS. Stow 751; *Corr.*, p. 305. For the fate of Steele's project, see below, p. 37. It should be underlined that no evidence has come to light for the belief that Bothmer recommended Steele directly to the King's favor. Aitken's statement (II, 37), repeated by other scholars since (e.g., *Corr.*, p. 304; Loftis, p. 51), was based on Macpherson's misreading of "Steele" for "Hill" in the *Original Papers*. See J. F. Chance, "Corrections to James Macpherson's 'Original Papers,'" *English Historical Review*, XIII (1898), 548. Bothmer may, of course, have recommended him.

[6] Alexander Lord Polwarth to his brother (and Steele's friend) Sir Andrew Hume of Kimmerghame, letter of 9 September 1714 in Edinburgh, Register House, Marchmont Papers (uncatalogued).

afford to. When the King arrived at last, on 18 September, all who could be called public figures had cast up their accounts, had gauged possible alliances, discussed places available with friends or, better, if they were prominent enough, with the Regents, or, best of all, had caught the ear of Bothmer or Robethon. As is usual in human affairs, many imagined that their future would be brighter than events proved it to be. Robert Harley, the Earl of Oxford, patron of Tory men of letters, who would be the principal target of Whig vengeance as leader of Queen Anne's last government, was hopeful or undaunted enough to appear at the landing of the King and receive his rebuff. Among Steele's Whig friends, some found marks of the King's pleasure immediately, while others were forced to wait their turn. Lord Cowper, who had prepared a judicious report on the political situation for the King's eyes, was created Lord Chancellor only three days later. The Duke of Marlborough, returned from voluntary exile in the Low Countries and once more Captain-General, was in Greenwich for the new King's arrival. "My lord Duke, I hope your troubles are now all over," [7] said King George. Other Junto Whigs straightway had their rewards: Lord Wharton took office as Keeper of the Privy Seal on 27 September, General James Stanhope as secretary of state for the southern department on the same day, joining Lord Townshend who had been appointed secretary for the northern department on 17 September. In the midst of this bounty, some of the Junto association were disappointed. Halifax, patron of literary Whigs, who expected to form the ministry and promised a secretaryship of state in his government to Addison,[8] became in mid-October only first lord of a treasury then in commission.

[7] Winston S. Churchill, *Marlborough: His Life and Times* (New York, 1933–1938), VI, 627.

[8] Eustace Budgell, *A Letter to Cleomenes King of Sparta, from Eustace Budgell, Esq* (London, 1731), pp. 208–209; Smithers, pp. 296–97.

In these days, trying yet exhilarating for the politically ambitious, Richard Steele reckoned his chances accurately enough. He was not on the trail of preferment in the ordinary sense of the word, that is, an administrative post in the government. He had little talent for the sort of administration in which his foster father, Henry Gascoigne, had excelled. Steele kept irregular hours, he was impatient of detail, and he was far too ready to announce his own opinions before gathering the opinions of others; all these were damaging qualities in an administrator. He had, on the other hand, good reason to believe that he would find royal favor, for he had served as the acknowledged principal author of Whig propaganda during the previous year, leading the attack on the citadel of a Tory ministry which numbered among its defenders Jonathan Swift and Daniel Defoe. His expulsion from the Parliament he and his fellow Whigs had fashioned into an example of devotion to the House of Hanover. He had been "loaded with Compliments" by the Lords Justices themselves. No doubt his imagination at times carried him, as it carried Halifax and Addison, to pomp and splendor, but, somewhat chastened by his expulsion from the House of Commons, Steele fixed his eyes on a realistic prize, one that would enable him to put his varied talents to work. He wanted to be governor of the theater in Drury Lane.[9]

Drury Lane was an important source of revenue and in that sense the equivalent of a place in the government, although totally lacking in social cachet. Taking the bad years with the good, the managers might expect to share three thousand

---

[9] On the subject of Steele's dissatisfaction with his rewards, I differ with both Aitken (II, 55) and Loftis (pp. 51–52). The letter to Lord Clare (*Corr.*, pp. 101–102), which is discussed below, pp. 40–41, appears to reflect Steele's caution at becoming involved with the ministry's propaganda effort in 1715 rather than dissatisfaction with his earlier rewards. There is little contemporary evidence to indicate that Steele was dissatisfied in the autumn of 1714 and the winter of 1714–1715, and much to indicate that his first objective was the one he achieved, the governorship of Drury Lane.

pounds' profit or more from an average season.[10] A manager who could supply an occasional play would be able to benefit not only as a shareholder in the enterprise but as the author. The day of the week and the month in the season when a play was produced, Steele had found during the first run of his *The Tender Husband,* could drastically affect the author's remuneration from the third and sixth night's performances; a theater manager could see to it that his play was produced at the right time and in the proper manner.[11] There can be no question, however, that Steele envisioned the governorship as much more than simply a route to increased earnings. No doubt he had gleaned during his association with the German advisers the fact that the monarch's son and daughter-in-law enjoyed the theater and that the King himself might sometimes grace a suitable entertainment with his presence. In contrast to Queen Anne, who viewed the professional stage with considerable suspicion, the new monarchy would perhaps exert a positive influence on the drama or at any rate encourage attendance by an appearance from time to time. So Steele would have reasoned.

If the stage wanted reforming, and there were very many who felt that it did, Steele regarded himself as amply qualified to superintend the necessary changes. Had he not written and seen produced three of his own plays, two of which were now staples of the repertory? Had he not served as a practicing critic for the past five years in the medium of his essay periodicals, pronouncing in one place or the other on almost every aspect of the stage? His Censorium project, which was quasi-

---

[10] During 1712–1713 the profit had been £4,000; 1713–1714, £3,600; and for the months of September–December, 1714, the net was £1,700 (*London Stage,* pp. 327–28). For the expectations of the company, see Colley Cibber, *An Apology for the Life of Colley Cibber,* ed. B.R.S. Fone (Ann Arbor, 1968), p. 271.

[11] See *The Tender Husband,* ed. C. Winton (Lincoln, Neb., 1967), pp. xii–xiv.

theatrical, would alone have been enough to demonstrate that Steele was a man of ideas who would not regard the governorship as a sinecure.

In addition to the stipend and the opportunity to see his thoughts on the drama put into practice, one other consideration might have suggested itself as an inducement for Steele to seek the governorship, and perhaps it was the strongest of all: the opportunity to use his pen in a task worthy of his talents. The great dawn of the half-sheet literary periodical was over and Steele, with his acute sense of the public taste, was among the first to realize the fact. The proliferating imitators of *The Spectator* probably had something to do with it. The comparative ease with which essay periodicals could be written, printed, and distributed was not lost on literary aspirants of the age, nor was the knowledge that Addison and Steele had received very large sums of money for their efforts in the genre. As more essay periodicals appeared it was less possible for any single one to dominate the scene. Addison was in the process of discovering this during the autumn of 1714 with his renewal of *The Spectator*,[12] and Steele had learned of the new situation the previous spring with his excellent but short-lived *Lover*. The day of the really large windfall profit in the conduct of a literary periodical had passed. The strife of parties was involved as well; wounds given and received during the succession crisis were far from healed. As it became clear that the fallen Tory leaders would be harried by the victorious Whigs, writers of Tory or Toryish sympathies like Pope and Swift were reluctant to collaborate with Addison and Steele, now associates of the ruling establishment. If the opportunities for a man of letters in the periodical press were not what they had been for reasons of economics and politics, there was still the stage.

It had been a commonplace among Tory pamphleteers during

---

[12] *The Spectator*, ed. Donald Bond (Oxford, 1965), I, lxxvi.

the winter and spring of 1713–1714, when the climactic propaganda battles were being fought over the question of the royal
succession, that Richard Steele wrote for bread. The charge
was unanswerable: he was a professional writer and his five
children ate bread daily. The implication that his pen was for
sale to the highest bidder did not, however, follow. For ten
months he had fought the Tories in signed pamphlet and periodical, at a time when the easy triumph of the Whigs after the
Queen's death was not at all predictable, when there was considerable risk, financial if not physical, for a man of restricted
means such as Steele in standing up to be counted. He had done
so and had been expelled from the House of Commons as a
result of his candor. But he did write for bread. Writing had
got him his seat in the House, writing had got him expelled,
writing had kept his family clothed and fed and sheltered. His
stage comedies *The Funeral* and *The Tender Husband* were
standard works in the repertory, revived almost every season.
In the autumn of 1714 Jacob Tonson bought back from Samuel
Buckley the copyright for reprints of *The Spectator,* for five
hundred pounds. At that particular moment Steele was probably, after Congreve, the best-known living writer in
English.[13]

The notion of Steele's fitness for the governorship of Drury
Lane was not his alone; in fact, a member of Oxford's ministry
had offered the post to him in 1712 or 1713, as an inducement,
presumably, for him to abate his zeal for party.[14] He had
declined the offer then, but after the death of the Queen the
actor-managers Barton Booth, Robert Wilks, and Colley Cibber approached Steele, urging him to apply for the governorship. He had assisted the company on many occasions by providing announcements in his periodicals and he was, as they

[13] Addison and Swift had, of course, published anonymously for the most
part.
[14] Loftis, pp. 25–33.

knew, well thought of among the Whig lords. As John Loftis has put the matter : "The managers were grateful for [Steele's] assistance in the past, and they hoped that it would be continued —they would gain much if in another periodical Steele would again write about the stage. They knew, moreover, the advantages of associating themselves with one in Steele's fortunate political position. . . ." [15] The arrangement would be mutually advantageous, for the writer as well as for the actors, and, some dared to hope, perhaps even for the theatergoers.

Steele set about his business forthwith, conferring with Cadogan on 4 August and again on the fifteenth about his farthing coinage scheme, but also no doubt about the governorship. Cadogan, as well as being a trusted adviser of Bothmer and Robethon on political matters, was the Duke of Marlborough's closest friend and the Duke was to be one of Steele's agents in approaching King George for the appointment. The Earl of Nottingham, "Old Dismal," a Hanover Tory now Lord President of the Council, was also invited to lend support to Steele's request.[16] Steele was orchestrating his quest for preferment with great care. A few days before the King's arrival Steele arranged an appointment with the Duchess of Marlborough, who had read Steele's propaganda during her voluntary exile and had approved of it. "I think all will do Well," Steele wrote his wife before the interview, employing one of his characteristic phrases. He presumably discussed not only the theater appointment at this meeting but also the biography of the great duke, proposals for which he had announced in *The Reader* the previous spring. Sarah Duchess of Marlborough was difficult to please and would have ended the transaction then and there if she had felt so inclined but Steele passed this test. Marlborough

[15] *Ibid.*, pp. 35–36. See Cibber, *Apology*, pp. 270–71.
[16] Cibber, *Apology*, p. 271. Nottingham's part in the appointment, hitherto unknown, is alluded to in Steele's letter to him of 16 January 1722, printed below, Appendix G.

or Nottingham moved quickly to put Steele's case before King George and Steele was in receipt of a message "from the King to know whether I was in earnest in desiring the Playhouse or that others thought of it for me—If I lik^d it I should have it as an earnest of His future favour." [17] This was encouragement indeed, even if one discounts the memorandum somewhat to balance Steele's ingrained habit of banking future earnings. On 18 October 1714 the Lord Chamberlain, the Duke of Shrewsbury, issued a license to Steele, Booth, Doggett, Wilks, and Cibber, empowering them to "form constitute and Establish . . . a Company of Comedians, with . . . Licence, to Act and Represent in any Convenient Place during Our Pleasure and no longer, and in such manner as any three or more of them shall think proper, all Comedys, Tragedies, and all other Theatricall performances (Musical Entertainments only excepted). . . ." [18] Steele's stipend was seven hundred pounds per annum, in effect a lifetime pension large enough according to Dr. Johnson's standard to maintain one in splendor. The appointment was not a sinecure in the strict sense, for some effort on Steele's part was expected by his colleagues, but it was certainly a substantial confirmation of the new King's favor.

The Steeles confirmed the appointment themselves, as it were, by moving their residence nearer the Court. Only two years after Steele had secured the "prettyest house to receive the Prettyest Woman" in Bloomsbury, the house was advertised as being "in very good Repair . . . to be Lett." [19] The size of the Steele family perhaps had something to do with the

[17] Quoted in Aitken, II, 48; not located at Blenheim in 1966.

[18] Aitken, II, 48. Doggett was eventually excluded.

[19] *The Daily Courant* (BM, Burney copy), 20 July 1714. Bloomsbury Square was among the Russell holdings, and after 1703 the forty-two year leases until then customary were falling in and being renewed with fines payable. It may be that Steele did not wish or was not able to raise the sum. See Gladys Scott Thomson, *The Russells in Bloomsbury, 1669–1771* (London, 1940), p. 186.

move, but one may conjecture that Steele assumed in July that the Hanoverians would succeed to the throne upon the death of Queen Anne and wished to be nearer the focus of political life. The area around St. James's Palace constituted that focus. Steele in fact had received the news of Queen Anne's death in St. James's Coffee House, where Mr. Spectator sometimes joined "the little Committee of Politicks in the Inner-Room. . . ." Steele looked over accommodations in the neighborhood and by October had leased No. 26 St. James's Street from Lady Vanderput and moved his family in. St. James's Coffee House was across the street and down the hill a few yards in the direction of the Palace at No. 87, White's at No. 69. It was a substantial neighborhood. Dr. Garth dwelled just across the way in a more prepossessing residence, paying rates of four pounds to Steele's one pound ten shillings, and the Marchioness of Halifax in Park Place opposite was assessed five pounds.[20] Steele had known this part of London since his days in the Life Guards; it was the center of the life he relished above all. It is safe to assume also that Prue approved the move if she did not indeed suggest it. Bloomsbury was still somewhat isolated, bounded on one side by farmland.[21] The couple had lived in St. James's soon after their marriage, and some time after their relocation there Lady Steele specified to her husband addresses which were possible: Pall Mall, St. James's Street, Gerrard Street, "or a Place near a Church." Prue's list of fashionable addresses serves as a reminder that Steele's desire for the approval of society was matched to some extent by his wife's similar feelings. They were both by origin outlanders, Irish and Welsh.

If the fact that Richard Steele had been born in Dublin and

[20] London, Westminster Public Library, parish rate books of St. James's, 1716; *Survey of London*, Vol. XXX: *The Parish of St. James Westminster*, Part One (London, 1960), p. 440.

[21] Thomson, *The Russells in Bloomsbury*, p. 184.

his wife in Wales constituted a disability in London society; if it caused him to seek that society's approval by living on the proper street and attending the fashionable church, it was also a source of strength in his career as a man of letters and, later, as a member of Parliament. Notoriously easy of access, Steele was addressed all his life by Welshmen, Scots, Irishmen, and colonials, who wrote or sought him out at home or in the coffeehouse, or recommended friends and kinsmen to his benevolence. As George Berkeley noted on his first meeting with him, Steele was very cheerful, with a conversation that "abounded with wit and good sense," but he was also a good listener. The stories these strangers told, the accounts they gave of their life elsewhere, the accents they spoke with, found their way into Steele's essays and plays here and there; the process contributed something toward the broadness of outlook that made the periodicals of Addison and Steele acceptable beyond the boundaries of Middlesex. "The most influential writers in [eighteenth-century America]," a scholar has recently judged, "were probably Joseph Addison and Richard Steele." [22] For Steele there was an interaction; he gave and he received. A correspondent addressed him that summer of 1714 from the other side of the world, Sumatra: "The *Bible* has the first Place in my Study, as teaching me the whole Compass of Duty. Mr. *Lock,* who first taught me to distinguish between Words, and Things, has the next Place; Those Writings [of yours], which have taught me a more easy and agreeable Manner of practicing Vertue itself, are my constant Companions: I hope the grateful Acknowledgments of an Honest Mind, for being made wiser and better, will not be unacceptable to One, who professes doing

[22] Louis B. Wright, "Colonial Literary Culture," in *Literary History of the United States,* ed. Robert E. Spiller *et al.* (New York, 1949), I, 19. See also Rae Blanchard, "Richard Steele and the Secretary of the SPCK," in *Restoration and Eighteenth-Century Literature,* ed. Carroll Camden (Chicago, 1963), pp. 287–95; and her "Richard Steele's Maryland Story," *American Quarterly,* X (1958), 78–82.

Good." [23] From the other hemisphere Steele received and answered a request for assistance. Jeremiah Dummer, graduate of Harvard and colonial agent for Massachusetts and Connecticut, was in 1714 assembling the first shipment of books for the Collegiate School in Connecticut, then an institution of some twenty students, better known now as Yale University. His method of collecting the library, in the case of living authors, was simply to approach the author himself and ask for a donation. Apparently the first donor, for his name heads all the rest in Dummer's catalogue, was Richard Steele, who responded with the deluxe eleven-volume set of the *Tatlers* and *Spectators* in royal paper, "neatly bound and gilt," which sold at retail for a guinea a volume.[24] The volumes were in distinguished company; Sir Isaac Newton responded with copies of the *Principia* and the *Optice,* and Dr. Richard Bentley contributed, among other writings, his *Dissertation upon the Epistles of Phalaris,* a work with which Swift was acquainted. In 1718 the trustees of the institution that had assumed the name of Yale College addressed a formal letter of thanks to Dummer and the donors for the "repeated instances of favour to our Infant School from generous Gentlemen. . . ." [25] One hopes that Dummer let Steele know about these thanks; few remarks would have pleased him more than this graceful reminder of his part in the spread of what he took to be enlightenment and reformed religion.

The aspect of Steele's work that was most praised in his own day, his efforts for the reform of manners and education, is that

[23] Joseph Collet, a London pepper merchant. Steele quotes the letter, deleting the direct reference to himself, in *Town-Talk* No. 7; see *Per. Jour.,* p. 236.

[24] Quoted in Anne Stokely Pratt, "The Books sent from England by Jeremiah Dummer to Yale College," in *Papers in Honor of Andrew Keogh* . . . (New Haven, 1938), p. 15. See also C. Winton, "Jeremiah Dummer: The 'First American'?" *William and Mary Quarterly,* 3d. Ser., XXVI (1969), 105–108.

[25] Pratt, "Books sent from England," in *Papers,* p. 24.

which the twentieth-century reader finds most difficult to accept. The age dislikes being told what to do, or indeed reading about others' being told in an earlier epoch, but there can be no doubt that in his own time Steele was chiefly valued for precisely this—for mixing ethical instruction and general enlightenment with entertainment, for acting, in his literary activities, as Isaac Bickerstaff, the Censor of Great Britain. His fellows, or at any rate those multitudes of his fellows who read the books and saw the plays he wrote, did in fact want to be, they insisted on being, told what to do, or as Bickerstaff had put it in the first *Tatler,* "what to think." In the long run the desire for instruction can be seen as part of that "colossal secularisation" to which Sir Herbert Butterfield has alluded, catered to in its early phases by guides to conduct such as the courtesy books of the Renaissance and evolving with the rise of literacy and the new science into a mood receptive to the Enlightenment itself.[26] In the short run of Richard Steele's life the public taste was revealed in a constant demand for more of the same from Steele. Sometimes his conscience troubled him about this profiting from ethical works; he was well aware that he did not exemplify in his own life the standards of conduct he appeared to advocate. His fellow officers in the brigade of Guards had brought the disparity between sermon and preacher to his attention years earlier when he had first published *The Christian Hero* with his name on the title page "in hopes that a standing Testimony against himself . . . might curb his Desires, and make him ashamed of understanding and seeming to feel what was Virtuous, and living so quite contrary a Life." [27] He had

[26] Butterfield, *The Origins of Modern Science, 1300–1800* (New York, 1957), p. 182. See also George C. Brauer, Jr., *The Education of a Gentleman* (New York, 1959), pp. 13–33; Peter Gay, *The Enlightenment: An Interpretation* (New York, 1966), pp. 256–68; C. Winton, "Addison and Steele in the English Enlightenment," *Studies on Voltaire and the Eighteenth Century,* XXVII (Geneva, 1963), 1901–1918.

[27] *Mr. Steele's Apology,* in *Tracts,* p. 339.

published *The Tatler* behind the mask of Isaac Bickerstaff, he explained in the last number of that paper, because he felt that his "life was, at best, but pardonable." Scruple as he might, the temptation to sell his views to a public ever ready to buy them continued strong. During that summer and autumn of 1714 he acquired new burdens for his conscience by lending his name to another work of popularized instruction.

The circumstances were these. Some time before the end of July, perhaps many months earlier, a manuscript came his way, as he put it, "upon the frequent mention in the *Spectator* of a Ladies Library." [28] Steele refers to the promises Mr. Spectator had given in No. 37 to recommend books "proper for the Improvement of the Sex" which he never fulfilled, although reminded of his failure by a correspondent in No. 528. The female compiler of the manuscript which came to Steele had collected and arranged excerpts from the works of various ethical writers in order to fix in "the Mind general Rules for Conduct in all the Circumstances of the Life of Woman. . . ." They were referred to him, Steele commented in the preface to the book, "as what were at first intended by the Compiler for a Guide to her own Conduct. . . ." Steele no doubt spent little time verifying the quotations in this manuscript which arrived during an especially busy period of his life, but the authorities, though not named, were impeccable: Jeremy Taylor's *Holy Living*, Fleetwood, Tillotson, *The Whole Duty of Man*. Locke was represented by copious extracts from his *Treatise on Education*.[29] The whole was, to borrow Parson Adams' judgment on another of Steele's works, solemn enough for a sermon. Steele was somewhat troubled at the thought of appearing without Bickerstaff's mask, and referred the compilation to a

---

[28] Preface, dated 21 July 1714, to *The Ladies Library* (London, 1714), signed by "R. Steele."

[29] An exhaustive analysis of sources, by G. A. Aitken, is in *The Athenaeum*, No. 2958 (1884), pp. 16–17.

"Reverend Gentleman" for his opinion. The reverend gentleman allayed Steele's uneasiness, noting that "its coming out
with my Name, would give an Expectation that I had assembled the thoughts of many ingenious Men on pious Subjects, as
I had heretofore on Matters of a different Nature: By this
means . . . the Work may come into the Hands of Persons
who take up no Book that has not Promises of Entertainment
in the first Page of it."

Steele having mastered his scruples on the point, Jacob Tonson issued the book in early October with the inscription on the
title page "Published by Mr. Steele." It is an attractive work in
three neat volumes, each with a good frontispiece by DuGuernier of ladies in different, appropriate activities: study, meditation, or the direction of a household. Volume II, for example,
with sections devoted to the instruction of The Daughter, The
Wife, The Mother, The Widow, and The Mistress (of a household, that is), has as its frontispiece DuGuernier's engraving of
a handsome widow contemplating a skull, presumably that of
the departed spouse, while suitors stand transfixed at the door.
The volume is dedicated to a friend of Steele's, Mrs. Catherine
Bovey, traditionally the prototype of Mr. Spectator's willful
widow.[30] The index is an outstanding piece of work, detailed for

[30] DuGuernier and Steele were fellow members of Sir Godfrey Kneller's
Academy for Drawing and Painting. See *Vertue Note Books,* Walpole
Society Publications, XVIII (Oxford, 1930), 2, 38.

It is in the realm of conjecture but it is possible that the "reverend
gentleman" may have been the Reverend George Berkeley and the compiler
could well have been Mrs. Bovey herself, who had assisted George Hickes in
his *Thesaurus* and to whom Steele refers in the dedication as possessing
knowledge "not inferior to the more Learned of [our sex]. . . ." If it is
assumed that the papers came into Steele's hands in 1713, when Berkeley was
assisting Steele on *The Guardian,* the possibility of his being the reverend
gentleman is somewhat strengthened. Finally, Berkeley knew Mrs. Bovey;
he paid an extended visit to her estate, Flaxley Abbey, in Gloucester in 1715.
See his letter to Sir John Percival of 23 July 1715 in *The Works of George
Berkeley Bishop of Cloyne,* ed. A. A. Luce and T. E. Jessop, Vol. VIII:
Letters (London, 1956), pp. 87–88.

instant reference by a lady on some troubled occasion. For example :

Shew, women misled by it, 444.
Silence in churches, enjoined women by the Gospel, 182.
    An excellent remedy against censure, 427.
Sin, the spitefulness of it, 208.

Tonson advertised the work in the *Daily Courant* as "proper for a New Year's gift for the ladies."

The index aside, there is little original work in the compilation : a phrase here and there, an occasional sentence amended or corrected so as to bring the content into harmony with its context. Steele did not maintain that he had done much with the volumes beyond writing the dedications (to the Countess of Burlington and to his wife, as well as that to Mrs. Bovey) and lending his name as "publisher," but the presence of that name on the title page was the source of another problem.

One Royston Meredith, grandson of Jeremy Taylor's printer Richard Royston, learned of the book and demanded compensation as holder of the copyright for *Holy Living,* which Steele, he alleged, had plundered "for a little dirty Money, which you Spend as Vainly, as you Get Idly." Well said, perhaps, but deficient in tact. Meredith then demanded satisfaction, as he put it, from Tonson, who replied, according to Meredith, "that he paid Copy-Money, and that I must apply myself to the Author for Redress; my Reply to him was, That the Law should then decide it." [31] "To which Mr. Tonson had the Assurance to say, It was better to be Doing than Talking; which Words I con-

[31] Meredith, *Mr. Steele Detected* . . . (London, 1714), p. 7. It should be noted that Meredith was politically hostile to Steele, who he writes was "deservedly Expelled the Honourable House of Commons for raising of groundless Fears and Jealousies in the Minds of the People" (p. 12). This is Tory rhetoric and it is possible that Meredith's tempest was raised or assisted by Tories to discredit Steele further.

ceive to imply an open Defiance to me, notwithstanding he
cannot be Ignorant, how that the Common-Law, the High
Court of Chancery, and even a late Act of Parliament, for
Securing the Right and Property of Booksellers to their Copies,
will all plead in my Behalf. . . ." "Two poor Orphans," he
wrote Steele, "have very little else to Subsist on. . . ." This
was a good line to take with Steele, the appeal to his charity,
but Meredith had already said too much. He wrote again and
Steele, having no doubt conferred with Tonson, replied:

> Sir,
>   I have a Second Letter from you. The Stile of the First was
> very harsh to one whom you are not at all Acquainted with; but
> there were Suggestions in it, which might give Excuse for being
> out of Humour at one, whom you might, perhaps, think was the
> Occasion of Damage to you. You mentioned also an Orphan,
> which Word was a Defence against any warm Reply; but since
> you are pleased to go on in an intemperate way of Talk, I shall
> give my self no more Trouble to enquire about what you Com-
> plain, but rest satisfied in doing all the good Offices I can to the
> Reverend Author's Grandchild, now in Town: Thus leaving you
> to contend about your Title to his Writings, and wishing you
> Success, if you have Justice on your Side; I beg you will give me
> no more ill Language, and you will Oblige,
>   Sir,
>   Your Humble Servant,
>   RICHARD STEELE

Meredith, for reasons best known to himself, had the exchange
of correspondence printed—though Steele appears to better advantage than he in the dispute—in a pamphlet grandly entitled
*Mr. Steele Detected: Or, the Poor and Oppressed Orphan's
Letters to the Great and Arbitrary Mr. Steele.* There the matter
rested, Meredith presumably having been advised by counsel
that he had small likelihood of recovery. Nevertheless, Steele,
with his unfailing instinct for controversy, had stumbled into

an area of the law which is still in dispute, and the positions of the principals in the dispute merit attention.

The question of copyright was, of course, crucially important in the development of a true profession of letters. A pirated edition of Steele's *Tatler* had appeared in London during the lifetime of that periodical, causing his publishers severe mental anguish and some financial discomfort.[32] Meredith, it will be noted, takes the position in his dispute with Steele that copyright was invested in the publisher, that the author's interest ceased when he handed over the copy to the publisher, and that the copyright was susceptible of inheritance, as constituting property, for an indefinite period, perhaps in perpetuity. The implication of this argument was that each book would belong to some publisher and his heirs, and thus, eventually, all books would belong to publishers. In fact, the various attempts at regulation of the publishing trade in England, most recently in the Copyright Act of 1710, had the effect of securing the rights of the publisher rather than any rights the author might possess in the work he had written.[33] Steele, an author himself though not properly speaking the author of *The Ladies Library,* promises that he will perform "all the good Offices I can to the Reverend Author's Grandchild," that is, the grandchild of Jeremy Taylor, the original author of the material quoted. He assumes that rights remaining in the work belong to the author and his descendants rather than to the publisher and his heirs. This defense of author's copyright is not revolutionary, but it is interesting to observe an author of Steele's prestige assert the position so emphatically. Tonson, who knew as much about copyrights as any man alive, in effect told Meredith to put his

---

[32] Richmond P. Bond, "The Pirate and the *Tatler,*" *The Library,* 5th Ser., XVIII (1963), 257–74.

[33] Harry H. Ransom, *The First Copyright Statute* (Austin, 1956), pp. 104–106. Cyprian Blagden, however, has directed attention to several references to author's copyright in the records of the English Stock before 1710, in his review of Ransom's book in *The Library,* 5th Ser., XII (1957), 66–69.

case to the courts; "better to be Doing than Talking" has a Tonsonian ring, and in fact the question was unresolved. Tonson offered sound advice but Meredith was not in a mood to be advised. In the meantime, *The Ladies Library* sold steadily and well; by Steele's death three editions had appeared in English and two, published in Amsterdam, in French. Tonson retained the English copyright.

Another work that had demanded some of Steele's energies during the spring and summer of 1714 appeared in October. *Mr. Steele's Apology for Himself and his Writings; Occasioned by his Expulsion from the House of Commons* had been printed before the Queen's death but publication had been delayed, probably because of the uncertain political situation.[34] If a ministry had been formed in the new reign which included moderate Tories, as some thought possible, then raking over these old ashes would have been impolitic. On the other hand, if, as had happened, the Whigs carried all before them, this tract might usefully serve as a reminder of the last administration's iniquities and would prepare public opinion for legal moves against the more prominent Tories. The original intention may have been, in Steele's words, only that of "rescuing my own Name from a seeming Disgrace of a Vote of the Commons," but he had by October something else in mind. The diction and tone of the preface and the dedication to Sir Robert Walpole, which were written after the Queen's death, contrast with that of the body of the tract. "You," Steele writes of Walpole, "have the Honour and Happiness to have eminently opposed all the Incursions which these guilty Men made upon the Greatness of the Crown and the Welfare of the Subject, by prostituting them both to their own selfish Designs, and destroying, as far as in them lay, the good Name of all Men of Virtue and Service." [35] Some of Steele's exultation derives from

---

[34] It had been advertised in *The Daily Courant* (BM, Burney copy) of 21 July 1714 as to be published "within a few Days."
[35] *Tracts*, p. 280.

the simple joy of victory, no doubt. It was good to have *The Examiner* silenced, especially inasmuch as Steele felt that his former friend Jonathan Swift had superintended the paper's attacks on himself, but the tone of preface and dedication, as well as the choice of dedicatee, argue that Steele was privy to the decision of certain Whigs to bring Oxford and Bolingbroke to the bar. Walpole himself had been expelled from the House in 1712, upon which occasion he had written his sister Dorothy, "I heartily despise what I shall one day revenge. . . ." [36] On the other hand, Halifax, long the patron of literary Whigs, had confided to Addison in September that as first minister he intended to pursue a policy of conciliation, and Addison had agreed.[37] Halifax did not become first minister and it is significant that Steele's rewards were proportionately greater than those of Addison during the first year of the new reign. Many Whigs were determined to pursue their advantage. Steele's tract may thus be seen not only as his apology for the expulsion affair (which, he was careful to demonstrate, really needed no apology) but more importantly as an early, if not the very earliest, public indication of the severe policy Walpole had in mind. Steele could reflect with some satisfaction, if he wished, that little more than a year earlier Defoe had begun the propaganda campaign on Oxford's behalf for Steele's expulsion; now the situation was altered.[38]

By presenting a capsule account of Steele's literary career, the *Apology* served also to remind anyone who required reminding that here was a writer of moment and substance, one well-deserving of another seat in Parliament by virtue not only of his party loyalty but also of his intrinsic merit. Steele probably told one or another of the Regents about his interest in re-entering Parliament when he discussed the governorship of

[36] J. H. Plumb, *Sir Robert Walpole: The Making of a Statesman* (London, 1956), p. 181.
[37] Eustace Budgell, *A Letter to Cleomenes,* pp. 209–10; Smithers, pp. 296–98.
[38] *CS,* pp. 181–82.

Drury Lane with them in August, for the theatrical license was framed in such a way as to leave the day-to-day routine to the actor-managers, with Steele at liberty to pursue his many other interests, including occupying a seat in the House if one should materialize for him. All factions were at work that autumn, canvassing the electors, buying votes, discussing and securing candidates, preparing in the eighteenth-century manner for the elections which would be held after writs were issued for the new Parliament in January. Someone, perhaps the Duke of Somerset, who was a Regent, suggested that Steele should contest a seat for Great Bedwin in Wiltshire. This was an undertaking decidedly fraught with risk. Somerset derived electoral influence in Wiltshire from his landholdings there but Great Bedwin was largely in the interest of the Earl of Ailesbury, whose father had refused to take the oaths for William and Mary and remained in exile until his death. Ailesbury's sympathies and those of the author of *The Christian Hero* were not likely to coincide. The Tories had carried the election of 1713 handily in Great Bedwin, though Ailesbury's agent grumbled that the freeholders had demanded five shillings and even seven shillings sixpence a vote. "Your Lordship's interest," he reported in September, 1714, "may be in some danger if two Whigs stand, and will be free of their money. . . ." Rumors persisted as late as December that Steele would stand. Great Bedwin, however, was a burgage borough, in which the votes were attached to pieces of property, and Steele's putative patron may have concluded that the effort of securing his election would not justify the necessary expenses, especially in the face of Ailesbury's well-compensated interest. The proposal in the end came to nothing.[39]

[39] Burgage boroughs: Robert Walcott, *English Politics in the Early Eighteenth Century* (Oxford, 1956), pp. 14n, 50, 55; information on Great Bedwin: HMC, *Ailesbury MSS.*, pp. 218–20. It is possible that Steele's friend Thomas Burnet, son of the Bishop of Sarum, suggested his looking into the seat at Great Bedwin. Burnet had been involved in an election

Robert Walpole in the meanwhile was reviewing candidates and prospects with a young nobleman who had recently inherited enormous landholdings and the opportunity for political activity which accompanied such holdings. Thomas Pelham-Holles, created Earl of Clare by the new King on 19 October, had relationships by blood and marriage with a constellation of substantial landed families: the Pierreponts, the Cavendishes, the Townshends, and of course the Pelhams.[40] He was proving to be, moreover, fascinated by those details of political life which bored or repelled many of his colleagues in the House of Lords. He was immensely rich and entirely willing to spend money in the service of party. His agents in Nottingham, for example, reported in November that they were in the process of speaking and giving money to every individual elector, in the interest of economy: "For less than seven hundred pounds the burrough [will be] in good hands for several years to come." [41] However devious he may have become later on in public life, young Lord Clare was direct with the multitude of his dependents; his methods and desires were as simple as one could wish: subordinates were to do precisely what he told them to do. Clare was no fool; in the sphere of national politics he realized that the world was not organized solely to do his bidding, but at home (and home included large holdings in Sussex and Nottingham, as well as property in Surrey and in London) he expected obedience. If tenants neglected to vote for his interest, for example, he did not fail to see that they were evicted immediately from their homes.[42]

---

quarrel there the previous year and reportedly had been locked up by the bishop to forestall a duel (*ibid.*).

[40] BM, Add. MSS., 32, 686, fo. 27. See also Stebelton H. Nulle, *Thomas Pelham-Holles, Duke of Newcastle: His Early Political Career 1693–1724* (Philadelphia, 1931), pp. 59–64.

[41] BM, Add. MSS., 32, 686, fo. 25, 26.

[42] *Records of a Yorkshire Manor,* ed. Sir Thomas Lawson-Tancred (London, 1937), p. 265. His successors were following the same practice as late as 1820 (p. 319).

From his uncle, the Duke of Newcastle, Clare had inherited property in Yorkshire which, though not large by his family's standards, had the advantage of including the adjoining boroughs of Aldborough and Boroughbridge, each returning two members to Parliament. With proper management these could be made safe franchises. Clare set about the business without delay, addressing a letter in August, 1714, to the electors of Aldborough.

> Gentlemen,
>   Being now in the quiet possession of the Estate devised to me by my late Uncle, the Duke of Newcastle's Will, I hope I shall meet with no opposition in your Town. I can assure you I shall be very proud whenever it lies in my power to do anything for your service. I shall never recommend anyone to you that is not entirely in the interest of his Country. I hope by your ready compliance with my desires you'll shew how well you deserve of me.[43]

In early December Lord Clare offered Richard Steele one of the two seats for Boroughbridge. The offer, probably made at the suggestion of Walpole, to whom he had dedicated his *Apology*, placed Steele in a difficult position. On the one hand, here was a seat almost for the asking, with a donor ready to assist in making up the considerable sum needed for election expenses, even in a borough well along the way toward a nobleman's pocket.[44] But again, serving as the dependent of a great man was not what Steele had in mind. His independence had been dearly bought, but it was his. The author of *Tatler, Spectator*, and *Guardian* need not make a leg. A seat in Parliament was desirable, but not essential, for the manager of Drury Lane. Steele, furthermore, knew Clare; they had been fellow members

---

[43] *Ibid.*, p. 269.
[44] As late as 1746, when Newcastle had complete control, election expenses were £182 (*ibid.*, p. 287).

of the Hanover Club in 1713–1714. He was fully able to sense the humorless pride of this ambitious politician twenty years his junior.

In the end, he could not refuse the opportunity. He decided to pick his way cautiously, impressing Clare with the fact that, though in a sense a dependent, Mr. Steele brought important advantages to the arrangement. He replied on the fourteenth of December:

> My Lord,
> I have received your Lordship's Generous offer. I am extremely at a losse how to expresse my self on such a surprise. The offers, in this kind, which have been made to Me are very precarious and uncertain. I am mightily perplexed to say something on this occasion which should be very well worth repeating, but indeed I am too much moved at your Goodnesse to be able to say any more than that I shall endeavour to answer Your inclinations on all incidents, and approve my self, My Lord
> Y^r Lordship's Most Obliged Most Obedient Humble Servant
> RICHARD STEELE.

Under the circumstances and considering the recipient of the letter, Steele could scarcely have said less. It is a most ambiguous letter. Expressing extreme surprise at someone's act of generosity is after all more candid than tactful. Steele conferred with William Jessop, one of Clare's candidates for Aldborough, and on the eighteenth dispatched another extraordinary letter to his patron in which he asserted that "the Opportunity of acting with uprightnesse in the Legislature is the most desirable Station in Humane life, and I know I shall expresse my Gratitude to you in the best manner by behaving my self with strict integrity. I am sorry I can promise You no other Qualities. . . ." Brave words for a dependent of the Earl of Clare. The relationship would be stormy: the young peer, accustomed from

birth to obedience, stationed near the center of things, attempting always to extend his power; the middle-aged man of letters,
struggling to escape the entangling webs of debt, custom, and
dependency that enfolded him. Several years later, when Clare,
then Duke of Newcastle, served as Lord Chamberlain, the
pretext of their decisive quarrel would be the theater in Drury
Lane but the quarrel had been building for a long time by then.

While Steele was arriving at his decision as to whether or
not he would return to Parliament the new theater season had
begun. Closed during August out of respect for the Queen
(August is a slow month in London anyway), Drury Lane
opened on 21 September, the day after King George's arrival in
the capitol. For the first production the managers had chosen a
reliable perennial, Farquhar's *Recruiting Officer,* to which
Steele contributed a prologue of conventional Whig panegyric,
raised briefly above the bathetic by his wit:

> Though great the Dearth of Comick Fools will be,
> And a thin Crop of Coxcombs we foresee;
> Though Sense is like to thrive throughout the Land,
> And all *French* Fopperies will be Contraband:
> We not despair. Some Ridicule may rise,
> Some modish Oddness, some bizarre Disguise. . . .[45]

Business had seldom been better, with place-hunters crowding
into town and seeking relief from their boredom at the theater.
During the autumn, furthermore, the Prince and Princess of
Wales had signified their interest by attending several performances.[46] Prosperity continued at Drury Lane until mid-December, when the brothers John and Christopher Rich reopened the
theater at Lincoln's Inn Fields and persuaded several of the
Drury Lane actors to join their troupe. Steele and his col-

[45] *Verse,* pp. 68–69.
[46] *London Stage,* I, 332–34.

leagues without success appealed to the Lord Chamberlain for compensation. Unable to produce some of their best plays because of the defection, the managers watched their profits evaporate by two-thirds. At a meeting of the managers called to deal with the crisis, Steele cheerfully agreed to accept a proportionate share of the profits rather than his stipend of seven hundred pounds and revealed a plan that would, they all felt, increase the managers' independence of the Lord Chamberlain. He would petition the King to allow the license, which was granted only during royal pleasure, to be "enlarg'd into a more ample, and durable Authority," a patent.[47] Such a patent would be something like those granted to D'Avenant and Killigrew by Charles II and would thus have not only legal but, of even greater importance in England, traditional substance. When Steele assured the actor-managers that their interests would be maintained, although the patent would be granted in his name only, his colleagues were well pleased to accede to the proposal. "This," Cibber later observed, "was what we had long wish'd for. . . ." The patent was endorsed favorably by the Attorney General on 12 January 1715 and had passed the Great Seal on the nineteenth. The celerity of the process, at a time when petitioners thronged the corridors of government, testifies to Steele's high standing. It also owes something to the fact that Steele, residing in St. James's Street, was located so as to be able to see each person concerned in the tortuous progress of the petition through the bureaucracy: from clerk to secretary to clerk again, each requiring a fee.[48] Being "well satisfied," the patent ran, "of the Ability and good Disposition of Our Trusty and Well-beloved *Richard Steele* Esq; for the promoting these

---

[47] Cibber, *Apology*, p. 275. For a full account, see Loftis, pp. 42–45.

[48] Although Lord Chancellor Cowper waived his fee as a gesture of friendship, there were many other expenses to be paid along the way. The passage of Sir Luke Schaub's patent for a pension in 1717 or 1718 required, for example, the payment of twenty-one separate fees, to a total of £42 5s 2d (PRO, SP 35/30/71).

Our Royal Purposes, not only from his Publick Services to Religion and Virtue, but his steady Adherence to the true Interest of his Country." [49]

On 12 January Steele received £500 from the Royal Bounty, presumably to assist with election expenses. "Steady adherence to the true interest" had produced rewards more tangible than the proverbial serene conscience. Only a year earlier Steele had approached a crisis in his career and perhaps in the history of the nation; now, six months after the death of Queen Anne, he found himself patentee of Drury Lane, recipient of the Bounty, "publisher" of a successful manual of instruction for ladies, and started on his way back, at least, to the House of Commons. Creditors had not disappeared, it is true; he put together a list of them in October with the amount he owed each of them, added the lot and made it out to be £2,798—in characteristic fashion he discounted the past: the correct total was £3,618.[50] He was, nevertheless, in a strong position. In a euphoric mood he addressed his wife, echoing the categories of *The Ladies Library:*

> To Mrs. Mary Steele
>   The Tender Mother
>   The Fond Wife
>   The Prudent Mistresse
>   The Frugall Housekeeper
>   The Chearful Companion
>   The Happy Slave to
>   Her Powerful Husband
>   RICHARD STEELE

[49] Original in PRO, LC 5/202/280–85. Steele later printed the patent in *Town-Talk* No. 6, which version is quoted here. See *Per. Jour.,* pp. 229–32.
[50] Aitken, II, 49.

CHAPTER II

Sir Richard

WHEN STEELE turned his attention to the contest at Borough-bridge, he discovered that the seat there was not going to be his for the asking. Clare's holdings in the region were substantial but not so large as to overwhelm local north country interests. His uncle, the Duke of Newcastle, had purchased the manor of Aldborough, nearby, and Clare's "quiet possession" of the title enabled him to intimidate the electors of Aldborough and choose candidates for their approval.[1] In Boroughbridge the situation was somewhat different. One of the seats had been held in the interest of an ancient Yorkshire family, the Stapyltons, since 1690. The incumbent, Sir Bryan Stapylton, had supported the Tories in the last government on at least two crucial issues: the Sacheverell trial and Steele's expulsion.[2] Clare's strategy was to make common cause with another Yorkshire family, the Wilkinsons, by appointing Charles Wilkinson his local agent. When control of the area had been achieved, the Stapyltons' candidate would be forced out. By an informal understanding, apparently never committed to writing, it was agreed that the Wilkinsons should thenceforth have the disposal of one of the four seats in the two boroughs of Aldborough and Boroughbridge, the other three being in the Earl of Clare's nomination, though all candidates must of

---

[1] *Records of a Yorkshire Manor,* ed. Sir Thomas Lawson-Tancred (London, 1937), p. 228.
[2] *A Collection of White and Black Lists* . . . (London, 1715), p. 18.

course be acceptable to Clare. This arrangement was intended to ensure a constant, sympathetic supervision of the absentee landlord's interest and in fact it operated to the mutual advantage of the principals, if not of the constituents, until the end of the century.³ Starting the arrangement was, however, Steele's immediate problem and he set about solving it.

Though unfamiliar with the north country, Steele knew the particulars of grassroots politics well enough, from his experience in the constituencies on the Isle of Wight and at Harwich on behalf of friends, and from his own brief service as candidate and Member for Stockbridge. He was to stand with Charles Wilkinson's nephew Thomas against Stapylton, the two candidates having the greatest number of votes to be declared elected to the two seats. On the advice of the elder Wilkinson, Steele sought a letter of endorsement from Clare in December, to be written, as Steele put it, "in Guarded terms." The situation was uncertain enough to make it profitable to avoid offending electors by a gross display of Clare's power. Perhaps Wilkinson had told Steele about the peer's high-handed treatment of the Aldborough electors. That would not do in Boroughbridge, at least at this stage.

On 5 January the Parliament of 1713 was dissolved and a new one called for by proclamation on 15 January. The Whig leadership, with the support of the King's German advisers, had no thought of losing this election. The Royal Proclamation calling the new Parliament was itself a party document: "[W]e were very much concerned, on Our Accession to the Crown, to find the publick Affairs of Our Kingdoms under the greatest Difficulties, as well in respect of Our Trade, and the Interruption of Our Navigation, as of the great Debts of the Nation, which We were surprized to observe, had been very much increased since the Conclusion of the last War." ⁴ In the event

³ *Records of a Yorkshire Manor,* pp. 228ff., 317.
⁴ *Journal of the House of Commons* (hereafter abbreviated *CJ*), XVIII, 14.

that a reader had missed the point, the proclamation closed with an exhortation to the voters to have "a particular Regard to such as shewed a Firmness to the Protestant Succession," conveying thus the usual Whig implication that all Tories were Jacobites under the skin. As if determined to oblige the Whigs, James III issued a royal proclamation on his own part, in which he reaffirmed his support of and belief in the doctrines of the Roman Catholic Church. It was to be a difficult election for Tories.[5]

No one had shown greater firmness to the Protestant succession than Richard Steele but he was more than ordinarily bedeviled that winter by lack of funds. He had traded away his seven-hundred-pound stipend at Drury Lane, it will be recalled, for a proportionate share of the profits but the theater was not making money. A seat in Parliament as such provided no remuneration and usually cost a considerable sum to secure. As late as the fifteenth of January Steele was still uncertain whether he could afford the luxury of standing and serving. If the patent for Drury Lane did not materialize, he told Wilkinson, he would have to resign from the House. Even though Steele had received the Royal Bounty and had borrowed eleven hundred pounds on the sixth of January he was in the course of borrowing still more from his acquaintance John Warner the goldsmith at the sign of the Golden Anchor, Temple Bar. In the end he was forced to appeal to William Jessop, candidate for one of the Aldborough seats, for a twenty-pound loan.[6] Elections demanded cash.

Boroughbridge, a cluster of houses on the road to Scotland, just eight miles north of York, was a burgage borough, with a

[5] For an interesting discussion of Whig strategy, see William T. Morgan, "Some Sidelights upon the General Election of 1715," in *Essays in Modern English History in Honor of Wilbur Cortez Abbott* (Cambridge, Mass., 1941), pp. 133–76. The Pretender's proclamation is printed in HMC, *Stuart MSS.*, I, 343–45.

[6] Aitken, II, 109; *Corr.*, pp. 308–309; *Calendar of Treasury Books*, ed. William Shaw (London, 1957), Vol. XXIX, Part 2, p. 328. The money order for the bounty was dated 10 January (*ibid.*).

presiding civic official called a bailiff. Members of Parliament were elected by the burgesses, owners of the "burgages" or pieces of property, each of which was endowed with a vote, and by the bailiff.[7] The key figures, then, indeed, the only persons worth attention at all unless one had in mind organizing a mob for some special purpose, were these electors, with the bailiff the most important of the lot. Asking Wilkinson to "suspend all unkind reflections" on his delay, Steele remained in London until the patent was safely in hand and then took the north-bound stage for Boroughbridge on 20 January accompanied by his wife. He left Prue at lodgings in York and set off for Boroughbridge, bearing her strict instructions to avoid the bottle. This was a difficult injunction to follow during an eighteenth-century election. One may be certain that Steele laid out a substantial amount on wine and spirits for the electors during the next several days, and of course Stapylton and his adherents did the same. Steele possessed the great advantage of having on his side two landowners, Clare and Wilkinson, both known by the local citizenry to be determined and ruthless. "I think I shall succeed," he reported to his wife on 27 January. The next day he felt even more sanguine:

Dear Prue:
I obey your directions exactly and avoid drinking and every thing else that might give you any trouble. The Precept for electing members for this place came hither to-day, and the election is to be on Wednesday. It looks with a good face on my side. . . . You and Yours, I fear, will make Me Covetous, I am sure you have made me value Wealth much more than I ever thought I should, but indeed I have a reason which makes it worth the pursuit, It will make me more agreeable to you.

I am indeed Prue Intirely yours
RICHARD STEELE

[7] John Owen, *Britannia Depicta, or Ogilby Improv'd* . . . (London, 1720), p. 18.

By this time, it appears, Steele knew that the bailiff had been won over. On 2 February the poll took place and Steele and Wilkinson were declared elected for Boroughbridge, with Sir Bryan Stapylton third in the ballot count. The following month Stapylton was to enter a complaint with the House of Commons alleging that the successful candidates had employed "threats, etc.," and that the bailiff had "arbitrarily rejected votes for the petitioner, and admitted others for the sitting members, and . . . notwithstanding the said practices, the petitioner was duly elected by a legal majority, and ought to have been returned. . . ." [8] All this may have been true enough, but it was not a good season for Tory petitions; Sir Bryan's complaint was referred to the committee on privileges and elections (of which Steele was a member), and there it remained.

The Whigs had won resoundingly. "So many Whiggs," wrote James Stanhope to Lord Stair, "have not been returned since the Revolution." Among Clare's nineteen candidates, only one failed to be elected. [9] Steele rejoined his wife in York and returned to London, to pay his respects to Lord Clare at the nobleman's magnificent estate, Claremont, in Surrey, and to be present for the opening ceremonies of the new Parliament on 17 March—just one year less a day after his expulsion.

The return was a personal triumph for Steele. Membership in the House satisfied certain persistent emotional longings on his part. No doubt these were in some measure due to a straightforward desire for personal aggrandizement: he wanted to cut a figure in public life. This was the accusation the Tory pamphleteers had leveled against him in the pamphlet campaign the year before. Of course it was partly true, not only of Steele but of

---

[8] Quoted in Thomas Carew, *An Historical Account of the Rights of Elections* . . . (London, 1755), I, 63.

[9] Stanhope quoted in W. T. Morgan (note 5 above), pp. 171–72. Clare's candidates: Stebelton H. Nulle, *Thomas Pelham-Holles, Duke of Newcastle* . . . (Philadelphia, 1931), p. 65. In August, 1715, Clare was created Duke of Newcastle-under-Lyme.

many other politicians of his time and some since. There was more to the matter, however, than Steele's hunger for renown. A smoldering desire to serve in the House of Commons was not a characteristic widespread among Steele's educated contemporaries, most of whom placed a higher value on land and titles. Literary fame, which Steele already possessed in large measure, was the solace of, for example, Alexander Pope and, after the Tories' catastrophe, Jonathan Swift. These men were in any event disabled by religion from serving in Parliament, but others who were not and who served as M.P.'s regarded membership principally as the stepping stone to further rewards. For Steele the House of Commons itself represented both the happy security of a gentleman's club and the guarantor of his social independence. "[I]n the House," he had written in the first number of *The Englishman* (6 October 1713), "and as a Member of Parliament, I am accountable to no Man, but the greatest Man in *England* is accountable to me." The House was, in his view, the most important element in that mixed structure of monarch, nobility, and commons which he and his contemporaries assumed to represent a true description of the national government; the guarantor of independence for subject and sovereign alike. "Her Majesty's Parliamentary Title," *The Crisis* had trumpeted, "is the Ark of God to *Great Britain,* and, like that of Old, carries Death to the profane Hand that shall dare to touch it." This is full-blown Whig rhetoric but Steele believed it, to the depths of his being. As much as any one man, indeed, he had been a creator of Whig rhetoric; more than any he had overseen its dissemination throughout the British Isles and the colonies. This rhetoric had as an initial assumption the sanctity of parliamentary government and thus played a part in reinforcing those convictions which the rhetorician Steele held to begin with.

The House was also the center of varied activity, which Steele's nature required; the bustle and talk of the place appealed to him. He came to enjoy debate in the House, and he assumed a large part in it until his health declined. He was a working member; he received his share of committee assignments and met his responsibilities with reasonable regularity, as is attested by the fact that he continued to be appointed and elected to these committees. Finally, and in this respect he was an unusual member indeed, he undertook to keep his constituency informed by writing weekly newsletters.[10]

It was to be a busy session. The King's address offered no quarter to the defeated Tory leadership and thanked those who had defended the Protestant succession "against all the open and secret practices that have been used to defeat it. . . ."[11] Steele was appointed to the committee to draw up the Commons' address of thanks to the sovereign, which spoke of the House's determination to trace out the sources of the Pretender's hopes and to bring the guilty to "condign punishment." On 9 April the government revealed the means by which it hoped to bring the offenders to the bar: Stanhope moved that day to form a Committee of Secrecy, to carry out the sentiments expressed in the address of thanks by investigating the negotiations for the Treaty of Utrecht. All this amounted to a declaration of war against the former ministry, of course, and on 15 April Bolingbroke threw in his hand and fled the country.

That Steele would have some part in the pursuit of the fallen Tories was a foregone conclusion among the Whigs; he was the most distinguished pamphleteer in their camp. In February his young friend Thomas Burnet was directed by the "higher Powers," as he put it, to publish over his name a most inflam-

[10] Though none of the actual letters have survived, a reference in *Corr.,* p. 101, indicates that he made at least a beginning on this project (the earliest of its kind?). In *The Importance of Dunkirk Consider'd* (1713) he had undertaken to report his conduct to John Snow, the bailiff of Stockbridge, "and at the same time to the whole Borough" (*Tracts,* p. 87).

[11] *CJ,* XVIII, 18. Written by Stanhope, now one of the members for Aldborough, and Walpole, in the opinion of J. H. Plumb. See his *Sir Robert Walpole: The Making of a Statesman* (London, 1956), p. 212.

matory pamphlet, *The Necessity of Impeaching the Late Ministry, In a Letter to the Earl of Hallifax,* in which Burnet
referred to "that honest *Englishman, Mr. Steele."* Steele
would, he hoped, pardon him "if I borrow his Phrase for once,
and assure your Lordship, that the *British Nation expect* the
speedy Impeachment of the late Ministry." Putting into circulation what was to become a favorite Whig jest, Burnet insisted
that the Tory leaders deserved "to be exalted to the *highest
Posts* in the Nation," that is, hanged. The phrase about the
British nation's expectations, borrowed from *Guardian* No.
128, touched a tender point with Daniel Defoe, who remembered Steele's part in the bitter Dunkirk controversy. Defoe
complained, in his pamphlet replying to Burnet's, that "to give
a seeming Weight to their Insolence, every Scribler now has
learnt of *St--l* to speak High, and say the Nation *expects it.*
. . ." [12] The question, then, was not whether Steele would
become involved in the propaganda battle but how soon and in
what way.

Various aspects of the business gave him pause. In the first
place, Steele was not by nature vindictive. In many an essay he
had counseled forgiveness, reconciliation, and brotherly love;
the remorseless punishment of a defeated foe did not appeal to
his temperament. Some of the victims were, moreover, unpleas-
antly well known to him. In opposition it had been enough to
hint of subtle, unnamed manipulators who were leading the
nation to ruin; now it was a question of dealing with persons:
Bolingbroke, Oxford, Ormonde. Bolingbroke was probably
only a nodding acquaintance of his but Steele had been on

[12] *Necessity,* 3d ed. (1715), pp. [5], 33. Eight thousand copies of this tract
were distributed within a few weeks; see *The Letters of Thomas Burnet to
George Duckett, 1712–1722,* ed. D. Nichol Smith (Oxford, 1914), pp. 79–81.
Defoe's pamphlet, printed and sold by the man who was to become Benjamin
Franklin's master, Samuel Keimer, is a remarkably able piece and deserves to
be better known: *Burnet and Bradbury, or the Confederacy of the Press and
the Pulpit for the Blood of the Last Ministry* (London, 1715).

friendly terms with Oxford, and the Duke of Ormonde was the grandson of the great first Duke, "the Memorable and Illustrious Patron" of Steele's infancy. He could not treat these men as abstractions. And then again, if Steele were to undertake journalism on behalf of the party, what would be the compensation for the unpleasant task? Men forget; how many times during the twenty years past had he heard noble lords promise what was never fulfilled? The Junto lords whom he had known and trusted were failing; Halifax died in April, much lamented by Addison, and Wharton in May. The Duke of Marlborough's role in active political life was dwindling to the vanishing point. Nottingham, a Hanover Tory, had assisted in getting Steele the license at Drury Lane when he still possessed some leverage, but this influence was fast disappearing. Would the emergent powers, Walpole, Stanhope, Townshend, Newcastle, deal fairly with Steele? He was full of doubts.

Portents were not favorable. His project for coining farthings had not got beyond the Treasury. On 17 June a parliamentary committee appointed to study the matter reported that the Treasury lords had decided further coinage of farthings and halfpence would be inconvenient, because, they predicted, great quantities of the heavy coppers would turn up in the receipts of the Excise and Post-office.[13] So ended that plan. Some minor patronage had, it is true, fluttered down to him from above: he was named Deputy Lieutenant of County Middlesex, and Surveyor of the Royal Stables at Hampton Court about the end of March.[14] There was a certain ironic congruence to the Stables preferment, which carried a stipend of one hundred and twenty pounds per annum [15] and involved reporting occasionally to the Board of the Works what repairs were needed. Steele had

[13] *CJ,* XVIII, 179.
[14] I have not been able to establish the precise dates of these appointments. *The Evening Post* (Bodleian, Nichols copy) for 26 to 29 March 1715 reports the Surveyorship appointment without a date.
[15] PRO, LS 13/44/21.

acquired a working acquaintanceship with these stables as a trooper in the Life Guards twenty years earlier. The Deputy Lieutenancy signified Steele's political reliability, of which no one had been in doubt, but the post was without direct financial compensation and it could be both expensive and time consuming. In April Steele was called upon in his new capacity by Lord Clare, the Lord Lieutenant, to draw up an Address of Loyalty to the King, for presentation at Court.

The ceremony was not routine, as it might at first appear. In the spring of 1715 the ministry sensed serious trouble ahead. The German King was in point of fact not the object of widespread adulation, and although the Whigs had seized control of the government with commendable efficiency, their very success in the recent general election ensured that there would be disaffected Tories in many parts looking for trouble. Men like Steele's opponent Sir Bryan Stapylton, for example, though out of office still had great influence in the counties and could turn a blind eye when Jacobites raised their standard. Mobs were easily formed in eighteenth-century England, and in the spring of that year some of the rioting had taken an especially ugly turn. It was in this context that Steele drew up the loyal address, in which he assured the King of the zeal and fidelity shared by the several deputy lieutenants: "[W]e solemnly promise, that we will faithfully execute the trust reposed in us; that we will be so far from encouraging or conniving at any of those riots and disorders which your Majesty has justly complained of, as the reproach of some late years, that no endeavours on our part shall be wanting, to prevent and suppress the least tendency to any commotion." [16] A casual reader might be surprised that the deputy lieutenants should think it necessary to assure the sovereign that they would not encourage riots, but these were extraordinary times and the address itself is a meas-

---

[16] Printed in *Corr.*, p. 526.

ure of how far the Whigs thought the situation had gone. The phrase, "the reproach of some late years," represents tact on Steele's part, to avoid revealing that there had been riots in King George's brief but happy reign. As the final step in the charade of loyal sentiments, Steele and the other deputy lieutenants accompanied Clare to St. James's, where the address was presented to the King. On that occasion, 9 April 1715, knighthood was bestowed on Richard Steele.[17]

This must have been a memorable day at No. 26 St. James's Street. If it was a routine event to the great world, it was not so to Richard and Prue. The Irish orphan had become a knight of the realm, the young Welsh woman was now styled Dame Mary. It was Mr. Addison, still, but Sir Richard Steele. Knowing Steele's affection for celebration, we may be sure that every member of the household at No. 26 had a treat of some kind on the ninth of April.

This was, of course, a political reward, and Sir Richard knew it. The knighthood was not bestowed on the essayist and dramatist but on the pamphleteer and Member of Parliament. The theater patent had in some measure represented a reward for his services to literature or at any rate his services to the stage, but he was Sir Richard because he was a Whig, as Jonathan Swift was Dean of St. Patrick's because he was a Tory. The question, in Steele's case, was whether the reward came for services rendered or to be rendered, and over this issue Steele and his new patron had the first of a long series of disagreements, culminating in their final, public quarrel.

From Clare's point of view the knighthood (of which he or Townshend, presumably, had solicited the King through his German advisers) was another step in binding Steele to his interest, the earlier steps having included assistance in securing the seat in Parliament, the deputy lieutenancy, and five hundred

---

[17] *The Evening Post* (Bodleian, Nichols copy), 12 April 1715. Robert Thornhill and George Cook were knighted on the same occasion.

pounds of Royal Bounty. In return for these favors Steele might display his gratitude by taking over a propaganda campaign in support of ministry policy, which greatly wanted supporting. Steele, for his part, looked on this patronage as reward for his faithful service during the last year of Queen Anne's life, service which he had recorded for posterity six months earlier in his *Apology* as "giving an Alarm to all honest Men, and disconcerting the Counsels of Men I thought ready to attempt anything. . . ." [18] He had, he felt, made his position clear to Clare in the letter of 18 December 1714 about the Boroughbridge seat, in which he had promised the nobleman only to behave himself "with strict integrity." But the phrase had a different meaning to the Earl of Clare. It was an arrangement ripe for misunderstanding.

As the spring of 1715 wore on, the political situation became more fragile. While Stanhope's Committee of Secrecy ransacked such of the late ministry's records as they could lay hold of, searching for incriminating statements, riots continued here and there. Ormonde's birthday was celebrated in Tory Oxford by a destructive mob. Thomas Hearne, antiquary and Jacobite, gleefully recorded the event in his diary: "The People run up and down crying King James the 3d, the true King, no Usurper . . . , every one at the same time Drank to a new Restauration. . . ." [19] At this juncture Townshend, secretary of state for the northern department, called on Steele to counter the mood of discontent with a new periodical supporting the ministry's position.

Steele's reply, in a letter to Clare, has been taken as a bill of complaint at his treatment.[20] It is more accurately seen, perhaps, as reflective of his caution in undertaking a difficult business

[18] *Tracts,* p. 286.

[19] *Remarks and Collections of Thomas Hearne,* ed. C. E. Doble *et al.* (Oxford, 1885–1921), V, 62. See also Morgan, "Some Sidelights upon the General Election of 1715," in *Essays,* p. 140.

[20] See above, p. 5, n. 9.

without a clear understanding about compensation. He points out to Clare that in the previous reign he had resigned his sinecures to stand for Parliament and support the Whigs, at a loss, he estimated, of £3,000. Putting it this way, he maintains, is not a demand for the lost income but "a reason why I will never hereafter do more than my part without knowing the terms I act upon. . . ." He would make it evident during the next winter that his accepting the patent for the theater was a great service to the Crown, but as for the journal, "before I enter upon the Argument I hope to receive 500l. or be excused from so painfull, so anxious, and so Unacceptable a Service." Why, Lady Steele no doubt was asking him, should Steele not profit from his fidelity to the Whiggish creed? Robert Walpole, a much greater political figure but no more devoted to the old cause than Steele, was well on his way to enormous wealth.[21] The new paper was to be entirely a party enterprise and why should not the party compensate him with something more negotiable than promises? Still, the letter, with its accent of independence, was not the sort of epistle the Earl of Clare was accustomed to receiving.

It will be noted that Steele separates his patent for Drury Lane from the calculations of profit and loss attributable to politics. He expected much of the theater patent, and much was expected of him. The managers looked to the next season (1715–1716) as an opportunity for recouping, a season for which they had time to lay plans with some care. Steele for his contribution agreed to write "plays & other performances" and to "Sollicite persons of Quality & other persons of distinction to resort" to Drury Lane.[22] The actor-managers would oversee the day-to-day activities but Steele would be in no sense merely a silent partner. He had good friends at Court to assist his solicitations of the quality. Mary Countess Cowper, wife of the Lord Chancellor, with whom Steele had been on friendly

[21] Plumb, *Sir Robert Walpole,* pp. 204–209.
[22] Steele's deposition of 23 June 1726, quoted in Loftis, p. 59.

though properly respectful terms for several years, was lady-in-waiting to the Princess of Wales. She had expressed her pleasure at Steele's appointment in her diary and had accompanied the royal couple in frequent attendance at Drury Lane during their first winter in England. In February 1715 both *The Funeral* and *The Tender Husband* were acted "by His Royal Highness' Command." [23] Receipts at the theater had not recovered fully from the reopening of Lincoln's Inn Fields but Drury Lane was regaining strength—by April so much so that one of the deserting actors, Pack, probably suborned by the rival management, slipped into the first night of Rowe's *Lady Jane Gray* and attempted to break up the performance by "ill-natur'd Gestures and frequent Hissings." [24] The play succeeded despite Pack's attempted sabotage. In fact, taking all in all, the partners at the end of their first season could look back with reasonable satisfaction. Steele had been too taken up with parliamentary business to write plays, but he was succeeding in attracting persons of quality, most especially the Prince and Princess of Wales. Some risk attended even this, however, because, as members of the Court soon discovered, George I disliked and distrusted his son; yet these were shoal waters through which Steele, with Lady Cowper's help, could steer the company if anyone could. Competition between the theaters had hurt profits, but Lincoln's Inn Fields had suffered more than Drury Lane. If the political fever would somehow abate, or not rise further, the managers could look forward to a good season. Considering everything, they decided to redecorate the house and spend more money on the productions in the repertory. [25]

In May Steele was able to realize one of his cherished

---

[23] Steele and Cowper: Rae Blanchard, "Richard Steele and William Lord Cowper: New Letters," *Publications of the Modern Language Association of America,* LXXX (1965), 303–306; *Diary of Mary Countess Cowper . . .* (London, 1864), pp. 46–47. Command performances: *London Stage,* I, 344–45.

[24] *London Stage,* I, 349–50.

[25] Loftis, p. 55.

dreams, when in celebration of the King's birthday (and, though he refrained from advertising this, in celebration of his own knighthood), he supervised the production of an evening's entertainment at his Censorium.[26] Entertainment is not an adequate term, for as Steele planned it this was to be the first of a continuing series for the edification of "a Hundred Gentlemen, and as many Ladies, of leading Taste in Politeness, Wit and Learning." The "Greatest Masters" of both the "Liberal and Mechanick Arts, in Conjunction, and in their Turn" would provide the substance of these evenings which would, Steele asserts, be cheaper than seeing an opera. The project, as has been pointed out, had its roots in the Renaissance, being modeled to some extent on the earlier Continental academies, but Steele's adaptation is marked by his own characteristic flair. It unmistakably possesses what Peter Gay has termed the Enlightenment style.[27] The inclusion of the "mechanic arts" indicated that scientific lectures and demonstrations would have their place along with performances of the fine arts. The fundamental purpose was instructive, as had been that of the *Tatler* and *Spectator;* men and women of leading taste were being taught "what to think." Men *and* women. The champion of education for women continued his advocacy; there must be the same number of ladies in attendance as there were men. Characteristic of Steele but not of his age, certainly, is his depreciation of opera. He is more restrained than in the days of *The Spectator,* because the King was known to be fond of opera, but Steele would fight the barbarous foreign import to the end. Perhaps his evenings of instruction and entertainment would accomplish what the arguments of Mr. Spectator had not been able to do, and put an end once and for all to the mindless fad.

[26] For Steele's earlier efforts on this project, see *CS,* pp. 134–36, 159–60; Loftis, pp. 98–118. Steele describes the Censorium in *Town-Talk* No. 4, printed in *Per. Jour.,* pp. 206–13.

[27] Gay, *The Enlightenment: An Interpretation* (New York, 1966), pp. 10–19; the quotation in Gay's book (p. 41) ascribed to Addison is, however, by Steele.

The entertainment on the evening of 28 May had been a long time coming and had cost Steele an inordinate amount of money. As early as 1713, George Berkeley's eyes had dazzled at the sight of the Great Room in York Buildings which Steele was then preparing for his Censorium. "[M]uch the finest chamber I have seen," is the description Berkeley had used then.[28] Steele had laid out a thousand pounds on refurbishing the room before the death of the Queen,[29] and more was required to put the place in order for the birthday celebration. About thirty-two feet square, the room had a twenty-one-foot ceiling. Upholstered seats were arranged around the room as in an amphitheatre, facing on one side a raised stage for the performers with a gallery opposite the stage "handsomely raild with Iron." [30] There were decorated columns, and the roof and side walls were adorned with painting executed, no doubt, by some of Steele's fellow members in the Academy of Painting. The lighting was placed so as to illuminate not only the lecturers or musicians but the bejeweled auditors as well; they became, as Steele later put it, "a more beautiful Scene than any they have ever before been presented with elsewhere." As he usually did, Steele knew his audience. These people of taste, these Whig aristocrats, would enjoy seeing an assemblage of themselves in the act of leading, a sort of animated conversation piece. If photography had been invented, Steele no doubt would have supplied each guest with a print of the occasion.

There is an anecdote which, though without supporting evidence, has the ring of truth, that tells of Steele's wandering into the Great Room sometime before work was completed, with a

[28] *The Works of George Berkeley Bishop of Cloyne,* ed. A. A. Luce and T. E. Jessop (London, 1948–1957), VIII, 62.

[29] See *Corr.,* pp. 113–15. Professor Loftis is surely correct in dating this letter before July, 1714 (Loftis, pp. 106–107n). The reference to the "Lord Treasurer," a title in disuse after the fall of the Tories, makes it virtually certain that Oxford is referred to and that the letter was written during his ministry.

[30] Described in *The Daily Post* (BM, Burney copy) of 17 August 1724.

theatrical professional's thought of testing the acoustics. He asked the master carpenter, at work with his crew on the interior, to ascend the rostrum placed at one end of the room and speak a few words. The carpenter climbed the steps but found himself tongue-tied, so Steele told him to say whatever came into his head. This reminded the tradesman. "Sir Richard Steele," thundered the carpenter from his commanding post, looking steadily at his auditor, "here has I, and these here men, been doing your work for three months, and never seen the colour of your money. When are you to pay us? I cannot pay my journeymen without money, and money I must have."

"I am in raptures with the eloquence," replied Steele, laughing, "but by no means admire the subject." [31]

Nothing so mundane as a dunning carpenter could be permitted to stand in the way of this important occasion. Musicians were hired, parts assigned, the guest list culled over; every detail was attended to. Admission seems to have been by special medals struck for the occasion, one of which came into the possession of Alexander Pope. [32] Steele was aware of Pope's incipient quarrel with Addison. If Pope was invited, as seems probable, the invitation was not only a recognition of his genius (to which Steele had been one of the earliest to pay tribute) but a gesture in the direction of reconciliation. *Suadere* was the motto of the evening, engraved on the medal, and Steele's thoughts dwelt on persuasion in this attempt at improving the public taste. As his spokesman put it later, in *Town-Talk* No. 4, "Most Men know what is Right, but they are come into the Practice of the contrary, with a certain Acknowledgement of their being in the Wrong, and Contempt of any Plan towards Amendment. For this Reason, it seems to be necessary, that he

[31] Nathan Drake, *Essays, Biographical, Critical, and Historical, Illustrative of the Tatler, Spectator, and Guardian* (London, 1805), I, 179–80.

[32] Sold from Pope's effects at Twickenham in May, 1802, and illustrated in *The Gentleman's Magazine*, Vol. LXII, Part II (1802), opposite p. 705.

who would succeed in this kind of Work, should take off all Severity from the Method he should propose." However quixotic may have been Steele's approach to enlightenment by the route of converting the English aristocracy, he was on—as he often was—to an important issue and his sentiments are by no means contemptible. In the short run Handel was better than bear-baiting, and if in the long run no solution has been found to the problem of "improving the public taste" the fact does not signify that the problem has disappeared. The significant word is "public"; Steele had in mind the spreading of enlightenment, the responsibility of society to see that the benefits of education are diffused.

He was determined not to let this important occasion slip. The prologue spoken by Miss Younger, an actress at Drury Lane, he composed himself, with compliment to the audience and a seasonable reminder of their responsibility: "The Land shall grow Polite from You, who sit/In chosen Ranks, *the Cabinet of Wit.*" [33] There was the required ode in honor of the royal family, there was an ode of Horace set and sung, there were other songs and instrumental numbers. For those of the audience who felt a trifle parched by the evening's cultural altitude there followed a collation: sweetmeats, burgundy, and champagne in profusion. Then the floor was cleared for the assembled Cabinet of Wit to perform country dances. An epilogue making jocular reference to such incidents in Steele's life as his search for the philosopher's stone and the Dunkirk controversy was recited by Wilks, to loud laughter. Steele never begrudged a joke on himself in a good cause, and the final laughter served to take off the severity, as he had suggested. [34]

This birthday celebration was the culmination of years of effort and expense, and the beginning, Steele hoped, of a new instrument of culture. The results did not measure up to his

[33] *Verse,* pp. 69–70, 108.
[34] *Town-Talk* No. 4, in *Per. Jour.,* pp. 206–13; Loftis, pp. 108–10.

grand expectations. Though he retained the Great Room until he left London permanently, in 1724, and though he contrived to provide from time to time entertainment and instruction like that on the King's birthday, he apparently never found his select group of one hundred men and as many ladies who preferred as a steady diet the delights of the Censorium to those of opera or farce.[35]

In the spring of 1715 he had little opportunity to arrange such performances, even if he had been able to collect the subscribers. He was, first of all, active in the management of Drury Lane. Then, sometime after Steele addressed the letter to Newcastle referred to earlier, the ministry met his terms and agreed to pay him five hundred pounds for undertaking a new periodical: reviving *The Englishman* for this occasion demanded thought and action on his part. He had a minor hand in publishing a new anti-Catholic book as part of the anti-Jacobite campaign. And he was deeply immersed in parliamentary business. During the first year of his service in the House he was appointed or elected to more than a dozen committees; one on naturalizing the Palatines (the "poor Palatines," German Protestant refugees on whose behalf Steele had pleaded in *The Tatler*) and one to consider the petition of merchants in sugar, ginger, oil, and sarsaparilla; one on relieving Quakers from the necessity of being sworn in legal proceedings and another to consider the petition of the colonists in South Carolina about Indian attacks.[36] The fare was as varied as that which Steele and Addison had provided in *The Spectator*. Thus, added to his general reluctance to take part in a vendetta against the former government, was the difficulty of finding the hours to edit and publish a new periodical. No one knew better than Steele the amount of mere labor involved in getting out an essay periodi-

[35] Loftis, pp. 115–16, gives evidence that the performances continued after 1721.
[36] *Corr.*, pp. 101, 106; *CJ*, Vol. XVIII, passim.

cal of any quality: the inexorable demands of writing and editing copy, of meeting printers' deadlines, of keeping an eye on distribution and sales. This would be the eighth periodical he had edited.

The ministry was pressing him hard. In May he lent his name to the publication of an anti-Catholic tract, *An Account of the State of the Roman-Catholic Religion throughout the World.* The volume was a sequel to *The Romish Ecclesiastical History of Late Years,* which he had published in May, 1714, and, as in that earlier book, the principal objective was to disable the Jacobites by associating their cause with that of Catholicism and of France. The enterprise was planned with the encouragement of Princess Caroline by Bishop Benjamin Hoadly.[37] That controversial prelate had in fact written the "large dedication to the present Pope" which appeared as the work of Sir Richard Steele. Hoadly's portion is broadly sarcastic, whereas Steele's own preface is temperate and straightforward, as if he felt some apology were needed for the tone of the dedication. Why, it may be asked, did he allow his name to be used as that of the author of the dedication? One conjectures that it was a gesture of loyalty on Steele's part, offered in the hope that he could still somehow avoid the disagreeable task of conducting the new periodical. Pressure was being exerted on Whig writers during the winter and spring of 1715 to announce loyal sentiments over their signature. Thomas Burnet, as has been seen, was forced to append his name to *The Necessity of Impeaching the Late Ministry, In a Letter to the Earl of Hallifax.* It is significant that Halifax agreed to the use of his name as the recipient of that inflammatory pamphlet, whereas he had earlier refused the dedication of Burnet's *A Second Tale of a Tub.*[38] Perhaps this was the price Halifax paid for the

[37] Cf. *CS,* pp. 209–10.

[38] Steele's dedication in *Tracts,* pp. 347–56; for Hoadly's part, see *Corr.,* p. 103. For Burnet and Halifax, see *The Letters of Thomas Burnet to George Duckett, 1712–1722* (note 12 above), pp. 73, 74, 77, 79.

earldom conferred upon him in March. He had begun his career as a writer, too, in partnership with the unfortunate Matthew Prior. Now Prior was one of the objects of Whig vengeance because he had served as a diplomatic representative at the negotiations for the Treaty of Utrecht, the "Tory peace."

There was really no way out for Steele. Sir Robert Walpole presented the report of the Committee of Secrecy on 9 June and the impeachment of Bolingbroke and Oxford was moved on the following day. Bolingbroke had discredited himself in the opinion of many by fleeing, but Oxford remained defiant. During the debate of that day Sir Joseph Jekyll, himself a member of the committee, expressed the opinion that he doubted whether there was sufficient evidence to convict Oxford of treason.[39] The case of Ormonde, who was a military hero in his own right, appeared even more daunting. After everything the Whigs had said about the iniquities of the Tory ministry, it was incumbent on them to back their words with proof, and proof, in the legal definition, was hard to find. A tumultuous spirit was evident in the country; the Austrian envoy, in a report to his government, estimated that two-thirds of the people were hostile to the royal family.[40] When Oxford was conveyed to the Tower on 12 July, having been indicted for high treason, a large crowd surged along the way, shouting "High Church and down with the Whigs." [41] Riots were not difficult to raise in Middlesex, and this one may have been staged, but it was a symptom of the obstacles the ministry faced.

Their bandwagon was being judiciously impeded by Daniel Defoe as well, who had given Richard Steele reason to remember that though Swift had retired to Ireland, the Earl of Oxford did not lack defenders. A pamphlet had recently appeared bearing the title *The Fears of the Pretender Turned into the Fears*

[39] [William] *Cobbett's Parliamentary History of England . . . ,* Vol. VII (London, 1811), p. 67.
[40] Wolfgang Michael, *Englische Geschichte im achtzenhnten Jahrhundert* (Berlin and Leipzig, 1921–1937), I, 488.
[41] HMC, *Portland MSS.,* V, 513.

of Debauchery. Propos'd, without Ceremony, to the Consider-
ation of the Lords Spiritual and Temporal; with a Hint to
Richard Steele, Esq. It is a minor masterpiece of political
pamphleteering. Defoe had defended Oxford's ministry elsewhere, most ably in *The Secret History of the White Staff,*
which, despite Swift's opinion to the contrary, was an effective tract. In the later pamphlet Defoe is on the attack, representing the Whig government as a sordid league of depraved
and vicious men; the Church is in danger from the vices of
the men of power. Steele's role, as portrayed by Defoe, has
been to encourage these vices, principally by "running up the
Humour of following Plays," which "has assisted to Debauch
the Morals of the People, especially about the Court." The
King, the author hopes, will discourage this debauchery and the
"appendices" thereto, *"Masquerades, Balls, Music Meetings,*
and all the Publick Resorts for Diversion." Queen Anne never
encouraged such things.

In a brief pamphlet, Defoe has stimulated the popular suspicion of the Court, contrasted the healthy days of the late
Queen's reign with the vile present, played on the fears of the
Church party, and associated Steele—who is treated with elaborate courtesy—with the noisome stew of the new government.
It is a pamphlet constructed to rouse the unease and ire of all
those who regarded with distaste a court dominated by foreigners, all those who felt that the drama was often indecent, all
those who suspected that the life of the aristocracy was one of
vice and debauchery. These categories, taken together, would
no doubt include a sizable fraction of the English population in
any period. Defoe had chosen the ground for his attack with
skill; his use of innuendo was seldom more effective.[42] It is a

___

[42] The inclusion of *"Music Meetings"* among the "appendices" of debauchery, referring to entertainments like those at the Censorium, provides further
indication that Defoe had Steele specifically in mind and that he knew or had
guessed of Steele's part in the forthcoming attack on Oxford. Defoe, of

nearly perfect example of political writing—sufficient notice for Richard Steele, even if it had not borne his name on the title page, of the difficulties ahead. Nevertheless, performing however reluctantly what he regarded as his duty, Steele began his new periodical on the eleventh of July, the day before Oxford was committed to the Tower.

---

course, genuinely disliked the stage, but in this pamphlet he is using the well-known affection of the Prince and Princess of Wales for the theater as an indication of the general debauchery of Court and ministry. Attendance at the theater by the royal couple had offended pious people, not all of them Puritans.

CHAPTER III

The Englishman and the '15

STEELE BEGAN his new paper by disassociating it from the earlier *Englishman:* "IT may appear unaccountable, that the Title of a Paper which was laid down with the Author's Name to it, should be reviv'd again by an unknown Writer. But to tell the honest Truth . . . this Name is assumed, because the Business of the World at present is much more proper to be considered under that Denomination than any other." So ran the opening lines of the new venture, as if to say that the readers should forget the author and think only of the issues; it seems unlikely that Steele hoped to conceal entirely his association with the paper.[1] It must be remembered that at this moment, in early July, 1715, the sole purpose of the revived *Englishman* was to justify the proceedings against members of the Tory ministry. As news of a full-scale rebellion became known later in the month, Steele's enthusiasm warmed to the changed task, but in the beginning his reluctance showed between the lines.

He had an assistant, presumably to take care of minor clerical work on the paper: making fair copies of the manuscript, seeing the paper through the press, proofreading, and so on. He was Leonard Welsted, a lesser man of letters who had sought Steele's attention by publishing in November, 1714, *An Epistle*

[1] Young Dudley Ryder identified the first number as "Steele's *Englishman*" in his diary. See *The Diary of Dudley Ryder, 1715–1716,* ed. William Matthews (London, 1939), p. 58 (under date of July, 1715).

to Mr. Steele, on the King's Accession to the Crown, in which he predicted that the new King's gratitude would shower upon those like Steele: "His skilful choice shall give Preferment grace,/ And with peculiar beauty Honours place." Welsted was responsible for many couplets of the same quality. American readers may remember him for his idiosyncratic views on learning, which, he felt "hereafter may possibly take her Flight into *America,* settle there, and flourish in that new-discovered World, even among Nations as yet unknown to us." [2] He is best recalled, however, for a brief appearance in the *Dunciad.* Beer, wrote Pope, was Welsted's inspiration and communicated its essence to his verse: "Tho' stale, not ripe; tho' thin, yet never clear."

Steele was very busy. The intention was that he would follow the course of the debates in Parliament and would lend support to the ministry as occasion demanded, in successive numbers of the paper. This required his constant attendance at Westminster for the sessions of Parliament, which often lasted into the late night. Since the paper was to appear twice weekly, writing the copy itself must have absorbed whatever time he had to spare. Consider the sequence of events: The second issue appeared on Friday, 15 July. The next day, Saturday, a committee from the House of Commons, to which Steele was appointed, was ordered to draft an address to the King on the necessity of the Riot Bill, the committee meeting at 5:00 P.M. On Monday the committee reported its bill out (and Steele published the third *Englishman*); on Wednesday the Royal Assent was given to the Act, and on Friday, 22 July, Steele published *Englishman* No. 4. This paper made mention of the civil disturbances and underscored the news that the government had intelligence of an invasion planned by the Pretender.

---

[2] From his critical treatise, the dedication to *Epistles, Odes, etc. Written on Various Subjects . . .* (London, 1724), p. xii.

Stanhope had received this information as recently as Wednesday, so Steele must have written his paper late Wednesday or Thursday after the sessions of the House. A busy week.

Most annoying to Steele, the ministry had still not shown him the color of their money. He kept the paper going by using his credit with Samuel Buckley, the printer, and, one assumes, with Welsted. Some people were buying the paper, an average of 382 customers for each issue in July, increasing to about 467 per issue in August as excitement mounted about the Pretender's invasion. This was enough to break even, but only just so;[3] no fortune would be made on this paper. Lady Steele, meanwhile, reminded him that their income would scarcely support their standard of living. Every weekday morning twenty or thirty creditors would gather at No. 26 St. James's, where they were always admitted most courteously to the entrance hallway. An argument regularly ensued among them as to who should have the right of approaching Steele first. "Till at last perhaps they inquire for Sir Richard and they are told he has been gone out these three hours. Or if he is caught coming downstairs they find him to be sure engaged in some very deep and earnest discourse with a friend that comes down with him, by which means he passes through the clamours of the multitude of duns without hearing a word they say."[4] He had nothing to reply. Except for his share of the Drury Lane profits and the tiny stipend of the Surveyor, they were living on the income from Prue's Welsh properties—and expectations. At the moment, though, Steele had good leverage for enforcing his contract with the ministry: he informed Townshend that he wanted to stop writing the paper and he wrote Clare of his decision. "I find that care of me is not to be taken, except I pass through sollicitations, which will take up more of my time, and

---

[3] Buckley's account in Aitken, II, 70–71n. Not located at Blenheim in 1966.
[4] *Diary of Dudley Ryder*, p. 368. Ryder apparently was told the story by Cornelius Wittenoom, a vinegar merchant.

quiet of mind than it is Worth." It was a bluff but it worked. The ministry needed, or believed it needed, the support Steele's paper could provide. Steele needed money. In August five hundred pounds was paid Leonard Welsted "without account: for our especiall service," for delivery to Steele from funds allocated to the Committee of Secrecy.[5] The impecunious husband relayed the news to his wife on 14 August by a letter addressed from the Speaker's Chambers.

> Dear Prue
>   I write this before I go to Ld Marleborough's to let You Know that there was no one at the Treasury but Kelsey, with Whome Welsted left the Order and He is to be at the Treasury again to-morrow between two and Three when, without doubt, the money will be payd. I have no hopes from that or any thing else but by Dint of Riches to get the government of y^r Ladyship.
>   Yrs
>   RICHARD STEELE

The outbreak of the rebellion put a different face on matters, as far as he was concerned. Instead of harrying defeated politicians, his task was now that of sounding the alarm. Bolingbroke had become the Pretender's Secretary of State, and by that action stood convicted of the charges against him, or so it seemed to Steele. In No. 7, for 1 August 1715, speaking much in his own voice, he addresses a note of warning to those not named in the indictments but who were associated with the late government, whom he terms collectively the "Parricides." He has Matthew Prior in mind and perhaps Jonathan Swift as well. He wishes, he writes, "they had Spirit enough to own what their own Hearts say to themselves . . . , that they were deceived and ensnared by the *Parricides*. . . . The pestilence is broke out upon the *Parricides;* it is impossible for their Friends

[5] *Calendar of Treasury Books,* ed. William Shaw (London, 1957), Vol. XXIX, Part II, p. 692. Money order dated 22 August.

to cure them, but they are sure to dye with them, if they abide any longer with them." Steele risked reprisal from his own employers for deviating from the root-and-branch condemnation agreed on by the Whig leadership, but did he ever speak to less effect? Was anything less likely to bring about repentance and remorse in Matthew Prior and Jonathan Swift than this exhortation, in biblical phraseology, from Richard Steele? He was carried away, it appears, by an exaggerated sense of his importance. He had enforced his contract with the Whig leadership, it is true, but this by no means signified that he was in a position to dictate party policy. From the ministry's point of view he was a useful writer, given to making trouble from time to time as writers generally do. Prior and Swift no doubt knew this better than Steele; for a year they had been learning the loser's side of the game.

Having characterized some of the Tories as misguided, Steele took his stand on the Duke of Ormonde's case and refused to condemn him at all. Personal associations with the Butlers were woven into the fabric of Steele's life: the first duke had known his grandfather in the court of Charles I, had secured preferment for his father, had found young Richard Steele a place at Charterhouse. The second duke had been his commanding officer when Steele had gone down from Oxford to join the Life Guards. In his paper, however, Steele defends Ormonde on public grounds: he was a soldier and had done what he was ordered to do. He "was not obliged to dive into the Motives of his Orders, but believed what he did was for the Good of his Queen and his Country. If he was so weak as to believe it, still he believed it, and the first Part of Treason, the evil Mind, is thereby not to be found." Let him, Steele advises, be punished by dependence on "an insolent and ingrateful Court for Bread."

This public defense of a man whom they were attempting to convict of treason the ministry must have thought somewhat extreme, on the part of a writer who was about to receive five hundred pounds for conducting a propaganda journal. Steele tempered his independence by consenting to print in the next number a letter of rebuttal but as late as the ensuing month, in No. 21, he still distinguished Ormonde's guilt from that of the other accused. Balancing the accounts to some extent, Steele paid a call on the Duke of Marlborough and in *Englishman* No. 12 presented what he termed a "sketch" of the Duke's character. That is to say, it was presumably intended as a preliminary study for the full-length portrait in a biography. Because Steele had spent a generous part of his career as a journalist extolling Marlborough, the essay is interesting both for what it says and for what it fails to say. As far as can be discovered, this was the first occasion upon which Steele had actually met his hero face to face in conversation. The interview took place at Marlborough House—Blenheim was not yet ready for the Duke and Duchess—and the strain upon the portraitist was evidently very great. Marlborough, the reader is informed, "is a person of the most exemplary Modesty. . . . His Manners are so gentle, and he enters so easily into ordinary Life, that a Man who had not a fine Taste would wonder he should ever have supported a Command; and a Man of Understanding would be as much astonished that he should ever have met with Opposition." Marlborough, that is, was courteous to his admirer and did not tell him much. Steele goes on to recount the iniquities of the Tory ministry in sacrificing Marlborough; "parricides" is the term he uses, once again. Steele's choice of the term reminds us how important Marlborough had seemed to him as a paternal figure: it had been Swift's attack on the Duke which caused Steele to put a full stop to their friendship. Swift had professed himself puzzled by the strength of Steele's feelings about Marlborough. It is worth reflection, however, that no single individual ever attracted Swift's wrath over so extended a period of time as Marlborough—and there were many who earned his animosity more than the Duke, who went from one year to another without mentioning Swift's name. It is suggested here that the intensity of feeling toward Marlborough, with Swift as with Steele, did not emerge simply from political events but had psychological roots extending deep into their characters. Both men had been left fatherless orphans.

Emotion, in the case of Steele, got in the way of the biographer's art. He had not developed the habit Boswell would bring to perfection, of objectifying, describing, and analyzing his own feelings; Marlborough's presence stuns him. "[The] *Reader,*" he comments unhelpfully at the end of his sketch, "may form to himself the Shades and Lights that are necessary to set the whole Figure in its proper View. . . ." On the other hand, working with the Duchess looking over one's shoulder, as it were, would not have been easy under the best of circumstances. Sarah had pronounced views on this subject as on almost everything else: a biography, she later stipulated, was to begin with the precise phrase, "I write the History of the Duke of Marlborough," and to continue with nothing but "short plain facts." [6]

As the summer of 1715 lengthened toward autumn and news of the rebellion reached London, it became apparent that proving the guilt or innocence of the Tory ministry was a matter of declining importance. Ormonde and Bolingbroke were with James in France; Oxford was safely locked up in the Tower. Civil war was at hand, and Steele straightway turned the paper toward the Whigs' most telling argument: James's Catholicism. Many of the lower clergy distrusted Whigs and were sympathetic to the Stuart cause, many ordinary Englishmen thought highly of the House of Stuart and had no regard for the German Hanoverians, but nothing like a majority could possibly be assembled in favor of a Catholic sovereign. Boling-

[6] David Green, *Sarah Duchess of Marlborough* (London, 1967), p. 298.

broke knew this and had attempted to persuade James that he should renounce his religion, if only in public. Fortunately for the Hanoverians, James was a man of principle, whatever his failings as a politician.

Pointing to the dangers of accepting a Catholic sovereign was an undertaking in which Steele had had experience and which he could conduct with zest. His fellow countryman George Berkeley observed to a friend that August: "What advantage some great men here out of employ may purpose from the Pretender's coming among us, they best know; but it is inconceivable what shadow of an advantage an Irish Protestant can fancy to himself from such a revolution." [7] In October Steele served as a Steward of the Irish Protestants residing in London, to organize an anniversary observance of the Confederate uprising in 1641. That had been the year, it will be remembered, in which the family of Steele's grandfather were trapped in Ballinakill during the siege. The Reverend Jonathan Smedley, a fire-breathing Whig parson, preached the anniversary sermon in Steele's parish church, St. James's, Westminster, and Steele gave the sermon a favorable notice in *Englishman* No. 34.[8] Steele has little new to say about Popery and the Pretender—it was a theme as worn by then as the demolition of Dunkirk had been two years earlier—but he tries to breathe life into the subject with letters to the editor, such as that of "Convert Hearty" in No. 33, who is a spy or deserter, according to Steele, from the enemy's camp. One issue (No. 29) is devoted to demonstrating that Roman Catholics are greater heretics and more dangerous than the Turk, but this, too, was a commonplace. Elsewhere (No. 30) he enjoins the "Worthier Sort" of English Catholics to remain loyal. More controversial

[7] *The Works of George Berkeley Bishop of Cloyne,* ed. A. A. Luce and T. E. Jessop (London, 1948–1957), VIII, 90.

[8] Smedley, later Dean of Killala, is generally held to be the author of works severely critical of Swift, collected as *Gulliveriana* (1728).

is his paper (No. 35) criticizing the English clergy who have
"suggested false Fears to the Multitude. . . ." "They loudly
pronounced the Church in Danger, when no Man else saw it;
they are silent now all the rest of the World acknowledge it."
Steele was an Erastian by conviction; it seemed to him natural
that a clergyman should be bound by his oaths of allegiance in
the same manner as a soldier, and that both soldier and parson
were subordinated to the legally constituted government. Many
clergymen found a problem where Steele saw none. What, they
asked, if the government by a policy of toleration for Dissent
were undermining the very institution of the Church itself? As
it became clear under Whig administrations that no priest who
had not been firm for the Hanoverian succession would receive
the miter, a large number of the lower clergy found their
ambitions effectively stifled. They raised the legitimate point
that this demonstrated the subjection of the Church to a party.
To a considerable extent this was true; Walpole later refined to
an art the process of selecting bishops who were politically
reliable. The men who became bishops by this route were in
many cases old friends of Richard Steele's. William Fleetwood,
White Kennett, Benjamin Hoadly: these he regarded as men of
sound learning and sound politics, tried and true over the years.
When they received preferment he rejoiced as sincerely as Swift
lamented.

   After September, 1715, little or nothing was written in *The
Englishman* about the original purpose of the paper, that is,
presenting the government's case against Oxford, Bolingbroke,
Ormonde, and Strafford. Several times, however, Steele refers
to the change of government in 1710, which brought in Harley
and St. John, as they were then, at the expense of the Godol-
phin-Marlborough-Junto Whig coalition. Swift, in Ireland,
was just now setting down his own recollections of the period:
*Memoirs, relating to That Change which happened in the
Queen's Ministry in the Year 1710,* and the continuation, *An
Enquiry into the Behaviour of the Queen's last Ministry.* Dur-

ing Queen Anne's lifetime Swift had petitioned for the post of historiographer royal; he was concerned to keep accounts settled, as he read them, for the sake of posterity. Steele, on the other island, was at that very time presenting material in his paper which supplements Swift's version. Swift, for example, describes how Harley persuaded the Queen that "she ought gradually to lessen the exorbitant power of the Duke and Duchess of Marlborough, and the Earl of Godolphin, by taking the disposition of employments into her own hands." [9] Swift goes on to relate how the Duke of Shrewsbury was removed while Godolphin was out of town and the removal presented to him on his return as an accomplished fact. Steele prints for the first time, in No. 32, the text of the letters that passed between the Queen and Godolphin in which the first minister warns the Queen: you are "suffering yourself to be guided to your own Ruin and Destruction, as fast as it is possible for them to compass it. . . ." Godolphin's example, Steele comments, is that of "Publick Spirit in a degenerate Age." Swift would have interpreted the letters differently. A conjecture is that the Duchess of Marlborough supplied Steele these important documents as part of the projected biography of her husband. At any rate, in 1715 Swift and Steele were re-enacting in their imagination, as it were, the events that five years earlier had doomed their friendship and changed their lives.

The defeat of a Jacobite army at Preston in early November signaled the beginning of the end for the rebels. With the prospect of another session of Parliament and a new season at Drury Lane before him, Steele ended the second *Englishman*'s life with the thirty-eighth number on 21 November 1715, discovering a final opportunity to warn his readers once again about the danger of indifference. If one assumes that the rebellion increased sales somewhat during the last two months of the

---

[9] Swift, *Political Tracts, 1713–1719*, ed. Herbert Davis and Irvin Ehrenpreis (Princeton, 1953), p. 116. Swift's memorial to the Queen requesting the post of historiographer is on p. 200.

paper's existence, then Steele realized a small profit over and above the five hundred pounds paid by the ministry.[10] The series had displayed sparks of imagination here and there, but only sporadically; in general it had the appearance of scissors-and-paste construction. Addison was to show greater verve in his new periodical, *The Freeholder,* which began publication in December. Steele had done his duty; apart from his tender treatment of Ormonde, the ministry had got what it paid for. Dudley Ryder, indeed, pronounced the paper "a very good antidote against that lukewarmness and coolness that appears in some people," but Steele was preaching, in Ryder's case, to the converted.[11]

Steele's principal role as a public spokesman during the rebellion of the '15 had been to reiterate and underline the legality of King George's title. The government proceeded with considerable effectiveness against overt rebellion: suppressing riots here and dispersing mobs there, sending the army to intercept organized bands of rebels. What force could do, force did; it was Steele's task to persuade those whom he could reach through his writing that not only might but right was on the Hanoverian side. Though the ministry prosecuted Jacobite propagandists when they could locate them, some effective opposition pamphlets appeared, one of the best being a reply to Steele's *Crisis* of the preceding year, entitled *A Letter to Richard*

---

[10] Buckley's accounts (Aitken, II, 70–71) show that an average of 920 copies per number were printed in July (against 382 average sold) and an average 757 printed in August against an average 467 sold. The printing operation was, that is, being adjusted to a more economical level and, although Steele owed £8 6s. at the end of August, the break-even point had been reached. Sales of 467 would yield approximately £2 18s., less approximately 19s. for the stamp tax and (Buckley's figure) £1 per number for paper and printing. Theoretically, the paper should have broken even at sales of precisely 240 per issue, assuming zero distribution costs, with a cost per sheet of one penny for paper and printing, and halfpence for the tax stamp. Breaking even at this low sales figure was an important element in the burgeoning popularity of the essay periodical.

[11] *Diary of Dudley Ryder,* p. 58.

Steele, Esq. This was a vigorous attack on the legality of William's title, and an affirmation that the oaths taken for James II were still binding. The tract, by "Philo-Basilius" (the name of course echoes the famous *Eikon Basilike*), was circulated surreptitiously.[12] The author hits at Steele's Lockeian assumption that government is for the convenience of the governed. "For if . . . People at first chose Kings to secure themselves from that *Confusion,* which naturally arises from *Equality,* then they may lay them aside for *Convenience* too, and erect any other sort of Government they shall think fit." Philo-Basilius, who asserts the divine origin of monarchy, has laid bare a possible consequence of Whiggery: the decline of monarchy, but Steele, as a Whig spokesman associated with the government of England, could not easily deal with such explosive material.[13]

There were many such tracts, but this was an especially able one and the government worked strenuously to run the printer and author to earth. In a proclamation of 25 July the principal Secretary of State offered a hundred-pound reward for information leading to the conviction of those responsible. The justices of the Middlesex Quarter Sessions Court expressed their corporate concern that "several . . . disorderly persons disaffected to his Majestie's government, in the public street, and also in the coffee houses, expose to sale many seditious books and pamphlets. . . ." The high constable was directed to be vigilant and to report in writing the success of his inquiries on the first day of every session.[14] A typical punishment meted out

[12] See *Englishman,* pp. 464–65.

[13] See the discussion of John Trenchard and Richard Gordon in Caroline Robbins, *The Eighteenth-Century Commonwealthman* (Cambridge, Mass., 1959), pp. 115–25.

[14] Middlesex Record Office, Court of Quarter Sessions Book, No. 732, p. 72 (Sessions of April, 1715). The printer and publisher of *A Letter* were discovered to be Edmond Powell and Thomas Atkins, and Henry Cheap was found guilty of having written it. See *Englishman,* p. 465. As Professor Blanchard indicates there, the true author was probably not discovered.

to those expressing agreement with Philo-Basilius was that given Thomas Nightingale, who was convicted of "wishing damnation to the King": he was to be fined three shillings fourpence, then to be stripped naked to the waist and whipped "till his body be bloody," then placed on good behavior for a year.[15] Steele was involved with these matters of crime and punishment in his capacity as Deputy Lieutenant of Middlesex, but he was much more concerned to counter the effects of Jacobite propaganda. In *Englishman* No. 22 (23 September 1715) he replied, over his own signature, to Philo-Basilius. His answer was evidently composed with great care. A society, Steele contends, is not bound to submit to its own ruin. "It is as if it should be said, That the Nature of a Guardianship requires, that the Children, for whose Good it was settled, must, without Limitation, submit, should a Guardian sell them to the Slavery of the Galleys." It was under such circumstances, with society facing total ruin, that the Prince of Orange came into England. James having fled to France, his departure "gave the *English* Nation Opportunity to say he Abdicated. . . ." The question of King William's title concerns only those who had attained majority before his accession; those who have come to manhood since are bound by the Revolution settlement. Steele gives a little ground to make good his final point, the legality of the present King's title: "King *William's* Title was partly his own Act; and his Arms and his Policy being employ'd in arriving at it, make the Glorious Work liable to Misinterpretations and Exceptions: But King *George* had no part in the Transaction which led him to the Throne, but accepts of an offered Crown for the Safety of Nations, which consulted their own Interest only in calling him to it." Steele is far indeed from supporting the divine origins of monarchy; his emphasis rests on the parliamentary gift of power, the crown offered to the new

[15] M.R.O., Sessions Book, No. 743, p. 50.

King. In the next number he briefly recapitulated his arguments and in No. 24 presented a jocular reply to Philo-Basilius,
in the form of a letter to the paper by one T.S. T.S. agrees with
Philo-Basilius that a king's title should go back to Adam but
reports difficulty in tracing the descent that far. Steele meanwhile was collecting several public addresses and a letter from
the Earl of Mar to the King for republication with *Englishman*
No. 22 as a sixpenny pamphlet entitled *The British Hero*. A
few days later, about 30 September, he published his most
important pamphlet of the year, *A Letter from the Earl of Mar
to the King, Before his Majesty's Arrival in England*. It was in
some sense his final answer to Philo-Basilius and the Jacobites.

The Earl of Mar had supported the Union in 1707 and was
in office as Secretary of State for Scotland at the time of Queen
Anne's death. On the sixth of September, 1715, he began the
rebellion by raising the standard on the Braes of Mar and
announcing to his tenants that their "rightful and natural King
James" had entrusted him with the command of his forces in
Scotland, sent to relieve their oppressions. Steele places this zeal
for the House of Stuart in a curious perspective by printing
Mar's manifesto in a column parallel to a letter he had written
just a year earlier to King George, who was at that time in
Holland on his way to England. Steele has, he writes, Mar's
original letter in his custody for the perusal of anyone who may
care to see it. It is a damning letter. "Your Majesty," Mar had
written to King George only twelve months earlier, "shall ever
find me as faithful and dutiful a Subject and Servant as ever
any of my Family have been to the Crown. . . . As your
Accession to the Crown hath been quiet and peaceable, may
Your Majesty's Reign be long and prosperous. . . ." [16] The
case of Mar, who had taken the oaths of allegiance and abjura-
tion, is much worse than that of the nonjurors, Steele asserts;

[16] Printed in *Tracts*, pp. 357–71.

because it casts doubt on the sincerity of all those who have taken the oaths, it attacks the mutual faith by which society exists. He recommends on the subject "a little pamphlet called, *Advice to the Tories who have taken the Oaths.* . . ." Though Steele does not identify him, the author of the pamphlet was George Berkeley.[17] Mar has laid aside his private faith and his public obligation and is now in rebellion against the king he has sworn to defend, working to introduce James, whom he has abjured under oath.

The publication of *The British Hero* (the title recalling Steele's famous *Christian Hero*), *A Letter from the Earl of Mar,* the *Account of . . . the Roman-Catholic Religion,* and the second series of *The Englishman* constituted Steele's considerable propaganda efforts during 1715 on behalf of the new regime. Though he undertook editing and writing the periodical with reluctance, when it appeared that his principal task would be to bring the former ministry to the bar, his concern increased with the realization that an invasion was underway; his writing during the late summer and autumn catches some of the tension of the times. He was, it bears repeating, unusually close to the day-to-day concerns of the government by reason of his service in a busy Parliament and his post as a Deputy Lieutenant of Middlesex. The regime was threatened from within and without; Steele found himself again, in a sense, in opposition. His mood and prose style always improved at the prospect of a struggle. Disorder might prevail elsewhere but not in Boroughbridge, he assured the King in a loyal address from the freeholders he represented. "Let treachery and imposture try their fate; let our adversaries contend for the glory of being successful traitors and prosperous enemies to their Country;

---

[17] See *Works,* ed. Luce and Jessop, VI, 49–65. Two London editions of Steele's tract, as well as one each in Edinburgh and Glasgow, all bearing date of 1715, have been noted. Publication was probably assisted by the ministry. See *Tracts,* p. 644.

while all honest men resolve to vindicate themselves from the infamy of transmitting chains to their posterity." [18]

He was not getting younger, though, and the wear and tear of politics and journalism caused him to long, from time to time, to leave Westminster, to throw up committee work and printers' deadlines and debates in the House. In September Thomas Burnet, the Master of the Charterhouse, died. Burnet, author of the celebrated *Sacred Theory of the Earth,* had been Master during Steele's days at the school. Steele put forward his candidacy for the post in a letter to Lord Cowper; the necessary qualities as he envisioned them for a Master were humaneness and "such a Tast of letters as may influence the Education of the Youth in that School." If this had indeed been all that was required for election, the prospects for Steele's appointment might have been good. He was, however, a well-known, indeed a notorious, Whig and the successful candidate required eight affirmative votes from a board of twelve governors most of whom were in the Tory interest. He was not a clergyman, as the Master traditionally had been, and he was married. In the face of these disabilities, Steele addressed persons who might be able to influence the election and went so far as to petition the King himself, ending one draft of the petition "et ce sera la dernier faveur qu'il demandera à Votre Majesté," but then he thought again and crossed out the explicit phrase. His candidacy generated interest in the press and hostile pamphleteers seized on it as another example of presumptuousness. Realizing the obstacles in his way, Steele withdrew his name before the election in November, at which the Reverend John King, chaplain at the Charterhouse, was voted Master.

Steele has been belabored so unanimously from his own day to ours for his temerity at seeking the post that one almost hesitates to point out that he was genuinely interested in educa-

---

[18] Printed in *Corr.,* pp. 527–28.

tion, as his many periodical essays on the subject attest, and that the qualities he mentioned to Lord Cowper, especially humaneness, are not undesirable ones in the head of a charitable and educational foundation. Can one be certain that the life of the pensioners was more comfortable, the education of the students more imaginative and humane under the mastership of the Reverend John King than would have been the case under the mastership of Sir Richard Steele? At any rate, the gates of the Charterhouse were closed to him.

CHAPTER IV

Town-Talk

THOUGH HE ended *The Englishman* in November, Steele was still living and supporting his family in the public world, the world of politics, journalism, and the theater. The attempted escape to Charterhouse Square had failed. His post in the royal household, as surveyor of the stables at Hampton Court, required little attention.[1] George I resided in seclusion, providing no encouragement for attendance at Court.[2] The new theater season opened at Drury Lane on 13 October, with a refurbished house, new costumes, and new settings; much was expected by the managers. Both *The Tender Husband* and *The Funeral* were produced during the first month but it was to be a disappointing season from the standpoint of profits. The uncertainty of the political situation perhaps contributed to the declining take; competition from Lincoln's Inn Fields certainly did.[3] Steele's duties as a manager included, it will be remembered, soliciting "persons of quality and other persons of distinction"

---

[1] Presumably resulting from one of Steele's surveys was the report by the Master of the Horse to the Board of Works on 4 July 1715 that "a great part of the buildings belonging to his Majesty's Stables are very much decayed and in an ruinous condition." *Calendar of Treasury Books,* ed. William Shaw (London, 1957), Vol. XXIX, Part II, p. 611.

[2] John M. Beattie, *The English Court in the Reign of George I* (Cambridge, 1967), p. 261.

[3] The profit for the entire season was only £878, of which Steele received one-fifth, to be compared with £3,600 in 1713–1714 (*London Stage,* I, 327, 367). Steele assisted in an undertaking to import two new actors from France; see Loftis, pp. 61–63.

to resort to Drury Lane. The actor-managers appreciated the power of Steele's pen. It may be that they asked him to resume writing on their behalf; at any rate he probably acquainted them with plans for his new periodical, to appear in December, 1715, and to be called *Town-Talk. In a Letter to a Lady in the Country.*

The new paper, designed, as he told John Hughes, "to be helpful to the stage," was a weekly. Even with Welsted's assistance, Steele may have felt it prudent to undertake a less demanding publication schedule. For *Town-Talk* he abandoned the trusted medium of the folio half-sheet and turned instead to the quarto pamphlet, to be sold for threepence.[4] The author of the periodical, who is not named, agreed to write his correspondent once a week, sending the news, that is, the chit-chat, of the preceding seven days. It would not be a newspaper as such, though it would carry news of theatrical events from Drury Lane. Steele immediately made good on his obligation to the theater by recommending a forthcoming production of *Hamlet*. The strange story of a blind gallant, also in the first number, may have been derived from the plot of a play he had read or heard discussed by the other managers. A legitimate topic for the paper, Steele judged, was theater reform. Part of the promised reform at Drury Lane was to be the production of works of artistic merit and in this respect the managers were at liberty to proceed with their plans: Otway's *Venice Preserved* and *Hamlet* were produced in December, followed by *Othello* in January and a total of eight more Shakespearean plays during the season. Later in the year, under a cloak of anonymity, the company would offer Addison's comedy *The Drummer*. The

---

[4] The nine numbers were paginated continuously, with the presumed intention of simplifying the publication of a "collected edition," which, however, did not appear. This is a very early, if not the earliest, instance of a new method of serial publication. It is of further interest that the first number was printed by Burleigh (against a favorable balance remaining in Steele's *Englishman* account?), whereas the rest were printed by J. Roberts.

production of Addison's play was in accordance with another aspect of reform, as described in *Town-Talk* No. 2, that is, encouragement of good living writers by presenting careful performances of their plays and by allowing them fair remuneration so as "to engage them steadily and heartily" in the interests of Drury Lane. Just compensation for the author was a cause that Steele always supported, but it was not a sentiment that found favor among theater managers generally. As the playwrights complained during the next several years, little came of Steele's hopes to reform the theater by encouraging new talent.[5] A third aspect of theater reform mentioned in the paper was that of theatrical independence. Steele and his fellows imagined that his patent represented a guarantee of freedom of action for the managers, and he reprinted the entire patent in *Town-Talk* No. 6. The patent, as has been pointed out, was a document in the movement toward stage reform but it did not ensure independence for the management. Among other requirements, the Crown stipulated "[T]hat, for the future, Our Theatre may be Instrumental to the Promotion of Virtue, and Instructive to Human Life, We do hereby Command and Enjoyn, That no New Play, or any Old or Revived Play be Acted under the Authority hereby Granted, containing any Passages or Expressions offensive to Piety and good Manners. . . ."[6]

Another instrument for improving public taste was Steele's Censorium, to which he alludes in No. 4 and No. 7. In the ninth paper he discusses Addison's *The Drummer* without identifying the author, who, he writes, "pleases you in every Part of it, but neglects to make you laugh in any." All in all, Steele's

---

[5] Loftis, pp. 84–91, presents a helpful discussion of the probable reasons for this: the difficulties of including new plays in the offering of a repertory company that presented fifty to seventy different plays a season; the dearth of genuine talent among the dramatic writers; and, most importantly, the competition from Lincoln's Inn Fields and the Haymarket, which strongly inhibited the managers from taking risks on new plays.

[6] *Per. Jour.*, p. 231; Loftis, pp. 46–47.

efforts in *Town-Talk* were primarily on behalf of Drury Lane. This was the time to promote the theater, for the patent was now his major source of income and he was desperately short of money.

There was simply no money coming into the Steele household beyond the rents from Prue's inherited property in Wales and the trickle of profits from Drury Lane, and the merchants and grocers, farriers and wigmakers met as usual at the entrance of No. 26 St. James's Street. During December and January the weather turned bitter cold, colder than it had been since the winter of 1709. As in that earlier time the Thames was frozen bank to bank and booths were set up on the ice in another winter "fair." In those days long gone Steele had looked forward to the future with confidence: he was in regular employment as gazetteer in 1709, he had the perquisites and pension of Gentleman Waiter, and the idea of *The Tatler* was germinating in his mind. He had then, furthermore, very little position to maintain, which may have been annoying but was certainly cheaper. In the winter of 1715–1716, on the other hand, he was encumbered with titles but, apart from the theater patent, his posts produced scant revenue. He was paying for the leases and upkeep of the house in St. James's, which his position demanded, and of the rooms in York Buildings as well. He had his country retreat, a house in rural Chelsea.[7] His outlook was less sanguine than it had been seven years earlier, but perhaps more philosophic. As 1716 approached, he noted in *Town-Talk* No. 2, "Every Body is preparing to repeat with fresh Vigour in the New Year the Follies and Vanities which make up the Account of the Old one."

The mood was disenchanted. Addison had vowed not to accept employment at a salary of less than one thousand pounds and on the twentieth of December 1715 had received appoint-

---

[7] For the traditions of its exact location (Paradise Row or Cheyne Walk), see *Corr.*, p. 314.

ment as a commissioner of trade and plantations at just that sum.[8] In *Town-Talk* No. 4 Steele describes the conversation of a gentleman "particularly Nice in his Discerning." The description and the sentiments expressed by the gentleman fit Addison, who, until his recent appointment, had undergone what his biographer calls a "year of bitterness." Men, said the gentleman, should practice only those virtues appropriate to their character and circumstances, for the wealthy take secret offense against those who contend that there are qualities superior to wealth and "contemn and suppress Men of low Fortunes, who have Qualities that would better befit the Condition of their Superiors." If it was Addison who made this observation, Steele was in humor to agree with him. But he was not prepared to give up the struggle. He wrote Dear Prue on the tenth of January:

> I have that in my Pockett which within a few days will be a great sum of money, besides what is growing at the Play-House. I prefer your ease to all things. I begg of you to send for Coals and all things necessary for this Week, and Keep Us only to the end of it out of [your] Abundance, and I shall ever add to it hereafter instead of attempting to diminish it. I cannot indeed get money immediately without appearing most scandalously indigent which I would avoid for the future.
>
> Ever Yrs,
RICHARD STEELE

Anxiety about money was beginning to sap even Steele's large reserves of good humor and self-confidence, and Prue was not making the situation easier. What Steele referred to as having in his pocket were two new pamphlets. He was determined to work his way out of their financial troubles. However envious he may have been of Addison's lucrative appointment, he kept

[8] Smithers, p. 331.

the feeling to himself and recommended *The Freeholder* in *Town-Talk* No. 4 as "Entertaining, Honest, and Instructive."

The pamphlets Steele had written were in answer to a Declaration recently issued in Britain by the Pretender. The Earl of Mar had fought to a draw at Sheriffmuir in November, while James's supporters in the north of England were losing the battle of Preston. James himself landed at Peterhead in early December, soon to learn that all hope of a successful rising had vanished. The ministry had ensured London's safety by stationing troops throughout the region: after the clash at Preston, England had nothing to fear. A well-equipped army of Dutch troops under the command of the Duke of Argyll had been put ashore in Scotland before the Pretender's arrival. By early February James and Mar had sailed away to France and it remained for the army to hunt down the fugitive clansmen in the hill fastnesses of Scotland. Because news traveled only as quickly as a horseman in those days, the fact that the uprising was effectively over could not be known in London. There continued all autumn and into the winter widespread fear about the chances of the Pretender's success; as George Berkeley expressed it, the scene was one of "every day opening and discovering new cause to apprehend a popish power, and all the dismal consequences of it." [9] To the Londoner, therefore, the appearance of a Declaration by "James VIII, By the Grace of God, of Scotland, England, France, and Ireland, King," was sensational news.

On Wednesday, 11 January, Steele took a room at Baldwin's Coffeehouse near Red Lion Square and settled in for a night-long stint of writing. The results appeared on Friday as *Town-Talk* No. 5, and, a few days later in somewhat altered form, as a folio half-sheet entitled *The British Subject's Answer to the Pretender's Declaration.*[10] In both of these publications Steele

---

[9] *The Works of George Berkeley Bishop of Cloyne,* ed. A. A. Luce and T. E. Jessop (London, 1948–1957), VIII, 95.
[10] Reprinted in *Tracts,* pp. 389–401.

printed the Declaration itself along with his discussion of it, thus giving circulation to the Pretender's treasonable remarks, as Steele's enemies were not slow in pointing out.[11] This was poor political judgment on Steele's part, perhaps, but good journalism. His strategy in both versions is to place James's Catholicism in relief; this he knew was a major obstacle, perhaps the only major obstacle, to Jacobite success. The earlier publication in *Town-Talk* is appropriately chatty. Steele gives over some space to a discussion of Bolingbroke's part in the uprising, and discovers in the Declaration "the Specious and Wordy Stile of our late Secretary. . . . An old Friend of Mr. Secretary's shews it about as a Piece of Wit and Eloquence of her Gallant. . . ." Steele was guessing accurately, for Bolingbroke had indeed rewritten the manifesto.[12] Ormonde and Oxford are treated by Steele in a conciliatory manner: "I must own I never have received greater Civilities, or more frank and disinterested Offers of Kindness and Favour, than from Friends of yours now in Arms, or in Custody for your Cause; I wish them all, from my Soul, in Heaven; and have no more Personal Provocation to be against any one of them, than *Brutus* had to the stabbing of *Caesar.*" Late hours at Baldwin's Coffeehouse, and the fact that Drury Lane was rehearsing *Julius Caesar,* would appear to have opened that vein of grandiosity which Swift delighted to mock. When Steele, continuing, condemns avarice and ambition, in the style of Cato Uticensis, even Prue must have felt that he had overstepped the bounds of decorum. The tract was, these purple passages aside, lively and

---

[11] See *The Annals of King George for the Year 1716* (London, 1717), pp. 176–77, as quoted in *Per. Jour.,* p. 304: "Even Sir Richard St--le himself gave just cause of offense by . . . printing in a paper call'd *Town-Talk,* the Pretender's Declaration. It is true he added some Remarks or Reflections, ridiculing and bantering the said Declaration; but, however, it spread also the Paper itself . . . and therefore there was good Reason why the printing it should be taken ill by the Government." See also Samuel Keimer's *The London Post* (BM, Burney copy), 14 to 21 January 1716, for a rebuke from a "Quaker" (by Defoe?).
[12] See his MS. notes in HMC, *Stuart MSS.,* I, 449.

readable. Steele's audience was by this time presumably accustomed to dilation upon the purity of his motives. Within the
year 1716 the public supported five printings of the pamphlet,
and one printing of the sober version in folio half-sheet. The
half-sheet is more temperate than the pamphlet: those who
advance the Pretender's interest are, in the main, only misguided, "our wavering and mistaken Fellow Subjects."

The military situation as reported in London was meanwhile
improving and by 3 February Steele felt confident enough to
advise his correspondent, in *Town-Talk* No. 8, to "lay aside all
Fears for a Great and Glorious People." When the seven rebel
lords captured at Preston were brought to London for trial in
early February, voices advocating clemency were immediately
raised. Among the earliest, and loudest, was that of Richard
Steele. He had indicated his changing mood in the tracts on the
Pretender's Declaration and in *Town-Talk*. The ninth and, as it
proved, the last *Town-Talk* told of the sentencing of the six
noblemen who had pleaded guilty. The ceremony took place in
Westminster Hall on 9 February. Steele describes the occasion
with proper reverence: the Lord High Steward (Cowper) un-
der a canopy of state, Garter King of Arms at one side and Black
Rod at the other; before him the Lords Spiritual and Temporal
in their robes and on the Lord High Steward's right hand the
Commons assembled. When silence was thrice proclaimed the
Lieutenant of the Tower brought forth the prisoners, of whom
Steele comments, "Their Quality, Change of Condition, the
Vigour of their Days, and the present Inability to offend fur-
ther, pleaded very strongly to a good natured, and generous
People, who are quick to Anger, but slow to Revenge." The
Lord High Steward pronounced the sentence of death.

Suddenly, and quite unexpectedly, Steele found himself in
opposition, at the head of an oddly assorted column all jostling
him to the front. This included the wives of the condemned
lords, who were preparing petitions to both Houses of Parlia-

ment. Out-and-out Tories naturally wished to see the lords saved and the Whig ministry discomfited. Hanover Tories such as the Finches (who had supported Steele's cause in the expulsion trial) asserted that it was wise to dampen party feeling and reduce the sources of friction, especially the many misunderstandings between Scotland and England. The ease with which a full-scale uprising had been raised in Scotland demonstrated, they argued, the strength of ill-will there. The generality of English people, if they thought about the matter at all, probably did not feel much animosity toward the rebel Scots; over the years they had come to associate rebellion with such tiresome foreigners. English history taught that foreigners rebelled against just English rule; what more could you expect of them? Even the ministry itself was split; Stanhope threatened to resign unless his Eton schoolfellow, Lord Nairn, was spared.[13] For these groups Richard Steele found himself elected spokesman *de facto*.

On the other side, Townshend and Walpole were pressing for a swift execution. Hesitation, they thought, would be regarded as weakness, and a rising public sentiment of compassion might enable traitors to escape the block.[14] Steele was feeling the saddle sores of office anyway; on the tenth of February, as patentee of Drury Lane, he directed a sharp reply to a letter of inquiry which Sir John Stanley, the Lord Chamberlain's secretary, had sent him, reminding Stanley of the Lord Chamberlain's failure to protect Drury Lane in the case of deserting actors.[15] At mid-month he and his friend Samuel Pargiter Fuller, M. P. for Petersfield, drove out to Chelsea to

[13] Basil Williams, *Stanhope* (Oxford, 1932), p. 195.
[14] J. H. Plumb, *Sir Robert Walpole: The Making of a Statesman* (London, 1956), pp. 218–20.
[15] As John Loftis points out, the actor-managers, taking their cue from Steele, were refusing to submit plays for approval to the master of the revels (a subordinate officer to the Lord Chamberlain) or to pay him the usual licensing fee (Loftis, pp. 49, 66–67).

"dine in the Air," as Steele described it, and to plan their
activities in Parliament. A few days later, on 22 February, the
wives of the condemned noblemen presented their petitions for
mercy, and Steele, after presenting a petition of his own composition, spoke on behalf of the rebels. Fuller seconded his speech
and so did William Shippen, Tory member for Newton, Lancs.
Walpole moved adjournment until 1 March, by which time the
condemned would have been executed. He managed to carry the
motion, by a slim majority. The next day sentence was carried
out in the prescribed manner on Derwentwater and Kenmure:
"The Executioner performed his office on the Earl of Derwentwater with one Blow, and the Lord Kenmure with two." [16]
The appearance of an unusually brilliant display of the aurora
borealis a few days later confirmed the government's iniquity in
the minds of the superstitious.

The excitement was almost over then. Two of the condemned
men escaped from the Tower and in the session of 1717 an Act
of Grace passed Parliament, under which the three remaining in
prison were released. In the end, the policy Steele had advocated prevailed, but in the meantime he had roused a hornet's
nest of difficulty for the ministry. He wanted disciplining. The
government periodical, *The St. James's Post,* on 2 March criticized the position of those who had counseled mercy and accused them flatly of having taken bribes from the Jacobites.
Names and places were given pseudo-Polish disguises, but
"Cavaliero Risko Chalybeski" was recognizable as Richard
Steele. On 6 March Steele published a reply in defense of his
conduct, in a letter to Spencer Compton, Speaker of the House.
Steele was eager to justify his actions on grounds of principle,
but in fact the reply is not convincing on those grounds. He had
taken a large part in the government propaganda effort during
the previous summer and autumn. Granting that he was moved

---

[16] *The News Letter* (BM, Burney copy), Saturday, 25 February 1716.

by pity at the plight of the condemned lords, was it necessary that he go to such lengths to create troubles for the ministry, on principle? Some exasperation on the part of Walpole and Townshend at this *volte-face* is understandable. Steele professes himself determined to maintain his freedom to act according to his conscience. "There are those every Day in your Eye," he informs the Speaker, "who have no further Views than doing their Duty in the Place where they stand before you. They know it their Duty without Vanity, Discontent, or Peevishness, in all that is for the Common Good, to support those who have the Honour to serve their Country in Great Stations: But as they are always inclined to act in Concert with them, they are always free to act in Opposition to them." [17] Here he articulates the platform of the "independent member" for those Whigs who did not wish to be associated in the public mind with Jacobitism but who, for various reasons, were dissatisfied with the government. Steele had neither the political acumen nor the family connections necessary for leadership in forming a true Opposition, but he gave voice to those who would serve as followers in the years ahead, when Robert Walpole, after being turned out, would provide that leadership. At the moment, however, he appeared merely to be stirring up trouble among those malcontents who were offering, from the ministry's viewpoint, aid and comfort to the Tories. There is no evidence that Steele accepted a bribe as assistance for his eloquence; if he had, the fact would probably have been used against him later. On the face of it, his tactics would seem to have been entirely futile and not at all likely to attract those rewards of place which he needed. But these were unusual times.

Underlining the determination to go his own way, at least for the present, Steele published the collected volume of the second *Englishman* in March, without any dedication. The

---

[17] *Tracts,* p. 413.

omission of a dedication to some prominent Whig, on the part
of a man who had supplied dedications to each separate volume
of *The Ladies Library,* is pointed. There is a brief preface in
which Steele alludes to the criticism he has received for advocating a policy of lenity to the rebels. It might possibly be, he
admits, that his heart failed him "against submissive Criminals,
though He has appeared determinate against Triumphant
Wickedness." The motto he adapts from the *Aeneid* expresses
his mood: "Learn from others about good luck; from me about
hard work."

Steele's mood of discontent and defiance that spring may
have been colored by the death of his son Richard. His name-
sake had certainly been alive in March of 1714 and was dead
before December, 1716.[18] The death of children was an ordinary
aspect of life in those days, but Richard Steele was more than
ordinarily fond of his children. He and Prue, moreover, were
concerned about their children's inheritance; they had married
relatively late and their good health was beginning to fade. The
plight of children left without money and without relations to
rear them was unspeakably grim in the eighteenth century.
Steele's only close relative was his sister Katherine, herself
mentally incapable and in his charge. Prue was the only child of
parents both long dead. The rents from her estate, their only
anchor to windward, were proving troublesome to collect. Seen
in this context, Richard Steele's frenzied efforts over the next
several years to establish his financial independence are understandable. Associated in his mind with financial independence
was moral independence, the freedom to chart his own course,
on which he set such store.

He was almost but not quite done with the rebellion of 1715.
Carefully hiding his identity, he wrote three issues of a new
periodical, *Chit-Chat,* in which the narrator defends the conduct

---

[18] *Corr.,* pp. 298, 318.

of Sir Richard Steele, "who has ever shewn himself a Friend to our Royal Family, a Patriot to our Country." [19] Though some were still reading or writing pamphlets about the rebellion in Scotland, most members of Parliament were more interested in the factional struggles at home.

The Whig leadership now put aside the last threads of any bipartisan disguise, bringing about Lord Nottingham's dismissal as Lord President of the Council on 28 February 1715/1716, and the removal of some of his dependents from place here and there. [20] Nottingham had been among the loudest advocates of clemency for the Scottish lords. Did the ministry's action against Nottingham, which reflected the personal sentiments of the King himself, [21] portend similar trouble for Steele? He had dedicated *The Romish Ecclesiastical History* to Nottingham's son Daniel Lord Finch. So may have been his reading of the attack on Cavaliero Risko Chalybeski in the *St. James's Post*. The government thereupon raised an issue in Parliament that served to smoke out the sentiments of Steele and other wavering members. In order to ensure a period of relative tranquility the repeal of the Triennial Act was proposed; under the new measure the term of the Parliament then sitting and of all subsequent Parliaments would be seven instead of three years. The proposal had obvious advantages for the party in power, and there was perhaps good reason for a breathing spell during which the popularity, or at least the acceptability, of the new royal family could be fostered. On the other hand, the notion of an elected legislative assembly extending its own tenure beyond the period for which it had been elected raised constitutional questions. Could such an assembly,

---

[19] So successful was he in masking his authorship that Aitken (II, 91) doubted he had written the papers. Professor Blanchard (*Per. Jour.*, pp. 309–11) argues convincingly for his authorship. A copy of *Chit-Chat* No. 1 has never been found.

[20] Beattie (note 2 above), p. 175n.

[21] *Diary of Mary Countess Cowper* . . . (London, 1864), p. 84.

having once done so, not extend its tenure indefinitely, the principle having been admitted? Addison prepared the way for the ministry by presenting the weaknesses of the Triennial Act in *Freeholder* No. 25 (16 March). Steele's first reaction was unfavorable; he began to write a periodical essay in reply to Addison's paper, expressing his fears about the constitutional problems involved and objecting to the *Freeholder*'s assertion that the English people are fickle in their political loyalties.[22] There was no personal animus involved. Steele during the month was overseeing the publication of Addison's comedy *The Drummer,* which he sold to Tonson on behalf of the author for the excellent price of fifty guineas. Steele had his suspicions about the trustworthiness of the ministry if not of Addison himself, perhaps; the allegation about taking the bribe certainly still rankled.

Something or someone served to change his mind on the Septennial Bill, because he spoke twice in its favor in the House. Three years is too little time for a government to accomplish its beneficent purposes, he argued. "The Ills that are to be done against single Persons or Communities are done by surprize, and on a sudden; but good Things are slow in their Progress, and must wait Occasion. Destruction is done with a Blow; but Reformation is brought about by leisurely Advances. . . ."[23] Steele spoke again for the bill on 26 April and the government got home with a sturdy majority, 264 to 121.[24]

In early June he was elected, by vote of the Commons, a commissioner of the estates belonging to the rebels of the '15, which had been forfeited to the Crown. The post, with a handsome stipend of one thousand pounds and allowance for travel-

[22] This may have been the fugitive periodical, *The Whig,* attributed to Steele in the eighteenth century, copies of which have never been found. For a full discussion and the text of Steele's unpublished essay, see *Per. Jour.,* pp. 330–32.

[23] [Richard Chandler], ed., *The History and Proceedings of the House of Commons of Great Britain . . . ,* I (London, 1741), 85–86.

[24] *Ibid.,* pp. 101, 105; Wolfgang Michael, *England Under George I: The Beginnings of the Hanoverian Dynasty* (London, 1936), pp. 217–19.

ing, would not have been his if the party leadership had objected to his election. What had brought about the reconciliation, only a few months after Steele had defended the rebel lords? It is in the realm of conjecture, but something like the following seems reasonable: that Steele showed Addison a draft of his essay opposing the repeal of the Triennial Act, that Addison remonstrated with him, convinced Steele of the Septennial Bill's worth (and in fact the Septennial Act proved its durability over almost two centuries until repeal in 1911), and interceded on Steele's behalf with one or another of the Whig leadership. Steele, for his part, was just then negotiating the sale of Addison's *Drummer* and superintending its production at Drury Lane, where it ran for three nights in March.[25] Lord Cowper, who had written the King's address to Parliament in which forfeiture of the rebels' estate was proposed and who looked favorably on Steele anyway,[26] may have been the point

---

[25] *London Stage,* I, 392–93; Steele, Dedication to *The Drummer,* in *Corr.,* pp. 505–18.

[26] Draft of address in Cowper's hand in Hertfordshire Record Office, Panshanger MSS. See Rae Blanchard, "Richard Steele and William Lord Cowper: New Letters," *Publications of the Modern Language Association of America,* LXXX (1965), 303–306. Lady Cowper had earlier assisted the Duchess of Marlborough in organizing a claque for Steele's play *The Tender Husband.* See the letters of the actor Richard Estcourt to Cowper in the Panshanger MSS. A letter from Steele to Cowper, hitherto unpublished, has recently come to light which underlines the warm feelings, at least on Steele's part. It is quoted here with the kind permission of the authorities of the James M. and Marie-Louise Osborn Collection, Yale University Library.

July 7th 1716
S[at]. James's Street

Dear S[r].

I was, this morning, looking over papers, and among them found a letter of yours on the subject of Going to M[r] Desaguilliers. As soon as I read it I immediately resolved to renew our Acquaintance. There are such obliging things said in Your letter, and those flowing from so worthy Sentiments that I earnestly desire to See You as soon as You can. I assure You I do not know in the world a greater pleasure than by conversing with Young men to inspire them with noble and Virtuous resolutions. Be pleased to See Me at Your first leisure and Know Me for, S[r], Y[r]. Sincere Freind &

Most Obedient Humble Ser[vt]
RICHARD STEELE

of contact. If this reconstruction of events is correct, Steele supported the ministry on the bill as a token of reconciliation and was granted the commissionership in due course.

Whatever the details of reconciliation may have been, it is certain that by June, 1716, Steele and the leadership were once more on speaking terms, that he had an assured increase in his income, and that a difficult winter was over. As a Member of Parliament, as a Commissioner of the Estates Forfeited to the Crown, or as a private citizen, however, Richard Steele would go his own way.

CHAPTER V

Dear Prue

SIR RICHARD'S election to the Commission for the Estates Forfeited to the Crown in June, 1716, provides an amusing afterpiece to the personal drama of the preceding twelve months. First he had spent his literary powers in rousing the nation to the dangers of Popery and rebellion. Then he had risked his place at Court by counseling leniency for some of the Popish rebels. Now he was charged with the just management of the property those rebels had forfeited by their rebellion. Under the terms of the act (I Geo. I, c. 50), a committee of thirteen was chosen by election in the House of Commons to oversee the estates.[1] Money derived from their sale or rental was to be used to repay the costs of suppressing the uprising, after the Commission's operating expenses had been deducted. A commissioner's stipend was set at one thousand pounds per annum but the act stipulated that the incumbent could not hold other remunerative employment under the Crown. This was a good stipend but not a lucrative place, and while he held it Steele would have to depend on Drury Lane or other sources of income to make ends meet. Accepting the appointment would require, that is, a thorough reassessment of the Steeles' financial position.

Suddenly his health gave way. During the winter of 1713–1714, the winter of *The Crisis* and of his expulsion from

---

[1] For information on sources, see Appendix A.

Parliament, he had suffered from attacks of what was diagnosed as the gout but he had not been incapacitated for any
length of time. In the spring of 1716, during another period of
extreme emotional tension, he was stricken with a severe attack
that left him helpless and immobile. His physician, Dr. John
Woodward, found him in great misery and diagnosed the problem as a return of the gout. Following the practice of the time,
as he advocated it, Woodward administered purgatives, unc-
tuous medicines, and clysters. In spite of the medication Steele
recovered quickly.[2] He was a hardy sort, but during the pros-
tration of his illness he must have thought with special urgency
about the necessity for putting his finances in order.

His situation was not all dark. The following autumn and
winter would, it is true, find him defendant in eight actions for
debt, totaling more than fourteen hundred pounds.[3] The queue
of creditors in the courts of justice, however, is a testimony to
Steele's credit rather than proof of his poverty, at least in the
ordinary sense of the term poverty. The creditors went to court
because they knew they could recover their money that way.
The statement bears repeating, and Steele was the author of it,
that he was very good at getting money. He could and did exert
himself to make money in order to support the kind of life he
thought that he and his family should live. "I never can . . . be
what they call, thoroughly, frugall," he once observed to Prue,
"but my Expence shall be at home in a plentifull supply of all
things for You and the Bratts, with regard to pleasures as well
as necessaries." [4] He lived by his beliefs, rejoiced in the company of his wife and children, and saw to it, by using his credit,
that they had the opportunity of enjoying life along with him.

[2] John Woodward, *Select Cases, and Consultations in Physick* (London,
1757), pp. 369–71.
[3] Suits summarized in Aitken, II, 109–12.
[4] *Corr.,* p. 356.

He had married for love and companionship, and the domestic values were important to him. "I would have You, intirely at Leisure to passe Your time with Me in diversions, in Books, in Entertainments, and no manner of Businesse intrude upon Us but at stated times. . . . I will work my brains and fingers to procure us plenty of all things, and demand nothing of you but to take delight in agreeable dresses, Chearfull discourses, and Gay sights attended by Me. . . . [I]f I throw away a little money in adorning my Brats I hope you will forgive Me" (*Corr.*, p. 355). This was the way he spent his money and it is an impertinence to say that he was unwise to do so.

Richard Steele was, nevertheless, a very poor manager of his capital, literary and financial. His financial judgment could hardly have been worse. In his private character he was honest, generous, and trusting—attributes the last of which at least is unsuited to sound dealing in the world of finance. Very large amounts of money came his way at different times in his life, but he was unduly careless in their disposition. The prospect of making a large sum in a single stroke, furthermore, seemed to paralyze his faculties of judgment. An instance of Steele's failure as a financial manager is provided by his actions in 1716.

Several years earlier, while observing the demonstration of an air pump (perhaps after a bad meal), Steele had begun meditating on ways of improving the method by which fish were conveyed to market. This was a period in English history during which agricultural productivity was rising and the vast London market for agricultural products was influencing, even revolutionizing, traditional methods of food production and distribution. New fortunes were being made in the process.[5] Steele's meditations culminated in the idea of a new type of

[5] Cf. E. A. Wrigley, "A Simple Model of London's Importance in Changing English Society and Economy 1650–1750," *Past and Present*, XXXVII (1967), 44–70.

well-vessel, to be called the Fish Pool, of which more will be heard later.[6] During the winter of 1716–1717 Steele was engaged in superintending the construction of a model vessel and it was no doubt with the thought of raising capital for this project, as well as of meeting the immediate demands of his creditors, that he took the extreme step of mortgaging his interest in the theater. The net result of a very complex financial agreement was that Steele delivered over almost all his income from the Drury Lane patent to a group of creditors in return for four thousand pounds, most of which was not in cash but in the form of a promissory note. A recent examination of the evidence indicates that Steele was the victim of an elaborate, and successful, conspiracy to defraud.[7] The revealing aspect of the matter, however, is the light-hearted spirit in which Steele could give up the certain income of the theater, just at a time when the profits at Drury Lane were beginning to rise once more. If this was the first result of his reassessment, it was an ominous beginning.

Within the family, the income from Lady Steele's estate, which had been estimated at five hundred pounds in 1713, was to be reserved to provide a portion for the girls. Steele, however, had drawn on this to the extent of about three hundred pounds over the preceding two years, and rents were not being collected efficiently.[8] Prue no doubt remembered the celerity with which Steele had gone through the inheritance of his first wife, a larger estate than hers. As a further step in ordering their finances it was decided that she should return to Wales

[6] Steele's *An Account of the Fish-Pool,* a promotional tract which presents the genesis of the plan, is reprinted in *Tracts,* pp. 419–52.

[7] Loftis, pp. 91–98. Steele's principal creditor, Edward Minshull, was found guilty in 1722 of defrauding a goldsmith and fled to Holland to escape prosecution (Aitken, II, 106).

[8] The figure for the income was George Berkeley's estimate. See *The Works of George Berkeley Bishop of Cloyne,* ed. A. A. Luce and T. E. Jessop (London, 1948–1957), VIII, 60. See also Lady Steele to Steele in *Corr.,* pp. 328–29.

and make certain that the management of her property was in good hands. Although this may have seemed a wise decision then, it had unhappy personal consequences, for Steele and his wife were separated during more than half the little time that still remained to Prue.

The decision of Lady Steele to return to Wales was brought about by the necessity for inspecting the property in person, but the timing of the journey probably had to do with Steele's election to the Commission for the Forfeited Estates. Soon after his initial election, as will be seen, he was voted membership on the division or "board," as they referred to it, of the Commission that would deal with the estates forfeited in Scotland.[9] This would require Steele's being in Scotland from time to time, to transact the business of the Commission there: presumably Prue's journey was to coincide with an initial trip to Edinburgh by Steele in the autumn of 1716. As it turned out, although Lady Steele did go to Wales, Steele was too pressed to get to Scotland that year. For the next five years his responsibilities to Parliament, to the theater at Drury Lane, to the Fish Pool project, and to the Commission were to conflict. Because of the criticism that has come down to us from one or another of those associated with him during this period, it may be felt that Sir Richard was resting on the honors bestowed after the King's accession, benignly drinking himself into the grave. This is the period, moreover, when many of the colorful anecdotes were minted, such as those passed along by Savage and Bishop Hoadly, and these support the image of a good-natured idler. It is certain that Steele drank more than was good for him but far from certain that he was drinking any more during those years than he had earlier. He was a notable figure in his own right now, however, and the stories of his debauches were preserved for posterity as they had not been when he was

---

[9] PRO, FEC 2/7. Meeting of 7 July.

mere Captain Steele. The charge of idleness will not bear examination. He spent too much time on the Fish Pool project in
view of the fact that it turned out to be a failure, but he of
course had no way of knowing this, and once he was well into
the project and had invested hundreds of pounds of capital there
it behove him to look after his interest. His partners at Drury
Lane were eventually to complain of his neglect, but these
complaints arose after his health gave way. Before 1722 they
had little reason to regret Steele's appointment to the patent,
even if he became less active in the day-to-day business of the
theater after 1716.[10] During these years he continued to bring
the theater to the attention of the public and of the royal family,
and to defend the independence of Drury Lane, as the managers
saw it, against encroachments by the Lord Chamberlain. In
1722 he provided a new play for the repertory, *The Conscious
Lovers,* which was to be one of the most popular comedies of
the century. In Parliament, Steele was regular in his attendance, served on many committees, and spoke often and well in
debate. He kept his own counsel and annoyed ministries by his
waywardness but he was a conscientious representative of Boroughbridge and a working member of the House. His duties on
the Commission were also more considerable than has been
realized, although in this case he did in fact for a time not bear
his full share. Steele's energies were stretched to the breaking
point in the years 1716–1721; he committed himself to more
than he could perform, but he was not idle.

The act providing for the Commission (I Geo. I, c. 50) had
left the method of operation and composition of staff entirely to
the decision of the commissioners, with the Treasury lords
exercising a supervisory power.[11] Parliament's general intent

[10] Loftis, pp. 213–30, sets 1721 as the beginning of the alienation between
Steele and his fellows, but it must be remembered that he supplied them *The
Conscious Lovers* the following year, from which all four made large profits.
[11] Danby Pickering, ed., *The Statutes at Large . . . ,* XIII (Cambridge,
1764), 299.

was that the Commission should be self-supporting, paying for its activities out of the funds realized from the estates. This implied that, within the bounds of discretion, the commissioners could ensure that their work was not impeded for want of staff. After taking the oaths they proceeded to plan substantial establishments, one for administering the estates in Scotland and one for those in England, Wales, and Ireland, each with nine professional staff members, sixteen clerks, and messengers, door-keepers, and housekeepers in proportion. The staff was, that is, nearly twice as numerous as the entire administrative office of the secretaries of state, who were charged with conducting much of the business of the realm.[12] An immediate task of the commissioners was getting Treasury approval for this comfortable establishment and Steele was one of five elected on 27 June to lay the plan before the Treasury lords, now acting under Sir Robert Walpole's direction. This was the sort of duty Steele, a member of the Kit-Cat Club with years of service around the Court, was able to render the Commission, most of the members of which were obscure Whig backbenchers. He was later to justify his failure to go to Scotland by contending that he was able to perform more valuable service in London than in Edinburgh. During the early days of the Commission there was justification for Steele's assertion: the conference with the Treasury was successful and the Commission proceeded to divide itself by ballot at its meeting of 7 July 1716, at which time Steele was elected to the board for Scotland, along with five others. This must have proved a disappointment to him, for whereas two of the five (Patrick Haldane and Robert Munro) were native Scots and another, Sir Henry Hoghton, had a seat near Preston in Lancashire, Steele's interests were in London or in Wales, and the journey would take him away

[12] Establishments in PRO, FEC 2/74/1. Mark Thomson, *The Secretaries of State, 1681–1782* (Oxford, 1932), p. 129, reports a total of ten clerks employed in both secretaries' offices in 1711, and only seventeen in 1758.

from his family and his projects, and from Drury Lane.[13] At the same meeting it was voted to allow a member of the board in Scotland to reside in England, "his necessary occasions so requiring." Steele was to take full advantage of this provision. The Commission had major patronage at its disposal and Steele may have helped his acquaintance William Moore of the Inner Temple, who had assisted him on *The Crisis,* to secure the important office of Master of References for the English board.[14] By the meeting of 19 July, when all nominees for the establishments in London and in Edinburgh had been approved by the full Commission, it was apparent that Steele's duties would call him to Scotland in the autumn. As has been noted, this was probably what precipitated Lady Steele's decision to travel to Wales in order to supervise the rent collection and transact other business having to do with her estate.

She intended to leave her children in London, Molly and Eugene, aged three and four, at home in care of nurses and Elizabeth, now seven, at a boarding school. Anyone who sets out to frame a biographical picture of Prue must pause at this point; there is no side-stepping an evaluation of her decision to leave three young children in the care of servants and guardians for more than a year. In fact, her trip to Wales is the most puzzling act of her life, as enigmatic as the abandonment by his mother of the infant Jonathan Swift. What is there to say about it, one may ask, that is not pure conjecture?

One may begin by saying that, as Irvin Ehrenpreis has pointed out in Swift's case, the custom of putting children in the care of foster nurses was not uncommon at the time. Infants

---

[13] Although the possibility exists that the John Sheils with whom he stayed in Edinburgh in 1717 (*Corr.,* p. 121) was a kinsman of Steele's mother, whose maiden name was Sheils or Sheills. The will of a John Sheills, clerk of the Excise Office in Edinburgh, who died in 1739, was proved in 1742. His next of kin and executrix was a Mrs. Alexander Cairns (Edinburgh, Register Office, Probate Records).

[14] Moore had also helped Steele with his Multiplication Table lottery project; see *CS,* pp. 148–49, 196, and *Corr.,* p. 60.

Lady Steele

A portrait by Sir Godfrey Kneller, probably done in 1715 or 1716. From the reproduction in George A. Aitken's *The Life of Richard Steele,* vol. ii.

were customarily boarded with wet nurses. Steele, however, had
protested the practice in *Spectator* No. 246, commenting, "The
Generation of the Infant is the Effect of Desire, but the Care of
it argues Virtue and Choice." [15] Even if Steele did not stand in
the way of Prue's making the trip, there can be no doubt that
such a long separation of mother from children was against
Steele's principles. In none of the many letters written to his
wife in Wales during the separation, however, does Steele insist
that she return. Writing after she had been gone almost a year,
while discussing her plans to come home he implies that her
decision to go to Wales had been preceded by disagreements
about money and sexual relations:

> I am Glad You resolve to live well on the road. As to the cold-
> nesse on this Subject I answer very sincerely that Your Lady-
> ship's coldnesse to Me as a Woman and a Wife has made me
> think it necessary to Supresse the expression of my Heart to-
> wards You, because it could not end in the pleasures and enjoy-
> ments I ought to expect from it, and which You oblig'd Me to
> Wean my self from, till I had so much money &c and I know not
> what impertinence. God be thanked this Whimsey has not been
> fatall to our Love.

If the decision had been Lady Steele's, she was in no hurry to
return, and she discouraged Steele from coming to Wales.
"[P]ray think not of coming," she wrote in February, 1717,
"till y° end of sommer to stay not above a monnth." Steele was
at the time dispatching letters in almost every post, many of
them full of praise and cheer and news of the family.

So much is certain. Since few of Lady Steele's letters to her
husband have survived, her attitude toward the separation can
only be established by reading Steele's letters in the mirror, as it
were. It is reasonable to surmise, however, that the marriage

[15] Ehrenpreis, *Swift: The Man, His Works and The Age,* Vol. I: *Mr.
Swift and his Contemporaries* (London, 1962), pp. 31–32.

went through a crisis in 1716, that Prue was in a deeply
depressed state (a condition perhaps brought on by the death of
her son Richard), and that she seized the pretext of a quarrel
over money to walk out, going to Wales to look after her
estates. There is no doubt that her estates needed looking after,
and certainly Steele could be trying when money was involved,
but the length of her stay and the manner in which she discouraged Steele's coming to see her lend strength to the assumption
that she had decided, consciously or unconsciously, on a separation and took such steps as were necessary to bring it about.
Consider the following letter, written before her departure, in
the light of an hypothesis that it was composed after a quarrel.
Is not the tone, slightly formal but genial, well chosen for
winning the heart of a vexed wife? Steele had of course made
goodnatured fun of ladies who read romances in *The Tender
Husband* and in his essay periodicals:

Dear Prue
    You may observe, in those Excellent Books which your Polite
Cousen reads to You, that necessaries are often wanting to the
Heroes and Heroines for want of stowing their Portmanteaus
with proper materialls.
    The bearer brings you, with this, a case of instruments for
eating and Drinking that may be upon the road both of Orna-
ment and Use to,

Madam,
Yr Obedient Husband
RICHARD STEELE

When she departed in mid-November, however, she left the
household without food or fuel, and her daughter Molly ill with
a disease that proved to be smallpox. For several months she
did not write Steele directly but communicated with him by
dictating to her cousin, Mrs. Bevan. "Mrs. Secretary," as
Steele referred to her, relayed questions and requests to him. In

these, one infers from Steele's replies, she complained of ill-treatment by her relations and of severe headaches.[16] Each of these actions is perhaps understandable, but viewed together they appear as the actions of a woman seriously disturbed, who has felt driven to cut the Gordian Knot by leaving her husband and children.

The causes of her decision are now past knowing, if they ever could have been known. Sexual disharmony must always be suspected first by any twentieth-century writer who does not wish to appear hopelessly outdated, and in truth a hint of frigidity does hover about the image of Prue. The nickname itself, though a term of affection, is obviously suggestive of "prude." [17] A few references in Steele's letters during their separation appear to corroborate this suggestion: "It is indeed as You observe a strange life we lead, and the Separation is painful to Me, for one reason more than it is to You." Or later, when he has heard that his wife has been afflicted with an ailment also troubling him, gout: "If Women are instigated with desire so much as men when they are Gouty we shall have [an] odd time of it, and you will, in your heart, at least be tractable to Me." [18] More compelling evidence than this is needed, however, before a verdict can be returned.

Certainly Mary Scurlock Steele strikes one as a lonely woman. Her only intimate friend in London appears to have been Hannah Maria Keck, who eventually assumed the guardianship of the Steele children. The fact that Prue was Welsh would have cut her off to some extent in London, but the impression gathered from the couple's correspondence during her sojourn in Wales is not that of a homesick provincial

[16] Steele's neighbor, Dr. Samuel Garth, the literary doctor, prescribed bathing the head with salt water as a headache cure (*Corr.,* p. 318).

[17] Steele refers to Lady Steele's friend Miss Keck, to whom he has just spoken, as "indeed, a very good Prue and tho I divert myself with Her Gravity and admonition I have a sincere respect for Her" (*Corr.,* p. 363).

[18] *Corr.,* pp. 370, 373.

returning to the bosom of a happy family. In spite of Steele's protestations to the contrary, she must have been a rather retiring person in public. Although wives were not expected to attract attention in this male-dominated society, the total absence of comment in the case of Lady Steele seems curious. George Berkeley, for example, who had been a guest in their house, might have been expected somewhere to remark on Steele's wife in his letters but he did not do so. Her desire for flattery, which Steele gratified in full measure, is also in accord with the impression of a shy woman, who, in her public role at any rate, lacked salt. Her personality does not bear comparison with that of other women who had played important parts in Steele's life: his aunt Katherine, Lady Mildmay, for example, or the flamboyant Mary Delarivière Manley or Lady Mary Wortley Montagu. Yet Steele loved her.

> Dear Prue
> Yours of the 25th is before Me: I am always Glad when you write a great deal, but do not hurt Your Eyes to scribble longer than is easy to You. Your kind expression is the most Welcome and pleasing thing which could possibly arrive at Me. Mr. Glanville of the Treasury asked Me the other day how my Wonderfull Girle did. There is, it seems, a Lady of His Acquaintance who visits Betty at School, and Cryes her up for a greater Wit than her Father; that is not much, but than Her Mother either. I am every day walking about the Offices to get our sallaryes paid that I might go into the Countrey, and particularly the Bath whence you shall direct Me further, that is, command My Motions. But if I find my limbs easy to Me I beleive I shall vigorously pursue my Journey to the Dearest of Women to the most Affectionate of Men.
> Poor Dear Angry Pleased Pretty Witty Silly Eve[ry]thing Prue
>
> Y[rs] Ever
> RICHARD STEELE

It must be said again, in Prue's defense, that the strains of living with Richard Steele were genuine ones. The clouds of dunning tradesmen around the entrance hall, sessions of Parliament that lasted into the small hours of the morning, printers' messengers hammering on the door for copy: No. 26 St. James's was scarcely an island of tranquility. The fact, too, that she preserved his notes and letters to her, even those written when she had withdrawn to Wales, argues strongly for her love.

The pretext for the continued separation had been, it will be recalled, a requirement on Lady Steele's part that Steele put their finances in order. This was a stiff provision indeed for Richard Steele and it came at a particularly unfortunate season, impelling him to bring to completion the Fish Pool project. The time spent on the Fish Pool, which perhaps resulted in loss rather than gain, though one cannot be sure, was in turn to prevent his fulfilling duties on the Commission, and this neglect was eventually to cost him five hundred pounds of his salary.

The full Commission met in London on 22 August 1716 and then adjourned until the first of September, the commissioners for England and Ireland to meet in Preston and those for Scotland in Edinburgh. It was not until the eleventh of September, however, that four of the commissioners held the first meeting in the Scottish city, where they ordered "that all the officers belonging to the Comm[ission] do attend during the time of the Sitting. . . ." [19] The command was addressed to Ingram and to Steele. The departure of Lady Steele, Molly's illness, and his responsibilities in getting the children settled detained him through November, but by early December he was making definite plans to begin the journey. He felt easy enough about Prue by Christmastide to chaff her gently about her insistence on righting the accounts between them: "Your man

[19] Edinburgh, Scottish Record Office, Forfeited Estates Papers 1715, Vol. 1 (Minute Book).

Sam owes me Three pence which must be deducted in the account between you and me, therefore pray take care to get it in, or stop it."

Pursuing his lucubrations on fresh fish, he was in touch with a mathematician, William Gillmore, to whom he related his plan of building a fishing boat that would bring fish to port alive in a well hold. Gillmore later said that he was not at first interested. Steele's discourse he "looked upon as a little too volatile." [20] The projector's enthusiasm soon won him over, however, for he was at work on the measurement calculations for the boat in mid-December, 1716, and by early January, 1717, Steele was able to inform his wife that Gillmore's work was finished. Steele had delayed his departure for Scotland for many weeks, during which time his fellow commissioners were meeting in Edinburgh. He was at work on their behalf, apparently serving as a liaison representative to the Treasury in an effort to secure payment of the stipends to the Commission and its staff.[21] This had been a disputed point from the beginning. Under the terms of the act authorizing the Commission, it will be recalled, it was stipulated that salaries and expenses incurred would be paid from funds derived from the forfeited estates. These funds could not, however, be turned on like water from a tap. Before the estates could be sold they must be surveyed and inventoried, outstanding claims determined, a date of sale set and advertised, and so forth. Rents from the estates were not forthcoming in the meantime either. Some landlords followed the practice of the Countess of Derwentwater, who ordered her tenants not to pay rents to the Commission's agents and promised to reimburse them for fines incurred.[22] In Scotland the Commission was obliged to learn the differences between Scot-

[20] Gillmore's statement in PRO, *Sansome versus Steele and Gillmore,* Chancery Proceedings, Reynardson, 1714–1758, No. 2363, as quoted in Aitken, II, 176.
[21] *Corr.,* p. 119.
[22] PRO, FEC 2/62.

tish and English legal theory, the one based on Roman juris-
prudence, the other on common law. The supreme judicial body
on the civil side, the Court of Session, moreover, was proving
difficult to deal with. Acting on their own initiative, the Court
of Session had ordered the rents from certain of the estates
sequestered, thus further reducing the Commission's income.[23]
The Commission, in short, required an advance to meet its bills
and to pay the stipends of the commissioners themselves, and
the Treasury was reluctant to let it have one. Walpole, now
Chancellor of the Exchequer, was in a mood of economy; he
had recently refused to pay the Duke of Argyll's pension.[24]
Some tactful persuasion was called for or the Commission
would be forced to live on tick for months to come. This was no
doubt the task set for Steele, and the justification for the
statement to his friend William Cleland in November that he
had "done as much in the commission as any man in it."

The situation in the government continued fragile. Taking
advantage of his access to the King's ear during the royal
sojourn in Hanover in the autumn of 1716, Stanhope managed
to persuade him to displace Townshend as Secretary of State by
naming him Lord Lieutenant of Ireland. Walpole, Townshend's ally, regarded this as treachery on Stanhope's part and
every quidnunc knew that there would be trouble after the
King's return, when the new session of Parliament met. These
maneuvers did not improve Walpole's temper nor make him
more disposed to bend Treasury regulations for the benefit of
the commissioners. At the end of the year the order for their
pay was still not signed, although they had been employed for
more than six months.

Steele had stayed on in London. Tempers were high

[23] *A Report from the Commissioners Appointed to Enquire of the Estates
of certain Traitors, &c. In that Part of Great-Britain called Scotland*
(Edinburgh, 1717). The so-called *First Report.*

[24] J. H. Plumb, *Sir Robert Walpole: The Making of a Statesman* (London, 1956), pp. 231–35.

during the summer and autumn of 1716. Mobs gathered to break windows and cry down the government despite threats from the Commission of Peace, and in the face of severe punishment, even execution from time to time. Whigs formed their own societies to drink loyal toasts and decry faction. Bishop Hoadly later recalled one such meeting at which Steele, full of loyal toasts and hobbled by the gout, was being lifted bodily into his coach by the waiters when a mob swept by, shouting the Tory slogan, "Down with the Rump!" "Down with the Rump!" "Up with the rump," cried Sir Richard to the waiters struggling beneath him, "or I shall not be at home tonight." [25]

Politics and fellowship, debts and Drury Lane, the Fish Pool and the forfeited estates: these occupied Steele's time during the autumn and winter of 1716 but they could not fill his life.

Christmas Day [1716]

Dear Prue

I went the other day to see Betty at Chelsea who represented to Me in Her pretty language that she seemed helplesse, and Freindlesse without any bodye's taking notice of Her at Christmas, when all the Children but she and two more were with their Relations. I have invited Her to dinner to day, with one of the Teachers, and they are here now in the room Betty and Moll very Noisy and Pleased together. Besse goes back again as soon as she has dined to Chelsea. I have stay'd in to get a very advantageous affair dispatched, for I assure you I Love money at present as well as Y^r L^p and am Intirely Yours

RICHARD STEELE

I told Betty I had writ to You and she Made me open My Letter again and give Her Humble Duty to Her Mother, and desire to Know when she shall have the Honour to see Her in Town. She gives Her Love to Mrs. Bevans and all Her Cousins.

---

[25] BM, Add. MSS., 32, 329, fo. 50. Spelling and punctuation here modernized.

On New Year's Day he wrote again :

Dear Dear Prue

I wish you from my soul an happy new Year, and many very different from what We have hitherto had. Inorder thereunto I have taken a resolution, which, by the blessing of God, I will stedfastly keep, to make my Children Partners with Me in all my future Gain, in the manner I have before described to You. That you may be convinced of this happy Change, You shall be Your self the Keeper of what I lay up for them by Quarterly portions from this day. I am, with the Tenderest affection,

Y^r Faithfull Husband & Most Humble Servant

RICHARD STEELE

S^{nt} James's Street
Y^r Children are all very Well.

CHAPTER VI

The Fish Pool

IT WAS a great age for investment. That it was also the age in
which the term "bubble" entered the ordinary person's vocabu-
lary as a synonym for visionary projects or fraudulent business
schemes should not lead one to overlook the fact that fortunes
were made as well as lost in the joint-stock companies. The year
1717 was a prosperous one; in 1717 twelve large English
companies had a share capitalization totaling more than twenty
million pounds, and this valuation had doubled in fifteen years.
Capital was available for starting new companies, interest was
low, investors were about, eager to back new schemes.[1] Years
earlier Steele had satirized, although gently, the craze for investment embodied in the character of Biddy Tipkin's Aunt
Barsheba in *The Tender Husband*, whose talk was all of
"stocks, Old and New Company, . . . partners for Sword
Blades, Chamber of London, banks for charity, and mine ad-
ventures. . . ."[2] Like her creator, Aunt Barsheba thought of
investments as roads to quick wealth. The notion that these
projects were for the betterment of mankind as well as the
enrichment of investors, the grandiose titles which promised
benefits to all, appealed to Steele's benevolent instincts.

With the double purpose in mind, then, of making a great
deal of money and of helping mankind, but perhaps principally

[1] William R. Scott, *The Constitution and Finance of English, Scottish and
Irish Joint-Stock Companies to 1720* (Cambridge, 1912), I, 393–96.
[2] *The Tender Husband,* ed. C. Winton (Lincoln, Neb., 1967), p. 39.

the former, Richard Steele pursued his Fish Pool project. For years to come he would pour energy, money, and time into the capacious well deck of the Fish Pool, working first to produce a model, then to secure letters patent for the invention, and finally to launch a formal joint-stock company. Steele made plans on a grand scale; when time came to form the joint-stock company he invited John Law, author of the Mississippi bubble in France, to come in as a partner.

It was, Steele later recalled, the thought that ships frequently admitted tons of water without sinking which first gave him the hint for a vessel that would carry nothing but water and fish, "whereby Fish might live commodiously, and such Water be admitted, and made to pass thro' at Will, and nevertheless the Ship to sail with Safety." [3] After Gillmore the mathematician had been induced to draw up plans, a model at a scale of one to thirty was constructed, with a little keel sixteen inches long representing a fishing boat of keel-length forty feet. This was to be exhibited to Parliament, to further the petition for a legislative patent, which would extend by twenty-one years the fourteen-year patent they expected to secure from the Crown. In the spring of 1717 Steele had persuaded his friend William Benson to lend moral and financial support, and the three partners were looking forward to approval of the patent and a speedy improvement in the quality of fish on London tables. A political and a personal crisis intervened.

By February, 1717, the Scottish board had adjourned their work in Edinburgh, so there was then no necessity for Steele's making the long journey until the following summer. The Treasury lords continued to refuse to pay the stipends of the commissioners. Debts that Steele had run up against his salary were coming due, he needed money to pay his daughter Elizabeth's bills at school, and yet his lobbying at the Treasury did

[3] *An Account of the Fish-Pool* in *Tracts*, p. 426.

no good.[4] The Chancellor of the Exchequer, Walpole, was wrestling behind the scenes with Stanhope and Sunderland. The situation that had threatened to be serious became a full-blown crisis after the King's return. Steele attended a meeting on 30 March 1717 of the Kit-Cat Club chaired by the Duke of Newcastle, which was meant to promote a reconciliation or at least some appearance of unity among the quarreling Whigs. Steele himself does not seem to have been much concerned with picking his way between factions at Court. The expense of dressing properly for Court appearance was a particular annoyance,[5] and he probably stayed away for that reason if for no other. Lady Steele, indeed, reported from Wales that she had heard he had become a Tory. Steele explained that he had on the same day spoken in Parliament in behalf of both the Dissenters and the Roman Catholics, thus offending extremists of both camps, but that he had not become a Tory. His speech on Roman Catholic relief, the opening of which he related to Prue, was acceptable to many Tories but Steele did not, then or later, worry about that consideration. Justice, he asserted, was involved:

> I cannot but be of Opinion that to put Severities upon men merely on account of Religion is a most greivous and Unwarrantable proceeding. But indeed the Roman Catholicks hold tenets which are inconsistent with the Being and safety of a Protestant People; For this reason we are Justifyed in laying upon them the Penalties which the Parliament has from time to time thought fitt to inflict, but, [Sir], Let Us not pursue Roman Catholicks with

[4] PRO, FEC 2/74/1, and *Calendar of Treasury Books,* ed. William Shaw (London, 1957), Vol. XXI, Part II (January–December, 1717), pp. 83, 503–504. Although ordered in January, payments appear not to have been made until April, and in August, 1717, the commissioners had received only half the sums due them.

[5] Cf. John M. Beattie, *The English Court in the Reign of George I* (Cambridge, 1967), p. 206.

the Spirit of Roman Catholicks, but Act towards them with the Temper of our own Religion.[6]

This was an enlightened opinion, but the speech represented a whimsicality that would not earn him place. When the old ministry fell, in April, and the new government of Stanhope and Sunderland came in, there were whisperings that Steele might get something. He hoped for the best but he did not credit the rumors and in the end nothing materialized. Addison was raised at last to the eminence of a secretaryship of state. Meanwhile the Fish Pool project had to wait for the dust of politics to settle somewhat.

On the face of it, the new political arrangement should have encouraged Steele. Sunderland had been an employer of his, years before, in *Gazette* days. Cadogan, whose interest was strong in the new government, was a friend of many years' standing. Joseph Addison as secretary commanded considerable administrative power, including the supervision of patents for projects such as the Fish Pool. The Duke of Newcastle was now Lord Chamberlain. For all this, Steele was drifting toward Walpole's Whig opposition, which was beginning to crystallize with the encouragement of the Prince of Wales. In March, the Prince and Princess had graced a revival of *The Tender Husband* with their presence at Drury Lane.[7] Steele found himself at odds with the ministry, in disagreements that culminated in the dispute of 1720 over the theater patent. The earliest indication of Steele's feelings, however, appears in his relationship with Addison.

The friendship cooled, unmistakably, in the spring of 1717. It apparently had never entirely recovered from the strains of the succession crisis in the winter of 1713–1714. One of the

[6] Quoted in *Corr.*, p. 338.
[7] *The Weekly-Journal* (BM, Burney copy) for 9 March 1716/1717.

indications of a rift is the fact that during that particular winter and spring their literary collaboration ceased. Addison helped Steele during the expulsion period with a few numbers of *The Lover,* but they did not collaborate after that. Addison came to rely upon his followers at Button's, on his cousin Eustace Budgell and his protégé, Thomas Tickell, who received an undersecretaryship in his office. Since the death of Halifax, Addison had been a follower of Sunderland's, and Steele never felt at ease around Sunderland. Finally, Addison was now immensely rich. He had married the Dowager Countess of Warwick in August, 1716, after years of courtship, and he was entitled to an official income estimated at about ten thousand pounds per annum.[8] It is only a conjecture, but one imagines the immediate cause of tension between the two friends in 1717 to have been an attempt on Steele's part to borrow money and a refusal on Addison's to lend it. Steele was critically short because the Treasury still refused to pay the commissioners' stipends, and he was forced to borrow at ruinous rates of interest. Even if Addison had at some earlier time refused him flatly, now was the hour for Steele to try again. No one knew more about this aspect of Steele's character than Addison, however, and he was embarrassingly hampered just then, as it happened, in his relationship with one of his undersecretaries, Temple Stanyan, by the fact that he had lent Stanyan money.[9] If Steele had asked him for a loan, he would have been disposed to refuse. Some such encounter probably preceded Steele's glum remark in a letter to Prue of 1 May 1717 that "I do not ask Mr. Secretary Addison any thing."

If he could not rely on Addison, he had little prospect of assistance from Stanhope or Sunderland. Why should they bother? Everything, he felt, depended on his own efforts; he would pursue an independent course in Parliament at the ex-

[8] Smithers, p. 370.
[9] Smithers, p. 371.

pense of being labeled a malcontent; he would build the Fish
Pool and make a fortune; he would get to work and finish the
comedy he had been thinking about and working on, sporadically, for so long. "Whenever I am a Malcontent," he assured
Lady Steele, "I will take care not to be a gloomy one, but hope
to keep some Stings of Wit and Humour in my own defence."

Ministers might frown, Treasury lords deny, old friends
forget, but Steele was determined to be cheerful in his relationships with his family, and to practice the doctrine he had often
preached, of domestic felicity.

Hampton-Court March 16th, 1716/7

Dear Prue

If you have written any thing to me which I should have received last night I begg Your pardon that I cannot answer till
the next post. The House of Commons will be very busie the
next Week and I had many things publick and private for which
I wanted four and twenty Hours retirement and therefore came
to visit your Son. I came out of Town yesterday being Friday
and shall return to morrow. Your Son at the present writing is
mighty well employed in Tumbling on the Floor of the room
and Sweeping the sand with a Feather. He grows a most de-
lightfull Child, and very full of Play and Spiritt. He is also a
very great Scholar. He can read His Primer, and I have brought
down my Virgil. He makes most shrewd remarks upon the Pic-
tures. We are very intimate Freinds and Play fellows. He
begins to be very ragged and I hope I shall be pardoned if I
equip Him with new Cloaths and Frocks or what Mrs. Evans
and I shall think for His Service.

I am, Dear Prue, Ever Yours
RICHARD STEELE

His best efforts could not banish sorrow at every hour. Prue
complained in her letters of unremitting headaches, and his own
gout, if that was the ailment, bothered him occasionally. His

imagination was full of thoughts about the children's future. In some moods, when the Fish Pool seemed certain to bring him immense profits in its well, he was expansive: "I am come to a resolution of making my Three Children my partners and will constantly lay up something out of all receipts of money for each of them in a Box bearing the name of the little one to whome it belongs." More often now, though, his mood was one of fore-boding mixed with disappointment and vexation: "[It] gives my imagination the severest wound when I consider that [Molly] or any of my Dear Innocents with nothing but their mere innocence to plead for them, should be exposed to that world which would not so much as repair the losses and Suffer-ings of their poor father. . . ." He promised his wife that he would be guided only by his conscience during the next session of Parliament.

Given Steele's opinions on the value of conscience as a guide and his inclination to latitudinarian views in religion, it was natural that he should agree with the doctrine of his friend Benjamin Hoadly, now Bishop of Bangor, when he preached his sermon before the King on 31 March 1717, *The Nature of the Kingdom or Church of Christ*. Selecting as his text "My Kingdom is not of this world" (John 18:36), Hoadly took the position in the sermon, which quickly became notorious, that Christ as law-giver was supreme. He drew as a consequence that the hierarchy of the visible church was without power. The drift of some latitudinarian preaching had been in this direction for a long time and during the reign of Queen Anne Whig controversialists had attacked the predominantly High Church hierarchy on these grounds. Steele himself had been one of them. Now that was past, bishops were certified for their Whig sentiments before appointment to the bench, and no one in authority preached the doctrine of passive obedience to the sovereign's will any longer, as Offspring Blackall, Bishop of

Exeter, had done in the years of *The Tatler*.[10] The fabric of the visible church, from the government's point of view, was in reliable hands. Now, however, Hoadly seemed to imply that a hierarchy, indeed any visible church or priesthood, was unnecessary. That there was some irony involved in the circumstances of a person advocating this view who was a principal beneficiary of the Anglican ecclesiastical system, wherein a bishop could be paid ten or a hundred times the salary of a curate, is beside the point. A cannonade of pamphlets was directed at Hoadly, scores of them, from every point in the spectrum of religious opinion. In May, 1717, a committee of the Convocation of Canterbury brought in a report on the sermon, characterizing it as heretical. To prevent the matter's turning into a confrontation between the clergy of the Lower House and the Whiggish Upper House of bishops, Convocation was prorogued. It did not sit again for the rest of the century, to the great detriment of the Established Church.[11] The pamphlet battle raged on, Hoadly himself contributing a round dozen.

Steele had a single opinion on the subject: "Mr. Hoadly the Bishop of Bangor," he wrote Prue, "has in the sermon for which He is so ill treated, done like an Apostle and asserted the True Dominion established by Our Blessed Saviour." If Steele contributed a pamphlet to the controversy, it has not been identified. Controversy interested him, but most of his work in theological polemic had treated the relationship between the visible church and the political system. His unqualified support for Hoadly is, however, significant. He had argued toleration for Dissent, in Parliament and in the tracts on the Schism Bill, contending that toleration was beneficial and persecution harm-

[10] See *CS*, pp. 113–14, and, for an account of the Bangorian controversy, see Gerald R. Cragg, *Reason and Authority in the Eighteenth Century* (Cambridge, 1964), pp. 194–200.
[11] With the exception of the abortive experiment in 1741, for which see Norman Sykes, *From Sheldon to Secker* (Cambridge, 1959), pp. 54–56.

ful to the body politic. He had voiced opposition to the Bishop of Exeter in *The Tatler* and to the Earl of Oxford in *The Lover* on the grounds that their actions involved an unwarranted intrusion of ecclesiastical power into the realm of politics. He based his criticism of the Roman Catholic Church on the same argument, that the activities of Catholics in the British Isles were directed toward political ends, and were a threat to British liberties. Nothing in this stand is original, but his arguments have a considerable consistency, and his statements bespeak a generosity of spirit that was often lacking in works of religious controversy. Hoadly himself sometimes resorted to heavy sarcasm and in controversy argued for victory. He was a friend and Steele overlooked his shortcomings, including the incongruity of Hoadly's depreciating a hierarchy in which, because of his Whiggish pen, he found such marked worldly success, achieving four bishoprics in nineteen years, each more lucrative than the preceding one. Steele admired Hoadly; he had recently sent to him a distich of appreciation, composed after an evening of drinking loyal toasts to the House of Hanover: "Virtue with so much ease on Bangor sits/All faults he pardons, though he none commits." [12] Steele's own religious position was not far from that of Hoadly; he was essentially a latitudinarian Low Churchman, no deist, but resonant to the appeal of natural religion, as many were in his century. His parish priest was Dr. Samuel Clarke, translator of Newton's Latin writings, whom Voltaire called "a reasoning machine." [13]

In point of fact, Steele's enthusiasm for hierarchies of every sort was draining away. In earlier days, when he was a young soldier, he had been a student of military leadership. *The Christian Hero,* which is about William III in his role as soldier-king and is dedicated to Lord Cutts, one of William's generals, reflected this admiration. Marlborough was for years the sub-

---

[12] *Corr.,* p. 117.
[13] Voltaire, *Lettres Philosophiques,* letter VII.

ject of economia in Steele's writings. In 1717 he felt different. The monarchy as such had never roused deep feelings of loyalty in Steele. Nobility was, he had learned through bitter experience, as nobility did. He was in no humor to render the obeisance and respect which young noblemen like the Duke of Newcastle regarded as a matter of obligation. It was very difficult, it was perhaps impossible to flourish independently within the establishment of upper-class English life, but he was going to continue the attempt. He assured Lady Steele in September : "I do hereby promise You never directly or indirectly to have any thing to do with the Court; for I am convinced there is nothing to be done, with those Poor Creatures called Great men, but by an Idolatry towards them which it is below the spirit of an Honest Free or Religious man to pay."

Worthy sentiments, but in eighteenth-century England it was still beyond the power of a gentleman without land to remain independent of the Court, in the larger sense of that term. Steele believed—no one more devoutly—in the spirit of English Whiggery but he found that the doctrine of personal liberty was a difficult one to maintain in practice. A man could join the army or navy but he could not rise in the military service without having something to do with the Court. Steele had no vocation for the Church, but if he had, he would have been reminded that preferment depended there too on one's relationship with the Court. A gentleman without land or noble connections had the liberty of remaining a junior officer in the army for his lifetime, like Sterne's father, or an impoverished country parson, like Parson Adams. There were, Steele found, for practical purposes only two routes to financial independence in his day that were not dependent on the Court's influence; one of these routes was writing, the other trade and commerce. One man of literary genius, Alexander Pope, at work on the great translation of Homer, was then approaching independence by means of his writing. Even Pope relied to a considerable extent on the favorable notice of noble persons, as had John Dryden before him. The occasion for Samuel Johnson's declaration of literary independence, his refusal of Chesterfield's patronage, was still many years in the future. Steele himself had achieved the position he enjoyed largely by virtue of his skill and fame as an author and editor. Most authors, even so gifted a man as Defoe (who made only a pretense of gentility), teetered on the brink of starvation if writing was their principal means of sustenance. It was possible to make a living as a writer, but just possible. The route to independence through trade had been open in England for a long time but, as with writing, if one lacked capital resources, success there depended on skill, perseverance, and luck. The qualities of temperament and mind that have enabled men to achieve literary eminence do not appear, on examination, to be those that have brought success in the world of trade and commerce, even if both activities have been avenues to the goal of personal freedom. It is this common goal, perhaps, which has led so many writers to try their hand at commerce, with the ensuing chronicles of failure enacting themselves like subplots in the stories of their lives: Defoe and his brickwork fiasco, Addison and the Irish shoe manufactories, Mark Twain and typewriters, and so on. Businessmen have on the whole been more discreet in their commercial ventures, and richer.

Steele was convinced that he could combine the two modes of life, writing and commerce, and win his freedom from that ubiquitous pandering to men of position which characterized political life in England. The Commission for the Forfeited Estates, once the money began flowing through the Treasury, operated with almost total autonomy and as a Parliamentary agency was only nominally under the control of the government. Drury Lane, the managers believed, had established its own freedom of action under Steele's royal patent. When Steele finished his new play Drury Lane would of course produce it, and as a partner he would be in a position to reap the financial rewards he had been denied earlier when he had been only the author. He could continue as a malcontent in Parliament, taking a stand on an issue when it pleased him, knowing as he did so that he was removed from consideration for favors in the ministry's gift. The Fish Pool would, he imagined, serve as the capstone to his independence and assure the comfort and safety of his children after his death.

The Fish Pool enterprise proceeded slowly. William Gillmore had been in poor health that winter and only by mid-April was he able to work again.[14] His other partner, Benson, was spending too much time paying his respects to the ministry. He complained to Prue in May that this was delaying the Fish Pool business, though it served to get Benson a lucrative appointment in November as Auditor of the Imprest. The trial of the Earl of Oxford further slowed their progress. Steele had lost interest in Oxford's fate, but he attended the debates and was irked by the maneuvering which the House of Lords employed to protect one of their own: "The Lords have been so carefull of that Great Patriot the Earle of Oxford as to acquit Him upon a pretence of Priviledge which they never exerted before. The Commons have much indignation at this usage and Address the King not to pardon Him, that they, the next session, may prosequute Him in a Parliamentary Way." In spite of all the drumbeating two years earlier, little that would incriminate Oxford had been found and prosecution was hampered by the lukewarm attitude of Walpole and Townshend, now in opposition. Lady Steele urged her husband to keep out of the debate, which finally came to nothing. Oxford was released from the Tower, and Steele in the following months regained some of the admiration he had once possessed for this

[14] For a most graphic description by his physician of his ailment and cure, see John Woodward, *Select Cases, and Consultations in Physick* (London, 1757), pp. 181–84.

enigmatic and powerful statesman who at one time or another attracted the fervent praise of so various a group of writers as Pope, Swift, Steele, and Defoe.

From time to time Steele retired to his house in Chelsea to work on the new comedy, which, he promised Prue, would bring a great deal of money in the next season. In Chelsea, too, he could visit his daughter Elizabeth at school and report on her progress. Under circumstances most unpromising for her psychological well-being, Elizabeth Steele was developing a character of great calm and fortitude. It would be her lot to survive her father, mother, sister, brothers, husband, and only child. Well did she learn the manner of arranging the dead for their final repose. Through it all she faced her trials as they arose, dealing with what lay before her, doing what had to be done. If Elizabeth Steele complained of her fate, no one ever recorded the fact.

Her father found it difficult to get away from his business, parliamentary and personal, in the spring and summer of 1717. He had committee work in the House to inch through, and the Forfeited Estates Commission was meeting frequently.[15] The first report of the Commission was presented to Parliament and published in July, but their continuing duties required Steele's attendance at Hampton Court and at "the most disagreeable place in the World, a great man's table." More precisely, Steele was lobbying for the Commission's interest, in opposition to that of the Scottish Court of Session, which had, it will be recalled, issued sequestration decrees on its own authority. In a long memorandum to the Treasury, Steele and his colleagues presented their side of the case, singling out the decrees "as the occasion of all the trouble and difficulty [which] hath occured in this whole affair." [16] Apparently the Treasury lords decided that another attempt should be made to resolve the matter by

[15] See Appendix A.
[16] Hertfordshire Record Office, Panshanger MSS.

conciliation, which implied that Steele would be required to go to Edinburgh in the autumn.

His health was troubling him somewhat, and he managed to get away for a long weekend to Tunbridge Wells with his neighbor Dr. Samuel Garth, who was attending the Duke and Duchess of Marlborough there. The waters of Tunbridge, which his aunt Katherine Mildmay had favored, worked such a cure that the former cavalryman got on a horse once again and assured his wife that he was able to ride thirty miles a day with ease. Although Tunbridge produced an improvement in his health, he was still not ready to leave London. He had not finished the new comedy. He had in mind moving from the house on St. James's Street to one in Covent Garden nearer the theater, for his greater convenience, but he had not done so by the end of the summer. Experiments with the Fish Pool occupied much of his time. A scale model of the boat ten inches long by the keel and five inches in the beam, with a well and a little glass deck, was constructed and loaded with a live cargo of one flounder and six gudgeons for the tests. (What, one wonders, became of this little boat?) Near Hackney the boat was moored in the race of a sawmill, where Steele and his partners observed "her Passengers very merry, which made us not a whit less contented." They left a young man in attendance, to keep a journal. Then came the crisis:

The Ignorant [Steele later wrote] are naturally malicious to any Thing they see out of the common Road, and we found the Weight of it in our first Essay; for a Servant of the Mill, tho' desir'd and brib'd to give Warning, when he should have Occasion to raise the Flood-gate, imagining he was able to do Mischief, open'd it upon our Vessel, which tore her from her Moorings; but she, tho' her proper Lading is but about one Pound, rid the Storm; and our trusty Pilate jump'd into the River, and took her up, where she was driven on the North of the Island of *Tresacre,* without having receiv'd the least Damage in her Hull or Cargo, from a greater Storm and Stress of weather than any Ship can possibly meet with at Sea.[17]

Here is a delightful eighteenth-century scene: the Lilliputian boat in peril because of a rascal servant; the matter-of-fact language of the story, with a proper philosophical remark on the malice of ignorance; the faintly blasphemous overtones of the project itself by which Steele, with his seven fishes, undertakes to feed the multitude.

The Treasury at last having consented to pay the commissioners' stipends, his health restored, and the Fish Pool model afloat, Steele was able to enjoy life in the summer of 1717. He welcomed a figure from the past back into his life, Mrs. Mary Delarivière Manley. Now down on her luck, Mrs. Manley came to him with a play, and Steele was prepared to forget the libels on him that she had written or commissioned during the years when she was concocting propaganda for the Earl of Oxford. She had been a friend, probably his mistress for a time,[18] but then had followed her conservative instincts into the Tory party. Now Steele had the power of decision. He approved her play *Lucius, the First Christian King of Britain* for production in May, 1717, and composed an interesting prologue for it which is principally about Nathaniel Lee's dramaturgical practices. Presumably Steele gathered the information from one of the Drury Lane company who had known Lee.

> NAT. LEE—for Buskins fam'd—would often say,
> To Stage-Success He had a certain Way;
> Something for all the People must be done,
> And, in some Circumstance, each Order won;
> This *He* thought easy, as to make a Treat,
> And for a Tragedy gave this Receipt:

[17] *Tracts,* pp. 427–28.
[18] He so referred to her in a letter to *Guardian* No. 53; see *CS,* p. 167.

Take me, said He, a Princess Young and Fair,
Then take a Blooming Victor flush'd with War;
Let him not owe, to vain Report, Renown,
But in the Lady's Sight cut Squadrons down;
Let Him whom they themselves saw win the Field,
Him to whose Sword they saw whole Armies yield,
Approach the Heroine with dread Surprize,
And own no Valour Proof against bright Eyes:
The Boxes are Your own—the Thing is hit; ⎫
And Ladies, as they near each other sit,   ⎬
Cry Ah, How movingly that Scene is writ!   ⎭
    For all the Rest, with Ease, Delights you'll shape,
Write for the Heroes in the Pit—a Rape:
Give the First Gallery a *Ghost*—on th'Upper,
Bestow, tho at this distance, a good *Supper*.
Thus, all their Fancies, working their own Way,
They're Pleas'd, and think they owe it to the Play.
    But the Ambitious Author of these Scenes,
With no low Arts to court your Favour means.
With Her Success, and Disappointment move,
On the just Laws of Empire, and of Love![19]

Mrs. Manley dedicated the play to Steele, and wrote in the dedication an end to their quarrels: "Be then the very Memory of disagreeable Things forgotten for ever. . . ." In another gesture of reconciliation, Matthew Prior contributed the epilogue to Mrs. Manley's tragedy.

It may have been about this time that Steele encountered another Tory, the ambitious young writer Richard Savage, who had been arrested for Jacobite activities during the '15.[20] The well-known story which Dr. Johnson relates in his *Life of Savage* could have taken place during this period. Steele and Savage, it will be remembered, repair to a tavern where Steele

[19] *Verse*, pp. 47–48.
[20] Clarence Tracy, *The Artificial Bastard* (Cambridge, Mass., 1953), p. 29.

dictates a pamphlet and sends him to the printer with the copy, seeking payment so that they can pay the bill for dinner. Steele has left home, Savage discovers, to avoid his creditors. Confidence in Savage's veracity is severely diminished by the fact that the next anecdote he related to Dr. Johnson, about Steele's using bailiffs as waiters for a dinner party, was certainly not true as he told it. As anecdotalists are fond of saying, it could have happened, but one must remember the strong Tory bias of Savage's political thought.

Steele was never again, in fact, to be on entirely easy terms with all of his Tory friends.[21] He was nevertheless working hard to restore some of the relationships, and it is true that the preponderance of the criticism directed at Steele during the remaining years of his life came from Whigs rather than from Tories: from Dennis, Tickell, the Duke of Newcastle. His friendship with Addison, moreover, was cooling just then in the summer of 1717 when Addison not only had offended by taking a rich wife and a high place in the ministry but by exerting his influence to puff Tickell's translation of Homer at the expense of Pope's. Steele's discontent with Addison would thus recommend him to Prior, Mrs. Manley, and, of course, Pope.

Life was happier for Steele in the summer of 1717. Prue suffered from what was diagnosed as gout, but had recovered sufficiently from her depression to write often and in her own hand, and was even able to face returning to London. "I have been a little intemperate, and discomposd with it," he confessed, "but I will be very Sober for the future, especially for the sake of the most amiable and most deserving Woman who has made Me Her Happy Slave and Obedient Husband." He

[21] See Bertrand Goldgar, *The Curse of Party* (Lincoln, Neb., 1961), pp. 166–67; and Robert Hopkins, "The John Dunton-Steel (?) Yoking in Pope's 'Sandys's Ghost,'" *Notes and Queries,* CCIX (1964), 53–55. But see also Richard B. Kline, "Tory Prior and Whig Steele: A Measure of Respect?" *Studies in English Literature,* IX (1969), 427–37.

was encouraging her to think of their family, and she was responding. In July he assured her of his renewed zeal for economy:

Dear Prue,

I have your Kind letter which expresses your fears that I do not take care of my self as to catching cold and the like. I am carefull enough when I am awake, but in the night the Cloaths are kicked on the Floor and I am exposed in the Damp till the Coolnesse awakes me. This I feel at present in my Arms and leggs, but will be carefully Tucked up hereafter. I wait with impatience for the receipt of money out of the Treasury to make farther payments. I believe when I have it, I shall wholly turn off my Coach-Horses for since I am at my study whole days together it is, I think, a senseless thing for Me to pay as if I was Gadding all that while, and showing myself to the World. I have sent your enclosed to Mrs. Keck. She came into the Dining roome to Me when I sent away [my] last letter, and We had some Tea and instead of such Chat, as should naturally arise between a great Gallant and a Fine Lady, she tooke upon Her to tell Me, that I did spend my money upon my Children, but that they ought to be better accommodated as to their dresse and the like. She is, indeed, a very good Prue and tho I divert myself with Her Gravity and admonition I have a sincere respect for Her.

I was last night so much enamoured with an Author I was reading, and some thoughts which I put together on that occasion that I was up till morning which makes me a little restive today. Your Daughter Moll has stole away my very Heart, but doubt not but Her Brother and Sister will recover their share when We are all together except their Mother robbs them of all of Him who is, Dear Prue,

                              Intirely yours,
                              RICHARD STEELE

The Fish Pool advanced. Gillmore was at work on the calculations concerning draught, capacity, and tonnage which had to

be presented with the application for a patent. It was going to
be necessary to make the trip to Edinburgh, however; three of
Steele's fellows on the Commission traveled as far as York and
refused to go further until he joined them. After many letters
back and forth between Wales and London, Steele thought of
sending a coach and horses, with a serving woman, to bring
Lady Steele back to London while he was in Scotland. The
family could live for a while longer in the house on St. James's
Street until they found new accommodations. "Now," he wrote
in September, while he was preparing to set out for Scotland,

> if I have health which, by the blessing of God, encreases to a
> Comfortable degree, this resolution of throwing away all pre-
> tensions from the Court, may, perhaps, fortify me to be the more
> usefull to my King and Country in Parliament and Every where
> else. The Children, God be thanked are all well: Now let Me
> answer to what you say that I have not expressed any thing
> about a desire of our meeting again. There is nothing upon earth
> I wish so much, provided always that You will be what you
> ought to be to Me and not let me burn for what ought to be free
> to Me, and that you will have the Children in the House with
> Us: For I am come to take great delight in them. When I return
> from Scotland we will never part more.[22]

[22] Does this imply that the children had not been in the house with them
before Prue's departure? During her absence Eugene seems to have been
placed at lodgings in Hampton and Elizabeth was at school in Chelsea. A
biographical enigma is posed by a letter in the Scottish Record Office,
Forfeited Estates Papers 1715, General Management No. 9A. Dated from
Edinburgh 26 November 1717, it is an unsigned, unaddressed office copy in
the hand of William Kennedy, Accountant General of the Scottish Commission. The unknown addressee is evidently a functionary of the Commission
then in London, because the letter is concerned with ordering account books
for the clerks. In closing, however, Kennedy writes: "Pray give my humble
Service [*lined through*] duty to Sir Rich[d] Steele & acquaint him that I saw
his boy on Sunday last who does very well the dressing is now taken off &
all appears to be right about him & I believe in two or three weeks he may be
able to walk, I am," [*letter ends*].
Sunday last would have been the twenty-fourth; Steele was to arrive back
in London from Edinburgh on the twenty-third. The boy, therefore, must

On the twenty-first of October Steele set out by stage coach for Edinburgh, taking as his travel companion a French minister in order to improve his accent, "for I find one cannot understand what passes without that Language." French, that is, was the language spoken by the King. Evidently Steele was having second thoughts about renouncing altogether the life of a courtier.

----

have been in or around Edinburgh. Did Steele take his son Eugene, who was in 1722 (*Corr.*, p. 396) afflicted with the stone, to Edinburgh for an operation? Or does the term "his boy" refer to a servant? I know of no other evidence regarding the matter.

CHAPTER VII

Milestones

THE JOURNEY to Edinburgh by way of Huntingdon, Stilton, Stamford, York, Newcastle, and Berwick was arduous under the best of circumstances, but Steele's gout seemed to improve with the rocking motion of the stage coach as it lurched over the road north to Scotland.[1] His traveling companion, M. Majon, enlivened the journey with his Gallic loquacity, "usual at His age, and inseparable from His nation," and made the long days in the coach and the nights spent at coaching inns pass quickly. A breakdown at Morpeth delayed their progress an extra day and forced Steele to give up plans for looking in on his constituency at Boroughbridge. About the first of November, after a journey of ten or a dozen days, which must have made the twenty-five-pound traveling allowance seem minimal indeed, Steele and Majon pulled into Edinburgh.

In those days Edinburgh was the Old Town, towering grey stone houses surrounding courts, clustered on the hill between the Castle and Holyrood Palace. The center of civic life was Parliament House, and the area within a few hundred yards of St. Giles's Church among the interlacing closes and cobbled alleys was without doubt where Steele began his acquaintance-ship with Scotland and the Scots. To the north, he could look

[1] *Corr.*, p. 382. For a description of the route, see John Owen, *Britannia Depicta, or Ogilby Improv'd* . . . (London, 1720).

across the Nor Loch, a small lake, to the hill now covered by the New Town but then pastureland.

He was well received in Edinburgh. He soon discovered, as have many visitors since, that "Scottish hospitality" is not an empty phrase, though whether it is a preferred treatment for gout is another question. As a commissioner he was of course a natural object of attention for those who had claims against one or another of the forfeited estates or who were interested in purchasing the properties of the rebels or who had other schemes afoot involving those properties. There were good economic reasons for cultivating his friendship. His friend William Moore, Receiver General of the English Commission, for example, had been set to work on the side, as it were, by Lord Chief Justice Parker himself to scout out estates with defective titles which Parker could obtain, in the manner of Chaucer's Man of Law "in fee simple" at bargain prices.[2] The actions of the Commission had to do with the redistribution of land, and in eighteenth-century Britain a redistribution of land was certain to attract speculators, great and small. There is no evidence that Steele misused his office for anyone's benefit, but who knew at the time that he proposed to execute his commission honestly?

Another and more generous motive for Steele's warm reception was the fact that he was well known for a spirit of forgiveness, lately displayed in his pleas for clemency toward the condemned rebel lords. His colleague on the board, Sir Henry Hoghton, by contrast, had led troops at Preston against the Jacobite invaders from the north and might be presumed a sterner judge.[3] Steele, too, was a celebrated figure in his own right, perhaps the most distinguished writer to visit Scotland

[2] BM, Add. MSS., 32,686, fo. 110–12; Stowe MS., 750, fo. 196–98, 204–205, 210–13, 262–63.
[3] [Abel Boyer], *The Political State of Great Britain* (London, 1716), X (July–December, 1715), 487. Hoghton commanded a militia regiment.

from England before Samuel Johnson and his companion made their journey to the Western Isles. His arrival was an event in itself. The commissioners were outlanders, they were up to no good, but nevertheless Steele himself was welcome. Alexander Pennecuik the merchant was moved to engross in heroic couplets Scotia's sentiments at the coming of the Commission:

With throbbing Breast, she dreads th' approaching ill;
Yet still SHE loves you, tho' you come to kill.
In midst of Fears and Wounds, which she doth feel,
Kisses the hurting Hand, smiles on the wounding STEELE.[4]

For his part, Steele, born in Ireland of a Celtic mother and married to a Welsh woman, was better attuned to Scotland than most Englishmen would have been. When he engaged a Scot to seek out well-attested instances of second sight in order to confute irreligious persons, he was at one with a culture that had produced Napier, who is said to have invented logarithms to prove the Pope was Antichrist. On the other hand, the legend that Steele endeavored to reintroduce the episcopacy into the Church of Scotland, undertaking many conferences with Presbyterian ministers to that end, does not ring true.[5] Steele was no special friend of the episcopacy as such; the story perhaps had its basis in Steele's efforts to assist the Scottish Society for Promoting Christian Knowledge in establishing charity schools. The previous year, 1716, the Society (which was at that time in friendly correspondence but not formally associated

---

[4] *Streams from Helicon: or, Poems on Various Subjects* (Edinburgh, 1720), p. 49. Pennecuik should not be, but often is, confused with Alexander Pennecuik, a physician and also a poet. See William Brown, "Writings of Alexander Pennecuik, M.D., and Alexander Pennecuik, merchant," in *Publications of the Edinburgh Bibliographical Society,* VI (Edinburgh, 1906), 117–31. I am indebted to Professor G. Ross Roy for guidance on these points.

[5] Second sight: "Theophilus Insulenus," *A Treatise on the Second Sight* (Edinburgh, 1763); Scottish episcopacy: *London Magazine,* XXIV (February, 1755), 82.

with the English society of the same name) had memorialized the Commission for the Forfeited Estates, proposing that some of the money derived from the sales be used to establish additional charity schools.[6] In the light of Richard Steele's many efforts on behalf of the charity schools, one may be certain that this proposal, which was eventually enacted into law, received his sympathetic attention.[7]

The principal reason for Steele's having been named to the Commission in the beginning was probably, as has been noted earlier, to secure the prestige and acquaintanceship he brought to a distasteful and difficult undertaking. Steele had a group of influential friends in Edinburgh, all of them, as it happened, Squadrone Whigs, engaged at the time in a factional dispute with the Duke of Argyll and his followers.[8] Sir Andrew Hume of Kimmerghame, younger son of the Earl of Marchmont, was the center of a wide circle that included George Baillie, a Treasury lord and M.P. for Berwick-on-Tweed, who was married to Sir Andrew's sister Grizell. Another good friend in the circle was Major William Cleland, whose son would write *Fanny Hill*. These men provided Steele's entree to Edinburgh society, and perhaps to the Masonic Order as well.[9] He was made an honorary member of the Corporation of Edinburgh. "You cannot imagine the Civilities and Honours I had done Me [in Edinburgh]," Steele reported to Prue. "[I] never lay better ate or drank better, or conversed with men of better sense than there."

Jollification was one aspect of the Commission's work. The act setting up the Commission had stipulated that the forfeited

[6] Edinburgh, Scottish Record Office, S.S.P.C.K. MSS., GD 95, Vol. 10, Nos. 62, 63.

[7] See Rae Blanchard, "Richard Steele and the Secretary of the SPCK," in *Restoration and Eighteenth-Century Literature,* ed. Carroll Camden (Chicago, 1963), pp. 287–95.

[8] Cf. Patrick W. J. Riley, *The English Ministers and Scotland, 1707–1727* (London, 1964), p. 267.

[9] See Appendix B.

estates were vested in the Crown, and the Court of Session interpreted this as meaning itself under Scottish law. Unhappily for Steele and his fellows, the Duke of Argyll's faction was strongly represented in the Court of Session, neutralizing the influence of the Squadrone Whigs.[10] If a majority of the Court, and especially Sir David Dalrymple, Lord President, could be brought around, then the Commission might at least begin to take some measurements on the dimensions of their task. Unless and until this could be done the Commission was hamstrung. Rents were not being paid, many claims against the estates appeared to be fraudulent, and some of the tenants had already gone so far as to throw the Commission's surveyors off the estates, thus preventing accurate assessments. These assessments were in themselves, the commissioners discovered, far more difficult to arrive at than they had anticipated because of the ancient Scottish custom of paying some rents in kind rather than cash. To an English landlord, twenty pounds meant twenty pounds, or four hundred shillings. In Scotland reckonings were different. A tenant might, for example, meet his obligations by supplying oatmeal for his laird's porridge. The Earl of Mar's estate, valued at £1,678 per annum, was found upon inquiry to yield £650 in money, but also two hundred and thirty-four pounds, five shillings sixpence and three farthings in oatmeal, calculated on four hundred and forty-nine bolls, three farlets, and one peck at ten shillings fivepence a boll. The "rent" of forty-two ducks at six and two-thirds pence was also gravely calculated, as was that of swine and other produce.[11] These calculations were difficult enough, but the really insurmountable obstacle remained the Court of Session. The Court was adamant. No amount of persuasion, by social or political means, could sway it. New legislation would be required. An impasse

[10] Riley, *The English Ministers*, p. 271.
[11] Scottish Record Office, FEP 1715, Abstracts of Rentals: 1719. Two pennies Scots equaled one-sixth of an English penny; hence the thirds. See *CJ*, XVIII, 425.

having been reached, the Scottish board adjourned its meetings in Edinburgh. Steele set out on the long return journey on 9 November, looking forward to the new session of Parliament and to Prue's return from Wales after so long an absence.

Prue was coming home. All through the autumn she had been undecided, had spun out objections and conditions, had hesitated and delayed. Steele was ready to agree to anything. Five of her letters reached him in Edinburgh, the first two full of business about her estates: "A third scrip, without date, says my letters are short, and so shall yours and concludes. Your fourth is in very pleasant Humour which you say you can support provided you do not want money and you have bespoke Gossips for y' next Child, &c. This is as it should be. Keep up this spirit and live and reign—you shall want nothing on my part towards it." On his way south from Edinburgh, he wrote proposing that he come himself to accompany her back: "I Grow very fond of waiting upon You, and bringing [you] from Wales when the House is adjourned for a few days and since you hear travelling agrees with Me I hope to receive your permission to attend You." In the end she set out without him, and Steele sent servants to meet her and accompany her home in triumph, as it were.

Wednesday Night, Dec^br 4, 1717

Dear Prue

Yours of Sunday was very late notice of Y' arrivall: Wilmot went to meet you that very day but least you should escape Him, I send Mr. Evans to Meet you on the day you hope to come. . . . You come in smiles and I will Sacrifice all to Y' Good Humour,

Obediently yours,

RICHARD STEELE

I am glad to find Journeying agrees with you as well as Me. I hope we shall never part more.

A few days later, presumably, Richard Steele and Prue were together again. Only a year remained to them.

The trip to Edinburgh and back had produced little in the way of accomplishment for the Scottish Commission but it had, Steele assured his wife, helped his gout. Remission of the gout appears to have induced one of those dangerous accesses of benevolence and confidence in mankind to which Steele was subject, which involved him, just before Prue's return in December, in another expensive and time-consuming lawsuit. The same commissioner who was zealous for the safety of public funds proved quite ready, once more, to jeopardize his own on a whim. The story began shortly after his arrival in London. One day turned up his old friend Woodes Rogers, the buccaneer captain, in the Tennis Court Coffeehouse.[12] Rogers, who had *rented* the Bahamas Islands from the Lords Proprietors in October, with the breathtaking ease of colonial days, had recently received appointment as governor of those islands. Taking coffee with him in the Tennis Court that day was a figure from Steele's past, John Sansome. Sansome had been at Charterhouse with Addison and Steele and had gone up from there to St. Catharine's College, Cambridge. For a while around the turn of the century his affairs had prospered. He had been in a position to lend Steele some six hundred pounds.[13] About 1702 he was Collector of Customs for Bristol but with this preferment his decline commenced. Discovered to be several thousand pounds in debt to the Crown, he sued Steele in 1705 for repayment of the debt and thus involved Steele (as possessor of assets due Sansome) in a debt to the Crown. Sansome then dropped out of sight; perhaps, so his acquaintanceship with Rogers might suggest, he sought temporary refuge in the British colonies across the Atlantic. Steele in 1705 had been a political and literary unknown at the beginning of his career in

[12] The following account is derived unless otherwise indicated from *Correspondence* and from the lawsuit (Chancery Proceedings, Reynardson, 1714–1758, No. 2363) summarized in Aitken, II, 161–79.

[13] See *CS,* p. 64. See also W. H. S. Jones, *A History of St. Catharine's College* . . . (Cambridge, 1936), p. 251.

London; when Sansome reappeared in 1717 Steele was a celebrity in the fullest sense. Sansome, still hopelessly in debt to the Crown, was apparently making ends meet by cadging money from those friends who would lend it. He was, in short, an adventurer, as Steele was to discover.

At the Tennis Court that day, however, Steele was much taken by Sansome's well-informed discourse. The three discussed trade and navigation and as they talked Steele's compassion was no doubt kindled for this old friend, intelligent but poor. Steele knew the rigors of genteel poverty. Next day the barmaid delivered a letter to Sansome when he appeared at the Tennis:

> Dear Jack,
>
> I take it very ill of you that you could think so meanly of me, to whom you have done ten thousand good offices, as never in the course of your perplexities to employ or make use of me in your service. I desire to know your affairs, and I shall to my utmost ability manifest myself your servant with my purse, my interest, and my time.
>
> RICH. STEELE [14]

Steele was an eloquent writer of letters when he chose and Sansome caught his drift well enough. At their next meeting, Sansome made himself so serviceable that the notion occurred to Steele of employing him as secretary for the Fish Pool project, at the considerable stipend of fifty guineas per annum plus expenses. So far so good. Steele arranged for Sansome to meet Gillmore and informed the mathematician that Sansome was to serve as his deputy while he was engaged in business at the House of Commons and the Commission.

---

[14] This letter, though not included in *Corr.*, was quoted in the suit (Aitken, II, 162–63) and admitted in Steele's brief (*ibid.*, p. 171) as genuine. The date given, 11 November 1717, appears to be incorrect, however, inasmuch as Steele was then in Edinburgh.

The Commission was then demanding a large slice of his time, meeting in December and January to put together a report that would stimulate the further legislation needed to break the deadlock in Scotland.[15] In January Gillmore acquiesced and Sansome began his employment. He drafted a petition to the King for a patent on a "Certain Vessel, which, by the Structure thereof, can bring Fish whereever caught, to any distant place Alive and in Health." The invention, His Majesty was informed, would "Greatly contribute to the accommodation of the Rich, the releif of the Poor, and the General Good of All Towns and Cityes in y^r Majesties Dominions." [16] Sansome was assuredly composing prose in his employer's idiom. Since he was actually working with Sansome on the project and because he was not blinded by the sentimental mist which Steele had cast around his old school friend, Gillmore soon began to have second thoughts about the broken gentleman. Steele, on the other hand, was delighted. He lavished rewards on Sansome. It would be proper indeed, he felt, to employ an attorney to draw up articles of a partnership which would ensure that Sansome as well as Gillmore profit directly from the undertaking, and he ordered Sansome to see that the articles were drawn. Sansome hired an attorney of his own choosing, who formulated articles that made Sansome's part in the undertaking the equal of Steele's with respect to profits and that stipulated mutual performance bonds of three thousand pounds each. Steele, however, was to bear all the expenses of the project. A day was appointed for signing the articles.

Here, surely, is a virtuoso effort of financial whimsy on Steele's part. Gillmore glanced over the articles and quite sensibly refused to sign, backing out of the room while Sansome and

[15] Steele attended meetings at Essex House on 14 and 24 December, and on 20, 28, and 31 January (PRO, FEC 2/3).
[16] *Corr.*, p. 531.

his lawyer threatened him and Steele attempted to persuade him to put pen to the agreement. As Gillmore pointed out later, he and Steele, having contributed technical skill and money, would be bound in partnership with Sansome, who had contributed little or nothing beyond a convincing line of talk. They might well be adjudged liable for his unsatisfied debts to the Crown. Nothing Steele could do or say would make Gillmore sign.

Sansome began to bully Steele about the breakdown of the understanding and Steele, as he later put it, "fearing Sansome would take too deeply to heart Gillmore's refusal to take him into partnership" went to Sansome's lodgings in Stockwell in April, taking Prue and his children with him. There they stayed for almost two weeks, until Sansome made threats of physical violence to Prue one day, at which point Steele and his family packed their luggage and returned to St. James's Street. Sansome threatened legal action in May and in July brought suit in Chancery to have the articles enforced.

Consider the point to which Steele's generosity and financial soft-headedness had brought him: on the basis of an agreement which he had not signed, he was being sued for a third share of the profits of an invention that had already cost him eight hundred pounds by the man whom he had paid to serve as his secretary. Before the storm broke he had been prepared to bind himself to the extent of three thousand pounds to a man whom he knew to be penniless and a debtor to the Crown. Fortunately for the sake of his children, Steele apparently won this suit.[17] The project having been rid of Sansome, work could continue. During the spring and summer of 1718 a full-size vessel was put together on the building ways at Rotherhithe, under Gillmore's supervision. In March the Attorney General gave his

---

[17] His reference in *The Theatre* No. 28 to "a late Judgment in my Favour, concerning a certain ridicul'd Invention" is plausibly taken to refer to this suit, though no record of a decision has been found.

favorable opinion of the patent, and on 10 June letters patent were granted to Steele and his assigns for a period of fourteen years. The Fish Pool was almost ready for the open sea.

Gillmore had stated in his Chancery brief that Steele's time was "taken up with matters of far greater importance," and it is true that the situation during the session of 1717–1718 required more attention than usual if Steele was to maintain his political equilibrium. Steele presented the report of the Forfeited Estates Commission, which he had helped to draft, to Commons on 16 January. It was on the whole favorably received and after considerable debate a new act (4 Geo. I, c. 8) received the royal assent. This measure specified that estates vested in the Crown were vested in the commissioners rather than the Court of Session, and authorized the Commission to summon the sequestrators and to establish forthwith sums payable the Crown. The act further authorized the expenditure of up to twenty thousand pounds from the proceeds for establishing additional charity schools in the highlands.[18] With this enacted, the work of the Commission in Scotland could at last proceed. On 26 March 1718 the full Commission met at Essex House, took the oaths again, and once more divided by ballot. The same commissioners were re-elected for Scotland and England.[19]

Other aspects of the parliamentary session were not so placid. Walpole, Townshend, and their supporters in opposition were creating trouble for the ministry wherever they could do so. Overshadowing parliamentary business was a most scandalous quarrel between the King and the Prince of Wales. This had been brewing for years, heated by the antipathy between father and son, and between father and daughter-in-law. A series of incidents during 1717 had culminated in the King's insistence

[18] *CJ,* XVIII, 669.
[19] PRO, FEC 2/11.

that the Duke of Newcastle serve as godfather to a son born to Princess Caroline in November, 1717. The Prince did not care for Newcastle in any capacity and heartily resented having him foisted on the royal child as godfather. At the christening the frustrated Prince insulted Newcastle by calling him "rascal," a term ordinarily reserved, of course, for use within classes of society or as a mode of address for a nobleman of a commoner.[20] Newcastle tattled to the King, who, furious at this treatment of a favorite, ordered the Prince to his apartment and commanded that he have no army officers in his household, with the implication that the Prince's loyalty could not be trusted. After a while, the Prince was released but banished from St. James's along with the Princess. The King retained his grandchildren in order to supervise their education. When the Prince of Wales set up his own establishment in Leicester House he provided a formal rallying place for dissidents of the regime, Whig and Tory, to which they flocked. Here Walpole and Townshend commenced building their base of support against the day when opportunity would once more be theirs.

Although Steele was drifting in the direction of Walpole's group because of his general dissatisfaction with the government, and although he was impelled further in this course by the quarrel with Newcastle over Drury Lane and by Addison's coolness, he was not ready decisively to cast his lot with the opposition. He and the actor-managers wanted large audiences at Drury Lane, whether Whig, Tory, or Jacobite. The theater had beyond a doubt profited from the patronage of the Prince and Princess of Wales, and the King himself was showing at least a tolerance for the English stage, which was to culminate in a series of performances during 1718 at Hampton Court. The fact that this new-found interest was part of a campaign to

---

[20] Among many reports of the incident is one in PRO, SPD 35/10/15.

improve the popular reputation of the monarch only argued caution more insistently on Steele's part.[21] There had been hope during 1717 that the company at Lincoln's Inn Fields might collapse, leaving Drury Lane a monopoly.[22] Steele, moreover, had pending the application for a patent on the Fish Pool. All these considerations spoke against his committing himself in a dynastic struggle; he cut too small a figure in the great world for that.

He would, instead, support the government when he chose and oppose its measure when it pleased him. During December, 1717, Walpole launched a strong attack on the supply bill for the army, strengthened by his knowledge of the facts gained when he had been Secretary-at-War. The army was expensive, he argued, badly organized and a threat to British liberties by its very existence. The large provision for officers on half-pay attracted his special criticism as a waste of public funds. The army was a subject of which Steele believed he, too, had special knowledge and he supported the Secretary-at-War, Craggs, in speeches on 9 December and 22 January. The government was, however, with the exception of Cadogan, suspicious of Steele and he continued to have the feeling that he had been fobbed off with a cheap title or two, and with the commissionership, which involved hard work.[23]

Whatever his feelings of discontent with the Stanhope-Sunderland ministry, in that winter of 1717 and spring of 1718 Steele could enjoy the satisfactions of a reunited family. He looked forward to the building and launching of the first Fish Pool vessel, and to continuing his service on the Commission and at Drury Lane. Although he had not managed to finish the

[21] John M. Beattie, *The English Court in the Reign of George I* (Cambridge, 1967), p. 274.

[22] *Corr.*, p. 353, and *London Stage*, I, 413.

[23] J. H. Plumb, *Sir Robert Walpole: The Making of a Statesman* (London, 1956), pp. 262–63; [Richard Chandler, ed.], *The History and Proceedings of the House of Commons of Great Britain . . .* I (London, 1741), 173.

comedy on which he had been at work for so long, he was evidently keeping an eye on the theater. He heard John Dennis had a new play in hand and arranged for a reading before the managers at his house in St. James's Street of Dennis' *Coriolanus, The Invader of his Country,*[24] which was accepted for production.

With the passage of the new legislation enabling it to proceed, and the proroguing of Parliament in March, 1718, the Commission for the Forfeited Estates made plans for a season of accomplishment. Steele in March engaged a house in Edinburgh from the antiquary James Anderson which Anderson assured him "will be to your lady's liking. . . ." It was to be furnished by the fifteenth of May. As usual, Steele's plans did not proceed smoothly to fulfillment. In April, Prue knew that she was pregnant once more.[25] During the same month, it will be recalled, he had ushered her and one or more of his children to Stockwell for the prolonged confrontation with Sansome. When Sansome attempted to delay submission of the patent, a hearing was ordered at Steele's request in the chambers of Justice Eyre, one of the justices of the Court of Chancery. The hearing was held on the thirteenth of May, the day on which the English Board of the Commission for the Forfeited Estates met and issued a letter to the members of the Commission for Scotland, tactfully urging their departure. "[It] would be needless to hint to you how desirous a set of People are to find fault. . . . We therefore know you will excuse our reminding you of the necessity of your speedy attendance at Edinburgh. . . ."[26] Steele was disturbed. He had intended conscientiously to do his duty in Scotland this year as he had the year before, but the patent had now been challenged and he foresaw the possibility

---

[24] Loftis, pp. 70–71.

[25] Steele's brief in the Sansome suit states that she was "then with child" (Aitken, II, 175).

[26] The letter, an office copy, is filed in PRO, FEC 2/62; the original has not been located. Full text appears in Appendix A.

of losing all the time and money he had invested.[27] His reply to the Commission's letter is an extraordinary document:

> I have received the honour of yours dated yesterday, and very frankly own to you that I am detained by what may be yet called my private business, tho' it is a matter which relates to the fishery of England.
>
> If there are not other properties in air, wood and water than are yet known it will not only be an ample fortune to me, but (what I sincerely much more value) make me the instrument of great good to others.
>
> The King has been pleased, as fast as due form will admit, to grant me a patent for a new invention of this importance.
>
> It is gone so far as a bill underwritten by Mr. Solicitor General for the King's hand, but I have been interrupted from a pretension formed by a gentleman who has made an artful use of a confidence I put him in, to come in for a third share of the benefit arising from the design.
>
> [He tells of Judge Eyre's decision.]
>
> This has been the main impediment to my going out of town, but I am to acknowledge others also, which are that by minding the business of mankind more than that of myself or family my fortune is in a very perplexed way. But as I have in me twice as much as I owe were I to die this moment, a little application will make all tight; in the mean time, tho' (besides what I have to leave behind) my present income is 2000 l. *per annum*.[28] I cannot this moment leave the town without almost irreparable detriment. A patriot (which I have been with all the faculties and opportunities in my power) must expect to bear the detraction of his friends and the revenge of his enemies. I have felt both as much as a private man ever did, and I will to my life's end, in

---

[27] From the omission of Benson's name in the lawsuit, it appears that by May he had dissolved his connection with the project.

[28] The total indicates that he expected to receive about a thousand pounds from Drury Lane and as income from his writings, in addition to his stipend as a Commissioner. Most of the income from the theater, however, was still entangled in the mortgage Steele had undertaken, and would be for years to come.

spite of both, go on in the same path. But I will hereafter be better prepared for it by taking care of my own fortune. I gave up for some years my quiet, my fame and my income, when contrary measures would have enlarged them all to a very high degree, and the end of all this is that the famous Richard Steele, Esqr. has no great man his friend but Sir Richard Steele, Knt.

Steele's recital of his personal finances for the benefit of his bemused colleagues is astonishing enough, but the letter casts in relief other important aspects of his character as well. There can be no question, first, that the idea of the Fish Pool as a benefit to mankind appealed strongly to him. It would be "the instrument of great good to others." Technology in the service of mankind, for private gain and public benefit, was not a novel idea in the unfolding age of enlightenment, but Steele was among the first to popularize it. "[S]o delicious a Food," he was to write a few months later, "as that of Sea-Animals, brought alive and in Health to our very Kitchins, wherever we reside, cannot but be as welcome and beneficial to all Mankind, as well as fortunate to the Undertakers, as any Invention that has been brought into Practice for many Ages." [29] To the twentieth-century ear this may sound like the work of an early advertising writer, and it was, but Steele believed his own copy.

The second aspect of Steele's letter to the commissioners which merits attention is the refrain of self-revelation. It is not enough to say that Steele often indulged in a public justification of his actions, and that the tone he characteristically employed in such an undertaking was pompous and offensive. This public discussion of one's private life is sufficiently unusual in an age and a culture where one kept private business in the background and employed a disguise even in replying to lampoons and libels. Steele went out of his way to introduce himself personally in his writings; he was constantly parading himself as his

[29] *Tracts,* p. 449.

own spokesman, bringing up matters of private concern (such as the discussion of his income in the letter) where they were inappropriate. An interesting contrast may be drawn with the practice of Jonathan Swift, whose compulsion was the opposite. Throughout his literary career Swift made elaborate, sometimes ludicrous attempts to conceal the authorship of his works, though he was not pleased to have them ascribed to others and was at pains to see that they were correctly printed. Steele, on the other hand, cared little about the manner in which his writing was published and seldom revised his works to any extent when they were reprinted. But he would freely affix his signature, even to compositions not his own, as he did to Hoadly's Dedication to *The State of the Roman Catholic Religion*. No one enjoyed seeing his name on a title page more than Richard Steele. These two attitudes, though different, stem from a similar cause, the pride of sensitive men—both orphans and both born in Ireland—who felt that their abilities were not properly recognized. Steele paraded his feelings before all the world, as if determined to gain his due by shouting. Swift burned inwardly, revealing his emotions indirectly in the great satires or very occasionally in a letter, such as that one cited by his recent biographer in which Swift complained of the ill usage of his first patron Sir William Temple and added: "This I will venture to say, that in the time when I had some little credit I did fifty times more for fifty people, from whom I never received the least service or assistance." [30] Swift's response is the more dignified and admirable, but he did not have a wife to remark on the ingratitude of great men.

Whatever its interest as biographical evidence, the letter failed to mollify his colleagues on the Commission, whose work was impeded by Steele's absence. In June, William Kennedy, the Accountant General of the Scottish board, observed to a

---

[30] Irvin Ehrenpreis, *Swift: The Man, His Works and the Age,* Vol. I: *Mr. Swift and His Contemporaries* (London, 1962), p. 263.

friend in London, "I shall not pretend to tell you how much our Commissioners are blamed that they have not before this fallen to business. You know very well . . . how the greatest part of this Country are disposed with respect to the Commission. . . ." [31] It was a time for the Commission to exercise diplomacy and their chief diplomat was building fishing boats.

ii

The Fish Pool obsessed Steele, but the theater was also getting in the way of his journey to Edinburgh in the summer of 1718. With another child expected it was necessary for him to redouble his struggles toward financial independence. Perhaps the Commission would accept his promises for a while, until he could get the Fish Pool launched and the special series of theatrical performances at Hampton Court behind him. His colleagues in Edinburgh had secured an office in Parliament Close, only a few yards from the Court of Session, and were settling in for a busy summer. "[I]t is thought," a London newspaper reported, "they will have Business enough upon their Hands to keep them employ'd for some Time." [32] They cursed and looked for Steele's coach in vain through July. In August he assured his landlord James Anderson that he would certainly be there soon and directed Anderson to find a caretaker for the house against his arrival. [33]

The Fish Pool was attracting a fair amount of attention, carefully fostered, no doubt, by its projector. The Duke of

[31] Scottish Record Office, MSS. FEP 1715, Forfeitures in General, No. 9A: Letters.

[32] [Mist's] *The Weekly-Journal: or, Saturday's Post* (BM, Burney copy), 26 July 1718.

[33] Edinburgh, National Library of Scotland, MSS. 29.1.2, letter of James Anderson to his son Patrick of 4 August 1718: "I have gott a most civil Letter from Sr Richd Steel^e who is yet necessarily detained but will certainly be here. He desires me to have Some Body on his Charge to take care of the House. For diversion I send you Lucky Spences last advice by Ramsay ye wigmaker who for Wit & old Scots is much esteem'd. . . ."

Chandos, for example, not a notably sentimental person, was impressed to the extent of granting Steele a loan. A crew was retained, more money was found somewhere, and on 18 August, after appropriate ceremony, the first well vessel was lauched before "many Gentlemen of Learning, Skill, and Experience who all concurr'd in the Opinion that the said Vessel would be of great Benefit to the Publick." [34] So *The Post Boy* reported the event. Londoners in the age of projecting were willing to be persuaded that wealth lay around the corner, in the next project. By the day of the first voyage, 13 September, the enterprise had cost £1,143.[35] With the exception of whatever contribution Benson had made, virtually all of the money was Steele's. There were many who believed in what he was doing, however. When Mist's *Weekly-Journal* directed a flippant criticism at the Fish Pool, "Mr. Tell-truth" replied indignantly in a letter to the paper "that there never was, and never will be found out a more ingenious Piece of Work. . . ." [36] If Steele could keep this sentiment stirring until he could incorporate a joint-stock company, the Fish Pool might yet turn out to be the well of gold he envisioned. In November, with sea trials safely logged, he published a long promotional tract on the vessel, dedicated to Sir John Ward, the newly elected Lord Mayor of London. The merchant, Steele affirmed in the dedication, should "by all be held in the first Esteem: It is he, who . . . extends the Offices, Advantages, and Civilities of Acquaintance and Neighbourhood to all Parts of the habitable World."

The views of course are those of Mr. Spectator, and the good opinion of Sir John Ward's city was essential to Steele in the new enterprise. It is significant, however, that more than three years had passed since he had last published a dedication to a politician. If political leaders worried about such things, one or

[34] Quoted in *Corr.*, p. 501.
[35] MS. memorandum of accounts, at Blenheim, quoted by Aitken, II, 160.
[36] BM, Burney copy, 29 November 1718.

another might have become annoyed at Steele's nomination of the merchant as first in the hearts of his countrymen. Politicians do not worry about such things; the concern of men in power is power and control. It was in this respect that Steele was threatened during the summer and autumn of 1718; his plans for political independence were at cross purposes with those of his titular patron, the Duke of Newcastle, who set about cutting Steele to size.

Steele's forebodings had been proved accurate. Newcastle was the worst sort of patron for a man of Steele's temperament. He was young, he was unsure of himself in politics, he was the more concerned, therefore, that his dependents demonstrate their loyalty. He had few or no intellectual interests and was not impressed by Steele's renown as an essayist and playwright. Steele's independence of mind unsettled him; it is easy to imagine a situation in which the outspoken Sunderland, for example, questioned Newcastle's ability to control his dependents when Steele voted against the Court. On the other hand, he had not proved to be an effective patron in that area in which Steele required assistance most urgently: he had steered very little money in Steele's direction. The title of Deputy Lieutenant and the knighthood were window-dressing; Drury Lane had been given him at the suggestion of Nottingham and Marlborough. Vast patronage was in Newcastle's hands now that he was Lord Chamberlain but none of it came Steele's way.[37] Although the ministry retained a veto in the proceedings, Steele had in fact been elected by his fellow members to the Commission for the Forfeited Estates. The more he thought about the situation the less his debt to Newcastle seemed to him. Newcastle, for his part, was unaccustomed to humoring dependents who forgot their obligations. The relationship had gone sour on both sides.

The tenants who had voted wrong in 1713 and had found

---

[37] Beattie (note 21 above), p. 133: "The lord chamberlain in particular disposed of dozens of honorific and financially attractive posts."

themselves evicted forthwith from their homes could testify that Newcastle had a strain of vindictiveness in his character. He was willing to exert himself in the business of bending underlings to his will. With the passage of the Septennial Act no election was in sight for several years to come, so there was little he could do about Steele's seat in Parliament, however much he disliked the waywardness of his votes. Stanhope and Sunderland, the centers of power in the government, were probably not unduly disturbed by Steele's conduct; they had known him for years and did not feel threatened by his impetuous gestures of independence. They were not prepared, of course, to work on Steele's behalf if he opposed their measures but they had seen ministries rise and fall before and, whatever the rhetoric they employed in the House, they did not regard independence on the part of a backbencher as equivalent to treason.[38] About the only quarter from which Newcastle could effectively reach Steele was that of the theater. Drury Lane came directly within Newcastle's purview as Lord Chamberlain and there was no reason for him to consult colleagues who might have advised restraint. Nor is there any evidence that he did.

Pinning Steele to the wall would be difficult, even for Newcastle, one of the few courtiers who had the King's ear. As part of a systematic program to reveal to his subjects a monarch who had for the first two years of his reign lived virtually as a recluse, the custom of Court theatrical performances was to be revived in the autumn of 1718. Plays were to be presented at Hampton Court by the Drury Lane company, at the King's command. This was a great coup for Drury Lane, which had enjoyed the patronage of the Prince of Wales and Princess Caroline but which until this occasion had not gained the favorable attention of King George himself. The plan had been to

[38] It should be remembered that at the next general election Sunderland assisted Steele in securing a seat for Wendover, Bucks.

build a stage in the Old Hall for performances twice a week during the summer, when the Court was in residence. Steele's crony William Benson had succeeded Sir Christopher Wren as Surveyor-General in April and plans for the stage no doubt owed something to the Benson-Steele collaboration. Perhaps the delays in construction did, too, for the hall was not ready until September and only seven plays were presented during the first "season." [39] It was at the opening performance, a presentation of *The Beaux Stratagem,* that Newcastle made his first move against Steele.

The leading literary artist associated with Drury Lane, as well as its governor, Steele felt called upon to prepare a prologue for the opening. He had already written one and delivered the copy to Robert Wilks so that the actor-manager could memorize it for delivery on the great occasion, when he discovered to his consternation that Newcastle had commissioned the serviceable Thomas Tickell to write the opening prologue. Worse was to come. Tickell had been kept on as an undersecretary after Addison's departure from office in April and Addison, in Bristol taking the waters, had read and emended his prologue. Steele interpreted the sudden appearance of Tickell's prologue as a calculated affront, accompanied as it was by Newcastle's direct command to Wilks—rather than to Steele, the governor—that it be read. He could scarcely have felt otherwise; he was the patentee of the company and Wilks had already memorized his prologue. Furthermore, Newcastle's action was a threat to the independence of the company, as the managers viewed that independence. An occasional request from the Lord Chamberlain was one thing, but a direct com-

[39] The stage was used only once in subsequent years. On 18 October 1731 a single performance was given for the Duke of Lorraine. The stage continued to block the hall until the reign of George III, when it was removed with the King's permission by James Wyatt, the arch-restorer, then Surveyor-General. See Ernest Law, *The History of Hampton Court Palace* (London, 1885–1891), III, 226–27, 240.

mand was quite another; it would constitute, in fact, a precedent for further encroachments on their freedom of action. Finally, if Steele learned of Addison's hand in the matter, he could not have failed to regard Addison's action as a personal rebuff from an old friend. Addison had been assisting both the literary and political careers of his protégé Tickell for some time, notably in the rival translation to Pope's Homer.

It is possible that Addison and Newcastle had in mind replacing Steele with the more tractable Tickell as theater patentee and hoped to humiliate Steele into resigning his office. Steele chose to move cautiously. In a letter as straightfaced as a lord justice, he remonstrated:

> My Lord
>   Before I knew that Mr Tickell had the Honour of your Grace's Commands to write a Prologue, I thought it my Duty to prepare one for the Occasion. Mr Wilks was perfect in this, when that very agreeable and Elegant peice of Tickell's came to His hands. As this has something solemn and respectfull in it, I fancy it might be a Prologue, and His a very pleasing desert to finish the entertainment. But I do assure your Grace I do not say this out of any arrogance of an Elder Poet but I submit this and things of much greater moment to Me, unreservedly to Your Grace. However, I thought it concern'd Me to Show, in a Circumstance wherein I have the happiness to be particularly under your command that I would omit no opportunity of appearing, My Lord,
>   Y^r Grace's Most Obedient and Most Devoted Humble Ser^{nt}
> Sep^{br} 21st 1718   RICHARD STEELE
> The Duke of Newcastle [40]

---

[40] Addison had known of Tickell's prologue before 22 September and might have been able to spare his old friend embarrassment by informing him of Newcastle's wishes, but he apparently did not do so. Does the phrase "very agreeable and Elegant peice" indicate that Steele knew of Addison's hand in the business? See R. E. Tickell, *Thomas Tickell and the Eighteenth Century Poets (1685–1740)* (London, 1931), pp. 70, 71.

Newcastle replied by forcing the issue: Steele's prologue was not heard at Hampton Court. In a few days the disagreement with Newcastle had advanced so far that Steele, solicited by some friends to seek a royal warrant from the Lord Chamberlain for a barge-builder, wrote to Jacob Tonson asking him to approach Newcastle on the friends' behalf.

Though his prologue was not read, Steele was very much in evidence at Hampton Court during the performances, which continued on into October. So were large numbers of courtiers, who attended the plays with the King.[41] The enterprise was a success; the King was pleased. He personally ordered all expenses paid and an extra two hundred pounds bestowed on the managers themselves, the whole grant totalling £547 1s 8d.[42] When Cibber thanked the Lord Chamberlain for the favor, Newcastle replied tersely that they had only the King himself to thank. One may be certain that in this case Newcastle was speaking the whole truth. Steele, with the King's money in his pocket, felt that he could afford a jibe now and then himself. Asked by a nobleman how the King liked the performance of *Henry VIII*, Steele replied, "So terribly well, my Lord, that I was afraid I should have lost all my Actors! For I was not sure, the King would not keep them to fill the Posts at Court, that he saw them so fit for in the Play." [43] In the context of Steele's quarrel with the Lord Chamberlain, who filled a large place in the Court, the remark has teeth. *Actors* would be better than these courtiers.

The first move had gone to Steele. He was higher in the

[41] [Mist's] *The Weekly-Journal: or, Saturday's Post,* 27 September 1718: "[O]n Tuesday Evening they acted the Play called, The Stratagem, where we hear that his Majesty and all the Nobility at Court were present"; on 20 September, the "Court was very numerous."

[42] *Calendar of Treasury Books,* ed. William Shaw (London, 1957), Vol. XXXII, Part II (January–December, 1718), p. 628.

[43] Colley Cibber, *An Apology for the Life of Colley Cibber,* ed. B. R. S. Fone (Ann Arbor, 1968), pp. 300, 301. Steele's statement is in italics.

King's favor than he had been for some time. Newcastle addressed a series of questions to Lechmere, the Attorney General, and a similar series to Thomas Pengelly, Serjeant-at-Law, seeking legal routes by which he could move against Steele, employing only his own authority as Lord Chamberlain: "whether his Majesty may not by the Chamberl[ain] of his Household make Orders from time to time for the good Governm[en]t and Regulation of the Players under Sr. Rich^d. Steele, any words or Clauses in his patent to the contrary notwth. Standing.

"In case of Disobedience to Such Orders, whither the Lord Chamberlain may not by his Majestys Command Silence the S[ai]d Company of players from further Acting, and whether Sr Rich^d. Steele's patent will not thereby be forfeited." [44]

Could the patent, that is, be circumvented by the authority delegated to the Lord Chamberlain, without invoking the King's authority as such? It was an interesting question. These were ominous words for the Company of Comedians at Drury Lane. Much depended still on at least the King's acquiescence. As Steele knew, although Newcastle had the monarch's confidence, there were others who detested him, with the Prince of Wales himself at the head of the list. Steele was not without resources, literary and political. Having received the replies from Lechmere and Pengelly,[45] Newcastle probably decided that he should await a more favorable tilt of the political balance of power before proceeding.

The Commission for the Forfeited Estates in the meanwhile had been getting on without Steele's assistance. The new legislation had released a logjam of business; at last the commissioners could accomplish something. More than three thousand claims were submitted for the Commission's adjudication;

[44] See Appendix C.
[45] For a draft of Pengelly's reply, hitherto undiscovered, see Appendix C. Lechmere's reply has apparently not survived. See Loftis, p. 126.

every commissioner was needed. By the time Steele got the performances at Hampton Court behind him in October, however, the board was concluding its meetings in Edinburgh for the year, anticipating the return to London for the opening of Parliament.[46] Something beyond persuasion would be necessary if Steele was to be got to Scotland.

The government's initiative in the new session was the daring course of moving for the relief of Dissent. The last months of Queen Anne's reign had seen the passage of the Schism Act under Bolingbroke's leadership. This measure was intended to hamstring the Dissenters' educational system and Steele had composed one of his most eloquent, if not one of his most effective, pamphlets in fruitless opposition to the act. When the Whigs gained power in the new reign, many Dissenters felt that the time had come to suspend the disabilities they lived under because of the Schism and the Occasional Conformity Acts. As delay lengthened from months into years they grew discontented. The feeling was widespread among nonconformists that the Whigs had welched on their commitments to the Dissenting interests, commitments given in return for their firm support of the Hanoverian succession.[47] On the other hand, life still remained in the High Flying Anglican position. Tory squires who were torpid from one grouse season to the next would stir and mutter at any suggestion of toleration for Dissent. It soon became clear from the temper of the new session

[46] *To the Honourable the House of Commons, a Further Report, Humbly Offered by the Commissioners and Trustees Who acted in Scotland . . .* (London, 1719). The so-called *Third Report.* See also Scottish Record Office, MSS. FEP 1715, Vol. 14: Minutes of the Commissioners. Although there is no record therein of formal adjournment, the minutes break off after 10 October and resume in July, 1719. It is just possible that Steele could have made a flying trip to Edinburgh in October but if he did so I have seen no evidence of it. He is not recorded as being present at any of the Commission's meetings in Scotland during 1718.

[47] See, for example, Dudley Ryder's reading of the situation in *The Diary of Dudley Ryder 1715–1716,* ed. William Matthews (London, 1939), p. 361.

that the Occasional Conformity and Schism Acts could not be repealed. "The Church in danger" had felled many a politician before this. Stanhope nevertheless introduced a bill of relief for Dissenters in December and had steered it through both houses by mid-January. Steele supported relief and voted with the ministry on the bill. It was his last act of parliamentary support for any major measure introduced by the Stanhope-Sunderland ministry.

His personal life had been unusually tranquil during 1718, as far as one can judge such matters. He was happy that the family had been reunited after their long separation. During the summer he had visited Hampton Court, his visit no doubt having to do with the building of the stage there or with his infrequent duties as Surveyor of the Stables. One day he had left Lady Steele and the children at Hampton while he went off on some business or another. On Monday morning, 23 June, he addressed the last letter which has been preserved of a series extending back over a decade. It does not differ substantially in tone from the first:

> Dear Prue
>
> I send this messenger to tell you that I shall not be with You till Eight of Clock tomorrow morning. At that hour, God Willing, I shall reach Hampton-Court, and hasten (as soon as I have taken up you and the rest of my Dear Cargo) to London, where it is necessary I should be in the forenoon. I am, Dear Prue
>
> Y^r Most Affectionate Most Obedient Husband & Servant
>
> RICHARD STEELE
>
> I was so pleased with my Son from His Lodging to Hampton, that I shall please God, take Him with Me to Scotland.

Prue was pregnant during the year. She was apprehensive by nature and her worries no doubt increased Steele's reluctance to make the journey to Edinburgh. She was not in a condition to travel or to be left alone. One imagines that Steele gathered his children together at the house in St. James's Street for Christmas that year, as he had two Christmases earlier. The day after Christmas, 26 December 1718, Prue died, perhaps of complications resulting from her pregnancy. Her husband wrote David Scurlock on 27 December :

> Dear Cousin
> This is to let You Know that my Dear and Honour'd Wife departed this life last night.
> I desire My Aunt Scurlock and Mrs Bevan and You Your self would immediately go into Mourning and place the Charge for such Mourning of those two Ladies and Your own to the account of, S^r,
>
> Y^r Most Affectionate Kinsman
& Most Humble Servant
RICHARD STEELE

It was not the moment for rhetoric. Steele knew that another chapter in his life had closed. Death was around the corner of every street in the eighteenth century, but the pain of loss and separation was real, however familiar it may have been. He would attempt the best for Prue in death, as he had, imperfectly perhaps, in life. On the thirtieth of December, 1718, Prue was buried in Westminster Abbey,[48] accompanied by the final, fervent prayers, one is sure, of Richard Steele. It may be that burial in the Abbey was a last promise on the part of her husband; Prue would have liked that.

If an objective observer, such as Mr. Spectator, had been watching the burial procession wind its way through the echoing Transept of the Abbey, where Prue's body would be laid to

---

[48] Abbey registers, cited in Aitken, II, 192. There is no record of the burial of a child with her.

rest, he might have asked if she had been worth all the bother. She was a pretty woman, to be sure, but beyond that fact, for which we have the evidence of Kneller's portrait, all testimonials to Mary Scurlock Steele's worth emanate from one source, her husband. On the other side of the ledger, she had not been a very efficient wife, she had been retiring and sensitive to a neurotic degree, she had left her family during a crisis in her children's health and her husband's fortunes. But the heart has its reasons unknown to the outside observer; though she annoyed Steele now and then, he loved her intensely, reassured her when she needed reassurance, and regarded himself as a fortunate man in possessing her. She had borne a great deal in the dozen years since they met at his first wife's funeral, and the years of living on the brink of a financial abyss surely took their toll, in her nerves if not in her health, and probably in both. Steele did not see marriage as a business of debits and credits; whether she was or was not neurotic, shy, or inefficient he loved her, from first to last. We must leave the couple there.

He caused a blue marble gravestone to be put over her grave in the middle of the South Transept, with an inscription the modesty of which is in marked contrast to the effusions on monuments nearby:

> Dame Mary Steele
> Wife of Sir Richard Steele Knight
> Daughter and sole heiress to
> Jonathan Scurlock Esq
> of the County of Carmarthen
> Died December the 26 1718
> Aged 40 years.
> Leaving issue one son and two daughters
> Eugene, Elizabeth and Mary.[49]

[49] Aitken, II, 192. The inscription, legible in Aitken's day, is now effaced.

In her lifetime Richard Steele had praised her, in public print and in private correspondence, but at her death he turns his back on the fashion of the age for storied urn and animated bust. It is as if he were saying that there are some feelings better left unexpressed. I shall go to her but she shall not return to me.

CHAPTER VIII

Victory and Defeat

No NEW YEAR could have dawned bleaker for Richard Steele than 1719. Work, however, is considered a potent antidote for grief and in the weeks and months following Prue's death Steele found his energies fully employed. No doubt he welcomed the activity. The children required his first attention. Eugene was settled in a school, apparently at Hammersmith,[1] and Hannah Keck, Mary Steele's closest friend, assumed the supervision of Elizabeth and Molly, for which she was reimbursed by their father. Soon after Prue died, Steele moved from the house on St. James's Street, with all its associations, to the rooms he had leased years before on Villiers Street in York Buildings. These were commodious : in addition to the Great Room or Oratory, where the Censorium held its sessions, there were two rooms on the ground floor, three on the first, six more rooms on the second, and seven garret rooms, with a kitchen and cellar.[2] This would be his London residence until his final departure for Wales, in 1724. As a virtual bachelor, Steele was able to be about his business. Parliament, his new play, the Fish Pool, Drury Lane, the Commission for the Forfeited Estates : all these demanded and received his attention in greater or lesser degree during the year after his wife's death. An unhappy

[1] *Biographia Britannica,* Vol. VI, Part I (London, 1763), s.v. Steele.
[2] Advertisement in *The Daily Post* (BM, Burney copy), 17 August 1724.

consequence of his activities in Parliament was a final quarrel with Addison. The old partners were never reconciled.

Edinburgh was farther away than Westminster or Drury Lane, and Steele continued to neglect his duties on the Commission. He intended to mend his ways, however, for he went to the plenary meeting of the Commission at Essex House on 20 April, where he was re-elected by unanimous vote to the Scottish board.[3] The commissioners agreed to meet at Edinburgh in May and this year his colleagues had prepared a strategy directed toward getting Steele to Edinburgh. Under the terms of an act passed during the last session (5 Geo. I, cap. 23), the Treasury was empowered to deduct five hundred pounds from the salary of any commissioner "absenting himself for three weeks without order or consent of four commissioners. . . ."[4] On the last day of June, Munro and Haldane reported to London that they were the only commissioners present in Edinburgh and requested the English board to make up a quorum. The English commissioners then addressed a letter, dated 9 July, to the members absent from their post, entreating them to repair to Edinburgh. Otherwise, they tactfully observed, the commissioners present "cannot refuse the Publick the justice to sign a Certificate of your Absence. . . ." Steele was reorganizing the Fish Pool project at just that time. He dispatched the following reply to the English board:

> Gentlemen,
>
> I received the Honour of Yours Yesterday, with the Enclosed from Edinburgh. All that has been urged in excuse of others I have to plead for myself in a more urgent Degree, but I frankly acknowledge to You, that I have been insensibly led on from time to time and one incident to another in the Design of the Fish-Pool and that this only has Suspended my Jurney.

---

[3] PRO, FEC 2/11.
[4] Danby Pickering, ed., *The Statutes at Large* . . . , XIV (Cambridge, 1765), 110–11.

That affair has, at last, come to a Successful Issue, and thô doing greater Service to the Publick than I could have done by being at my Post be no defence, Yet I hope, it will be thought such an alleviation of my Fault [to] preserve me from any violent resentments.

I cannot leave this Town without ruining all that I have been doing till the 20th Inst. but will be, God willing, at Edinburgh on the 6th of August.

After I have with this unreservedness told You the true occasion of my Stay here, I must take the liberty to say that [were] I now at Edinburgh I would not Join in one Publick Act till the Arrivall of Mr. Woolfe with the Records of Convictions, and I believe I have been of Some use in the Expediting that Work, tho' it is not Yet wholly dispatched. The plain of the Matter is that I have for some Weeks been y° only Commiss.ʳˢ of Scotland Who has done anything at all and my outmost Crime is that I have chose to be doing some little good at London, than to be doing nothing at all at Edinburgh, All which is Submitted by

> Gentlemen,
> Your most obedᵗ. & most
> humble Servᵗ.

Yorkbuildings
July 10ᵗʰ, 1719   RICHARD STEELE [5]

Steele's promises were then being received skeptically. On 17 July an order was issued commanding him to attend the lords of the Treasury. On 23 July Steele appeared before the lords assembled and promised "to set out in a few days and to make amends for his former neglect by his future diligence." [6] Steele may in fact have set out for Scotland in 1719, traveling by way of Wales.

---

[5] Commission's letter (an office copy) is in PRO, FEC 2/63 (for full text see Appendix A). Steele's, also an office copy, in scribe's hand is in FEC 2/64. John Wolfe, not identified in *Corr.*, p. 537, and Aitken, II, 185, 249, was Register of the Scottish Board.
[6] PRO, T 29/24, Part 1.

He was in Carmarthen in October [7] but he did not get as far as Edinburgh. In December, 1719, and January, 1720, he and his colleague Grantham were excluded from the stipend payments for the quarters ending Michaelmas and Christmas, 1719, "having forfeited & lost their Allow[ances] for ye said Quar[ters] by Absenting themselves from ye Office without the Order consent or Allow[ance] of the other Com[missioners]." [8] After this treatment, Steele was punctilious in discharging his duties on the Commission and attended meetings in Edinburgh annually, until he withdrew from the Scottish board in March, 1723.[9]

The Fish Pool, as Steele had indicated to his colleagues on the Commission, was in operation, at sea. After another trial voyage down the Thames on 4 May, carrying a shipful of passengers invited for the occasion, the well vessel cleared Gravesend on the sixth. The next morning she returned with a tankful of fish ("as Live as ever," according to the shipmaster) and set forth on her first regular commercial voyage. By late July Steele was able to send fresh fish to his creditor the Duke of Chandos, who pronounced the lot "as good as any I ever tasted. . . ." Steele and Gillmore were the sole partners in the enterprise, but Steele had plans afoot for forming a joint-stock company and to this end consulted Chandos, Robert Knight, cashier of the South Sea Company, and John Law. The mind reels at the thought of the advice Steele could have derived from such a trio of free-wheeling speculators as these. Law, indeed, was invited to share in the letters patent, it being "well know," Steele wrote him, "How ill Paris and other parts of France are Supply'd with [fish]. . . ." By the end of the next year Knight's South Sea Company and Law's Mississippi System

[7] See below, p. 165.
[8] PRO, T 60/10, p. 387: Treasury Order Book. The order was signed by John Aislabie.
[9] See below, p. 223.

would be in financial ruin, but who could know that in 1719, when the price of shares was rising? Steele's daughter Elizabeth sent him a purse as a present, perhaps on his birthday, and he thanked her for it, enjoining her that "if you and I Live till this day Twelve-month You are to ask Me for it again full of Gold." The incident brings to mind Ike McCaslin's cupful of gold pieces in *Go Down, Moses.*

Steele's decision to cast in with Walpole and the opposition that year, during the Peerage Bill controversy, would appear at first sight to have been nothing more than another in his long series of quixotic gestures. Opposing a government that had the confidence of the sovereign was still dangerous for a member without fortune or family influence. Newcastle was, he knew, already maneuvering for an opportunity to deprive him of the Drury Lane patent. Why, then, did he choose to take a part, and a very prominent part, in one of the most important debates of eighteenth-century British parliamentary history?

Vexation at Newcastle's treatment of him was probably an element. Steele felt that the ministry in general and Newcastle in particular owed him something and had delivered precious little. The calculated humiliation of Tickell's prologue, followed by Newcastle's movements toward legal action—of which Steele was certain to have had wind from any one of many sources around the Court—did nothing to increase his affection for Newcastle.

Steele, moreover, had come increasingly to respect Robert Walpole's ability and to have confidence in his future success. Even when opposing Walpole's plan for reducing the public debt in 1717 he had confided to his wife, "I believe the Scheme will take place, and if it does, Walpole must be a very great man." In 1722 Walpole achieved control of the government. The promptness with which he then restored Steele to full powers as governor of Drury Lane, after Newcastle's schemes to remove him had succeeded, lends strength to the feeling that

Steele's price might have been Walpole's agreement to support him in the theater controversy which he saw ahead.

Finally, he was impelled to go into opposition on the Peerage Bill because he opposed it on principle. He opposed the bill's passage on constitutional grounds, grounds which may be seen as tolerably consistent with the burden of his earlier political views. In summary, the government's proposal was this: the House of Lords would be limited to some two hundred and thirty-five members, with the King's prerogative of creating peers restricted to filling vacant titles only.[10] This would of course in time have the effect of drastically limiting the sovereign's power, an effect which the ministry, who knew that the Prince of Wales was hostile, were working to bring about. By playing on George I's hatred of his son and his relative ignorance of British affairs, they succeeded in securing the necessary waiver of prerogative from the King. Winning the support of a majority of the House of Lords was easily accomplished by hinting to the peers how greatly amplified would be the influence of those already holding seats: the membership of their club would be permanently limited, with little danger of nouveaux peers clambering over the battlements to invade their sanctuary. It was arranged to have the measure introduced on 28 February, 1719, by the Duke of Somerset, premier Protestant peer, who was careful to cite as a pretext for the measure the "occasional peers" created in Oxford's famous packing maneuver of 1712.[11] If the measure passed, Oxford's scheme could not be repeated. On 2 March a message from the King was read to the Lords expressing his approval of the bill and formally waiving the prerogative. Opposition was voiced by an oddly assorted pair, Oxford and Cowper, but they seemed to be

[10] Still the starting point for a discussion of the bill is Edward R. Turner, "The Peerage Bill of 1719," *English Historical Review*, XXVIII (1913), 243–59.

[11] [William] *Cobbett's Parliamentary History of England . . .* , Vol. VII (London, 1811), p. 589.

isolated: the measure appeared safely on its way to passage. On 14 March the bill was given its first reading, however, and a battle was joined; it proved to be far more spirited than the ministry had anticipated, and drew Addison and Steele into their last, and most acrimonious, disagreement.

On that day, obviously primed by information from Walpole, Steele opened a pamphlet battle that was to involve an unusual array of talent. He chose once again the medium in which he had truly found his strength, the periodical, publishing a weekly written "by a Member of the House of Commons" and entitled *The Plebeian.* The first number is one of the two or three most eloquent and effective of Steele's many political pamphlets. If readers had any question about the authorship of the tract, their doubts would have been dispelled by an early paragraph in which the proprietor of the Fish Pool applies the metaphor of stagnation to the House of Lords envisioned by the government: "THE shutting up the Door of the House of Lords in the manner talk'd of, cannot but prove a great Discouragement to virtuous Actions, to Learning and Industry, and very detrimental to the House of Peers itself, by preventing such frequent Supplies from going into it, as the Nature of such a Body requires; for want of which, it may in time become corrupt and offensive, like a stagnated Pool, which hitherto has been preserv'd wholesome and pure by the fresh Streams that pass continually into it." [12] Much more dangerous to the nation as a whole, however, than the stagnation of the House of Lords—or so Steele thought—was the threatened imbalance of constitutional powers. The royal prerogative, once so menacing, was now much diminished and would be reduced still further by the bill. On the other hand, the power of the lords would be significantly increased, introducing the possibility of an oligarchy of "two or three great Families." "[T]he Milk such Nobles are

[12] *Tracts,* pp. 460–61.

nursed up with, is Hatred and Contempt for every Human Creature but those of their own imaginary Dignity." It is difficult not to feel that Steele has Newcastle in mind, though of course his readers would not have made the application. "WHIGGISM," Steele defines as "a Desire of Liberty and Spirit of Opposition to all Exorbitant Power in any part of the Constitution." The danger of altering the balance of power in a limited monarchy, Steele demonstrates by reference to the history of Sparta.

All this is good, mainstream Whig talk of course, and even then somewhat out of date, if judged in strictly historical terms; [13] but the first *Plebeian* served the purpose. It ushered the debate into the House of Commons, it provided a good exposition of points that were disturbing many members, Whig and Tory, and it smoked out the government's position. Within a week forceful pamphlets were appearing in defense of the bill. *The Patrician,* perhaps by Robert Molesworth, testified on 21 March to the effectiveness of Steele's pamphlet: "The PLEBEIAN just published . . . has doubtless as much alarmed the Friends to the Government, as the presumption of its Author (to say no worse) has surprized those who so wisely steer the helm of it; and though it [is] written in a style as lofty as the end proposed in publishing it is vile and low. . . ." [14] Joseph Addison, although now in his final decline, was called upon to present the government's case in a new periodical, *The Old Whig,* the first number of which appeared on 19 March. Addison's title is intended to rally the Whigs to the true cause, somewhat as if the date were 1680 and the monarch Charles II.

---

[13] See J. H. Plumb, *The Growth of Political Stability in England 1675–1725* (London, 1967), p. 135; and J. W. Gough, *Fundamental Law in English Constitutional History* (Oxford, 1955), pp. 174–91.

[14] *The Patrician* No. 1, is reprinted in *The Town-Talk* . . . , ed. John Nichols, 2d ed. (London, 1790), pp. 403–12. For Molesworth, see Caroline Robbins, *The Eighteenth-Century Commonwealthman* (Cambridge, Mass., 1959), pp. 102–103.

Addison represents the peerage measure as preventing a further abuse of the royal prerogative and as ensuring that men of wealth would continue to find places in the House of Commons. This line of argument required literary tact of an extraordinary degree, inasmuch as the argument emanated from the Court party. Addison's apparent clarity is here, as it had been in *The Freeholder,* only apparent, concealing more than it revealed. There is always, though, the appearance of order, the Addisonian tone which speaks with unquestionable authority.

The debate between Addison and Steele grew sharper. Steele knew well who the Old Whig was, and in the second *Plebeian* his comment that the author of the rival paper "is us'd to Masquerading" was, as Addison's biographer points out, an acid reminder of the many times Steele had protected Addison's anonymity. The reference to masquerading extends beyond Addison's use of anonymity, however; Steele means that Addison is masquerading as a Whig: "I am afraid he is so *old a Whig,* that he has quite *forgot his Principles."* He goes further. In the first *Plebeian* he had mentioned the rulers of Sparta as examples of the dangers of oligarchy. What he had in mind, he explains in the second paper, was their practice of pederasty : he had not been more explicit "to avoid the least Appearance of personal Reflection." Is this a general reference to the sexual practices of members of the Court party or is it directed at Addison himself? [15] Addison chose not to reply directly to the charge—what reply could he make?—but he referred in the second and last *Old Whig* (of 2 April) to the author of the *Plebeian* as "a son of *Grub-Street.* . . ." The accusation that Steele would sell out his principles for bread, so long employed by Tory pamphleteers, is revived by Addison. In the closing paragraph, however, he tempers his attack: "I must own, however, that the writer of the PLEBEIAN has made the most of a

---

[15] Cf. Smithers, p. 437; see Appendix D below.

weak cause, and do believe that a good one would shine in his hands. . . ." [16]

Steele would not be entirely quieted. "This Author's Menaces," he wrote in the final *Plebeian* (No. 4), "are as vain, as his Compassion in another part of his Pamphlet is insolent." At the end of the paper he relents, asks the world to judge the Old Whig by his earlier works, and closes with a quotation:

> Remember, O my Friends, the Laws, the Rights,
> The gen'rous Plan of Power, deliver'd down
> From Age to Age by your renown'd Fore-fathers,
> (So dearly bought, the Price of so much Blood.)
> O let it never perish in your Hands!
> But piously transmit it to your Children.
> *Mr.* Addison's *Cato* [17]

The breach between the two friends which had opened two years or more earlier, the separation which had its beginnings not long after Steele's expulsion from Parliament, was made permanent by the exchange between *Plebeian* and *Old Whig*. As if enacting one of Dr. Johnson's melancholy essays on the fragility of friendship, Joseph Addison and Richard Steele ended their relationship of more than thirty years' duration in a wretched political wrangle. By eighteenth-century standards, it is true, the personal attacks in *Plebeian* and *Old Whig* were not strong; both writers adhered largely to the issues. But that Addison and Steele should have turned on one another in public print is a literary scandal that demands comment. One can dismiss the issues themselves without hesitation: they were important but not important enough to precipitate the final quarrel. The source of the bitterness was, it seems probable, the attacks of the one man on the public image of the other. Each

---

[16] Reprinted in *The Town-Talk*, pp. 317–38.
[17] *Tracts*, p. 496; italics reversed.

had a conception of himself as a public figure and in both cases this image was important to the man's self-esteem. Every controversialist knew that this was true of Steele, and used the fact to divert attention from the issues to the man. Steele was one of the few close enough to Addison (Alexander Pope was another) to realize that his studied self-effacement concealed an enduring concern that the public see him as he wanted to be seen. Steele had been a witness of Addison's terror during the opening performance of *Cato*. He knew that Addison's passion for anonymity stemmed less from modesty than from a reluctance to entrust his reputation to the rude hands of the public. He knew that Addison, reflective in the final degree, realized this as well as he, and Steele's public attack on Addison's preference for masquerading was probing dangerously deep into Addison's inner defenses. Some dreams are for one's own dreaming, after all; it was not his public image as such that troubled Addison in this last controversy, one imagines, but the fact that Steele revealed to all England that he, Addison, was concerned about the figure he cut in the world.

For Steele, Addison's appearance on the side of the government was a reminder that Addison considered the obligations of their friendship at an end. Many a time, he knew, Addison had pleaded neutrality on crucial issues, many a time Addison had avoided committing himself because he wished to avoid partisan squabbles. Now, however, he was willing to return from retirement, responding to an exclusively partisan issue that involved attacking his oldest friend in public print. Could Addison not, Steele might have asked himself, have entered one more plea of impartiality on this occasion? He was retired from administrative service, he was renowned, he was very rich. To Steele, Addison's entry into the pamphlet war must have seemed as unnecessary as it was wounding.

Little time remained for reconciliation. Addison's health was failing. He was stung to the bone by Steele's attack. On the fourth of June he named James Craggs ("young Craggs"), who had succeeded him as Secretary of State, as his literary executor, knowing that Craggs' undersecretary, Thomas Tickell, could be relied upon to treat his literary remains with respect. On the sixth he was said to be dangerously ill; on 17 June he was dead, having summoned Tickell and his stepson, Lord Warwick, to "see in what peace a Christian can die." [18] Steele was not present. Although the recent quarrel probably led Addison to appoint Craggs his literary executor, a most public affront to Steele, the literary partnership had not worked satisfactorily since 1713, since the date, precisely, when Steele was elected to Parliament and became a public figure in his own name during the Dunkirk controversy. Until that time Addison and Steele could maintain a symbiotic relationship, with Steele cast as the playwright and editor of periodicals and Addison as literary adviser and *arbiter elegantiarum*.[19] Addison could view the relationship *de haut en bas,* and in truth Steele required and profited from Addison's advice, as he was given to testifying. When Addison's junior partner came into his own as Richard Steele, M.P., however, the friendship weakened, and Addison began to devote more time to other relationships in which he occupied the position he had maintained with Steele, encouraging, guiding, and advising literary aspirants. Thus Eustace Budgell, Edward Young, Thomas Tickell answered Addison's, if not literature's, purposes.

Addison's body was laid in a vault in Westminster Abbey, next to that of his former patron and friend, Charles Montagu, Earl of Halifax. Addison was dead but Steele smarted from the quarrel and from events that followed. Reading the *Daily Courant* in July, he discovered that Tonson planned to publish an edition of Addison's collected works. Steele reminded Ton-

[18] Smithers, p. 448.
[19] It is significant that the only published letter from Addison to Steele consists entirely of literary advice (*Corr.,* p. 39).

son in a letter that he had purchased the copyright of Addison's *Tatler* essays, in which he and his heirs had a residual interest. "Mr Addison is the last man who shall be patiently suffer'd in doing unreasonable things (that He has you must know) to Y^r Most Humble Ser^nt." A few months later he would be enough himself again to print a handsome tribute to Addison in his new *Theatre* paper, No. 12. But in the summer of 1719 the wounds of his wife's death, of the quarrel with Addison, and of Addison's death were still new.

The outcry over the Peerage Bill continued unabated during Addison's last days. Plans were afoot, it was said, to stage a public burning of the bill in a pan of charcoal.[20] In order to calm the situation, the ministry moved the adjournment of Parliament, though indicating in the King's speech at the close that the bill had not been forgotten and would be passed in the next session. In May Steele published an audacious reply to the King's speech, entitled *The Joint and Humble Address of the Tories and Whigs Concerning the Bill of Peerage*.[21] Both parties, Steele contends, look with "Contempt and Hatred" on those who asked that the sovereign give up his prerogative. "[W]e shall always be ready to oppose the Designs of such Audacious and Wicked Men. . . ." As the title of the pamphlet reveals, Walpole was rallying Tories and dissident Whigs for the struggle against the measure in the ensuing session. Steele's was but one among dozens of pamphlets, including two by Walpole himself, which appeared during the months of debate. Some Whigs were troubled by the issue raised: was the measure or was it not in accordance with true Whig principles, whatever they were? Others disliked seeing all chance slip away of their or their descendants' wearing ermine in the Lords. The Tories, who were by tradition distrustful of limiting a sover-

---

[20] The Marquess of Granby to the Duke of Rutland, as quoted in Turner, "The Peerage Bill of 1719," *English Historical Review*, pp. 248–49n.

[21] *Tracts*, pp. 497–500.

eign's prerogative, were of course also delighted to see any Whig government embarrassed.[22] The strength of the opposition led the ministry to redoubled efforts toward ensuring passage at the next session; threats and promises were distributed with a generous hand, and tempers ran high. When Stanhope and Sunderland accompanied the King on his accustomed lengthy visit to Hanover—though the term "visit" may be more accurately applied to his sojourns in England during this period—Newcastle was left to manage the government's interests at home.

With unfortunate timing, Colley Cibber chose to publish in September his *Ximena,* prefaced by an epistle dedicatory to Steele, praising him for his independence and for his refusal to follow leaders in a bad cause. This reference to Newcastle was anonymous but unmistakable. The dedication also contained an unfavorable comparison of Addison to Steele, which in the context of the recent *Old Whig–Plebeian* controversy and the circumstances of Addison's death gave a handle to Steele's enemies they were quick to grasp.[23]

In the King's absence Steele had time to visit Wales and to finish or almost finish his new play, even if he could not get as far north as Edinburgh. His visit to Carmarthen, where he was admitted a burgess of the county borough of Carmarthen on 5 October, must have been a brief one but perhaps Steele took the occasion then to present a reading of the play.[24] Rumors were abroad in London that it would be presented during the season 1719–1720.[25] A visiting Swiss scholar, the Reverend Henry Ott, heard Steele quote Indiana's song, "From Place to Place

[22] It may be noted that Steele never during the Peerage Bill controversy defended Oxford's action in naming "occasional peers." His position was that, although the prerogative had been abused on that occasion and might be so again, it should not be restricted for that reason.

[23] Loftis, p. 132n., cites a number of allusions that appeared over the next several months.

[24] *Corr.,* p. 390.

[25] Loftis, p. 190.

forlorn I go," during a convivial gathering at Dr. Woodward's that included Sir Richard Blackmore.[26] The discussion had been about poetic inspiration; Steele may have needed to remind himself that he had been a writer before he had become a Member of Parliament; it was difficult to keep this in mind.

With the return of the King from Hanover and the opening of the new session in November, the ministry felt reasonably confident of success. Newcastle complained of their having the "whole Jacobite Party against them, joined by that of ye P[rince]," but expressed his confidence of being able to swing sixteen votes to the government in Parliament himself.[27] Presumably Steele's vote was included in the total. Newcastle was having legal action prepared against Steele's theater patent, which would be available for use as leverage if Steele continued to be stubborn. The peerage measure was reintroduced and passed the Lords easily. On 1 December it was brought to Commons. Here Walpole's efforts to rally disaffected Whigs and Tories were succeeding. On 8 December, the day on which Commons was to debate the measure. Steele published a new pamphlet that emphasized in its title and content the direction of the opposition's efforts. *A Letter to the Earl of O[xfor]d, Concerning the Bill of Peerage* was addressed to the statesman whose conduct Steele had criticized in many issues of *The Englishman.* He apologizes for the virulence with which he had attacked Oxford, but insists that he believed Oxford's "very Virtue was dangerous. . . ." "I transgress'd, my Lord, against you when you could make twelve Peers in a Day; I ask your Pardon, when you are a private Nobleman. . . ." [28] In the body of the pamphlet, which is unusually well-organized and no

---

[26] BM, Add. MSS., 27, 616, fo. 98ᵛ. This is in a long entry bearing the date 9 October but apparently containing information from several different dates. The meeting, then, must have taken place on or after 9 October. Ott, incidentally, was impressed to the extent of reading all the collected *Tatlers* during the next several months (*ibid.,* fo. 105, 106, 108).

[27] BM, Add. MSS., 32, 686, fo. 88, 152.

[28] *Tracts,* p. 525.

doubt benefited from Walpole's scrutiny, Steele reiterates the advantages of the bill for a comparatively small group of lords and its corresponding disadvantages for everyone else. It "is made," he writes, "for an Aristocracy, and, indeed, it seems to me calculated for nothing else; nay, it has not so much as the Appearance of any thing else. . . ." This was a line that would appeal to the backbenchers, who dreamed of coronets and now saw their dreams disappearing. There was some lingering resentment present in the Commons, moreover, which stemmed from the way the lords had handled or mishandled Oxford's trial, and Steele's pamphlet was meant to recall that fiasco.

Steele opened the debate for the opposition, restating in his speech the arguments of the *Letter* and in fact using entire phrases from the pamphlet.[29] James Craggs defended the position of the government, which found itself at a certain disadvantage because of the concentration of its leadership in the Lords. Walpole rose to the occasion with one of his greatest efforts, a speech Speaker Onslow later described as having "as much of natural eloquence and of genius in it as had been heard by any of the audience within those walls." [30] At a quarter past eight in the evening the question was put and the opposition carried it, 269 to 177. Although ministries did not resign when defeated in those days, Stanhope and Sunderland's government was badly shaken. Steele had been a leader in the triumph of what he thought a good cause.[31] He had exerted himself in the months following his wife's death to the extent of writing six,

[29] Speech reported in [Richard Chandler, ed.], *The History and Proceedings of the House of Commons of Great Britain* . . . , I (London, 1741), 202–209.

[30] HMC, *Onslow MSS.*, p. 459. Onslow was not Speaker at the time, of course.

[31] It may in fact have been a good cause. E. R. Turner ("The Peerage Bill of 1719," *English Historical Review*, p. 259) takes the position that had "the Peerage Bill become law, probably the sinister results predicted by Walpole and by Steele would have come to pass." For similar judgments, see A. S. Turberville, *The House of Lords in the XVIIIth Century* (Oxford, 1927), p. 189; and Basil Williams, *Stanhope* (Oxford, 1932), p. 417.

or perhaps nine tracts on the Peerage Bill, totaling more than one hundred printed pages.[32] Certainly he had worked to good effect in the lobbies before the debate, exercising his knowledge of men's motivations and his wide acquaintanceship to swing votes. His health was good, his energies undiminished.[33] It may be unfortunate that his literary talent was squandered on political pamphlets about issues long dead and buried, but in 1719 Steele's principal vocation was Parliament. He could still write; indeed, he had written a good deal that year, and the play still beckoned. But for the present, politics dominated his life.

[32] Edward A. and Lillian Bloom have recently argued, on the basis of internal evidence, that Steele was author of three other pseudonymous tracts, in "Steele in 1719: Additions to the Canon," *Huntington Library Quarterly,* XXXI (1968), 123–51.

[33] A minor but amusing literary and scientific scuffle which claimed Steele's attention in 1719 was the so-called Physician's War. Steele's own doctor, John Woodward, a somewhat metaphysical physician who had previously written *An Essay toward The Natural History of the Earth . . . , with an Account of the Universal Deluge . . .* (1695), had in 1718 published an account of his medical theories in *The State of Physick and of Diseases.* . . . In this, given over largely to a consideration of smallpox, Woodward recommended the use of emetics in treating the disease. This theory was opposed by such other prominent physicians as John Freind and Richard Mead, who recommended purging in smallpox cases. The wits joined the fray at once, addressing facetious replies to Woodward, and Freind wrote one entitled *A Letter to the Learned Dr. Woodward by Dr. Byfield.* Someone wrote a *Letter from the Facetious Dr. Andrew Tripe, at Bath, to his loving brother the profound Greshamite . . .* [i.e., Woodward]. The tide was running against Woodward when Steele and Ambrose Philips, who was at the time editing *The Free-Thinker,* entered the controversy. In *The Antidote, in a Letter to the Free-Thinker* (*Tracts,* pp. 501–10), published in June, 1719, Steele defends Woodward's personal character and deplores the abusive and undignified conduct of those contesting Woodward's theories. Soon after this pamphlet appeared, Mead and Woodward, meeting outside the gate of Gresham College, were involved in a brief exchange of blows during which Woodward drew his ceremonial sword and made several ineffective passes at Mead. The encounter was inflated by the press into a duel. Steele, the ancient foe of dueling, could not refrain from writing *The Antidote,* No. II (*Tracts,* pp. 511–19), in which he counseled forgiveness and deprecated vengeance. The participants lost interest in the controversy and Woodward and Mead presumably continued treating smallpox with, respectively, emetics and purges. For a recent discussion of the affair, see Marjorie Nicolson and George S. Rousseau, *"This Long Disease, My Life" . . .* (Princeton, 1968), pp. 119–26.

ii

In December it was time to pay the piper. The glorious victory of the opposition asked for retribution, and Steele was a natural target for harassment. Much later Steele expressed the opinion that Stanhope and Craggs had instigated the Duke of Newcastle's actions against him,[34] but surely a peer who turned his tenants out of their cottages for voting wrong needed no guidance when it came to vengeance. Newcastle detested Walpole's group anyway. He had been stalking the Royal Company of Comedians for some time, and Cibber's dedication to *Ximena,* with its pointed and unmistakable reference to Newcastle, would have tried his forbearance. The company had more than once thwarted or defied the Lord Chamberlain's wishes: as recently as November, 1719, when Steele, acting for the managers, had flatly refused to deliver a detailed accounting of salaries paid which had been requested.[35] The revocation of Steele's license as manager was an act of political retribution; the most surprising aspect is that Newcastle waited so long in getting about it. No doubt Steele's part in defeating the ministry on the Peerage Bill shocked Newcastle into action.

Although he later cast himself in the role of persecuted martyr and played the part in public to the hilt, Steele knew a blow was coming. He underestimated the ability of Newcastle's lawyers, principally Thomas Pengelly, Serjeant-at-Law, and overestimated the security of a royal patent. He grossly overrated the effect his own journalism would have in arousing public sympathy for his case. Once battle was joined he lost every skirmish. Then, by virtue of a convolution of politics, he won the war.[36]

[34] In his journal, reprinted in *Corr.,* p. 541, but see below, p. 198.
[35] *Corr.,* p. 145.
[36] The dispute is thoroughly described and analyzed in Loftis, pp. 119–80. I disagree with his conclusion, however, stated in the introduction to his edition of *The Theatre* (p. x), that the quarrel was "essentially a jurisdictional one. . . ."

The theater dispute was of such byzantine complexity, attracted so numerous a swarm of controversialists, and generated so much personal animosity that it has no doubt received more attention than it deserves. The complexity arose not only from the fact that Steele's personal financial interests were entwined with those of Drury Lane but that the true nature of a theatrical patent was not then and never became entirely clarified. Among the principal controversialists, moreover, was Steele's friend and foe, John Dennis, a man quick to anger, who injected a strain of personal abuse into the dispute which led Steele into much defensive posturing and some abuse of his own. Meanwhile, both in print and in Parliament, Steele stepped into separate controversies on the fabric trade and the South Sea Company. The acrimony and the documents generated by all this have contributed to the impression that the theatrical dispute provided a sort of volcanic climax to Steele's life, after which he retired to Wales and died. In truth, the basic plot line of the drama was simple enough and Steele emerged from the excitement virtually untouched except in his purse, the area in which he usually received his wounds.

What took place, in essence, was this: Newcastle, after considering a move against Steele's patent,[37] decided on the advice of his lawyers to revoke the license of the Drury Lane managers —rather than to recover Steele's patent as such—and then to issue a new license in the King's name to Cibber, Wilks, and Booth. Steele thus retained his patent but had no voice in the company and received no financial benefits. When Walpole regained power in the spring of 1721 he saw to it that Newcastle issued a warrant ordering the actor managers to "Account with the said Sr. Richard Steele for all past and future Share[s] Arising from the Profits of the Theatre as he would have been

[37] See Appendix C.

Entitled to. . . ." [38] This, shorn of the rhetoric, fustian, and fanfare is essentially what happened.

Alert as ever to capitalize on matters of topical interest, Steele began what was to be the last of his periodicals, *The Theatre,* on the second day of January. By then he knew that the payments of his stipend on the Commission for the Forfeited Estates for the quarters ending Michaelmas and Christmas had been stopped,[39] and he realized that bad weather was ahead for Drury Lane, because Cibber had been silenced by Newcastle's order on 19 December. A new periodical would be helpful in holding off the creditors. The opening number was promising. The narrator, Sir John Edgar, a gentleman of mature years who has recently renewed his interest in the theater at his son Harry's instance, ushers in the usual circle of the periodical club: Sophronia, a "Lady of great Quality and Merit," Lysetta, a widow, and Sophonisba, a "dependant Relation" who frequently reads to Sophronia. All these "are great Patronesses, and Advocates for the Theatre." [40] The paper was to appear twice a week, on Tuesdays and Saturdays. In the second number Sir John compared the British theater with that of the Continental countries, vastly to Britain's advantage. Striking a note reminiscent of *The Tatler,* Sir John noted that "as the Stage is a Representation of the World, so is the World but a more extended Stage," and proposed himself as *"Auditor-General of the real and imaginary Theatres. . . ."*

Steele was in excellent form. The new paper in the new year succeeded beyond the printer's expectations; the first impression of several numbers sold out and more had to be printed to meet the demand.[41] With expertise derived from years in the

---

[38] PRO, LC 5/157/415–16.

[39] See above, p. 155.

[40] All references are to the edition of *The Theatre* by John Loftis (Oxford, 1962).

[41] See Bibliographical Note in *Theatre,* p. xxvii.

editor's chair, Steele built his audience, mingling anecdote and comment in the manner he knew best, of all living men. In No. 2 he promised to employ spirit and industry with his pen whenever the service of his country should call him; this was an eighteenth-century way of saying that he would deal with political issues if he chose. In opposition once more, Steele was writing well. His essays (Nos. 4 and 5) on the distinction between "whimsical" and "wrongheaded" men of affairs are based on his own experience, as the knowing would realize, but the comments are appropriate to Steele's spokesman Sir John Edgar, who applauds the whimsicality of "a Person who governs himself according to his own Understanding, in Disobedience to that of others, who are more in Fashion than himself." The story of Leucippe (No. 6), lured by her false lover to her virtue's destruction in a bawdy house under the impression that it was his mother's home, would have stirred the sensibilities of Richardson or Fielding.[42] Steele was attracting a sympathetic audience before which he might try his and Drury Lane's case.

On the twenty-third of January, in the seventh number of the new paper, Steele praised Cibber, who was still under an order of silence, and attacked false counselors who offer their sovereign poor advice. This is prologue to a defense of the stage's independence. The author cannot but express his surprise that anybody "of great Fortune and Quality should desire a Jurisdiction over Players, who cannot possibly be govern'd, as to their Oeconomy, their Accommodation on the Stage, their Salaries and Assignments of their Parts, but by themselves and those of acknowledg'd Superiority amongst them. . . ." This

---

[42] It had appeared earlier as a separate half-sheet; see *Theatre*, p. 128. Interestingly enough, Leucippe indicates that the practice of assigning names and titles to the whores, which practice both she and Clarissa found so confusing, was a standard one. "It is the Manner of those Houses to give each other the Names and Titles of such Women of Beauty and Quality, as they resemble in Air, Shape, and Stature; and upon Novices and Foreigners they impose 'em as the real Persons."

summarizes the theater company's side of the basic controversy: that the stage should be run by persons who know the stage, rather than by government officials. Steele continues: the actors "could not have Capacity for their Business, were they not fuller of Sensibilities, or had they not quicker Tastes of Pains and Pleasures than other men. I don't say a Word here of the Women amongst them, but omit to say, that they are like all other *English* Ladies, whose Dispensation is, that they are rather humor'd than govern'd."

Here is the defense of a man of the theater, who has known actors and the stage for two decades and more. The theater cannot be managed, he asserts, either as an ordinary business is managed, or as a department of the state. The independence of the stage is a condition of its continued healthy existence, a necessary guarantee of its creativity. Surely in the larger sense Steele is right or, if he is wrong, instances will have to be produced of flourishing theaters run on strict principles of accounting or under rigid governmental control.

In the immediate foreground, however, there were many who did not agree with him, most especially authors and politicians. Steele's argument is from the point of view of the theatrical company, not the dramatic author. Authors complained, in his day and since, that the companies were unduly timid about producing new plays, were too concerned with box office receipts, catered to the debased preferences of the audiences, were stingy in compensating playwrights. No doubt authors have had a legitimate basis for complaints: Steele himself should have known, inasmuch as he had written one of the staples of the repertory, *The Tender Husband,* and had never received twopence for the performances until he came to share the profits as a manager.[43] One author who was aggrieved, and who was never behindhand in making his grievances known, was John

[43] See *The Tender Husband,* ed. C. Winton (Lincoln, Neb., 1967), p. xiv.

Dennis. His adaptation of *Coriolanus,* entitled *The Invader of his Country,* which he had read to the Drury Lane managers assembled at Steele's house, had opened at last in November, 1719, and closed three short nights later, a failure.[44] Dennis was morally certain that the managers had conspired against him to ensure the play's rejection by the public, as he argued at length in the dedication of the printed version to the Duke of Newcastle. Whether Dennis was suborned by Newcastle or not is arguable; perhaps his wounded pride and general sense of outrage was enough to induce him to launch a very abusive attack on Steele in an anonymous pamphlet entitled *The Characters and Conduct of Sir John Edgar, Call'd by Himself Sole Monarch of the Stage in Drury-Lane; and His Three Deputy-Governors. In Two Letters to Sir John Edgar.*[45] In addition to attacking Steele and the actor-managers personally, Dennis went after the independence of the theater itself, as the title of his pamphlet indicates, on the grounds that it was in the hands of the ignorant and should be brought under the control of the Lord Chamberlain. Other authors added their voices in agreement. Charles Gildon, presumably, writing under the pseudonym of Sir Andrew Artlove in a prose satire entitled *The Battle of the Authors,* portrays Drury Lane as a miasmic sink of ignorance. Dennis, John Loftis has observed, is cast there as

[44] See above, p. 135, and *London Stage,* II, 555.
[45] Dennis's pamphlet is reprinted in *The Critical Writings of John Dennis,* ed. Edward N. Hooker (Baltimore, 1939–1943), II, 181–99. Hooker (II, 476) deprecates the notion that Dennis was paid to write the pamphlet, and Loftis (p. 163n.) adds "there is no evidence to support Aitken's assumption (*Life,* II, 231) that *The Characters and Conduct* was a 'hireling' pamphlet." Perhaps no direct documentary evidence in the form of a receipt from Dennis, but surely the coincidences run together in multitudes: Dennis, who as late as September had said in a letter to Steele that it "is a pleasure to write thus to one who has done so much good in the same cause, the Cause of Liberty . . . ," chose the moment of Steele's discomfiture in the Drury Lane dispute three months later to launch an abusive personal attack, and in March dedicated to Newcastle the continuation of the pamphlet, *The . . . Third and Fourth Letter to the Knight.* Steele asserted flatly that Dennis had been bought (*Theatre,* Nos. 11 and 12).

leader of the forces of light.[46] Only firm direction by the government, Artlove insists, could alter the situation for the better. Not far below the surface of these attacks on the theater and the calls for ministerial intervention is the assumption that the Lord Chamberlain would see that the right plays, the plays, that is, of the complaining authors, are produced. In Gildon's case at any rate there is documentary evidence that he called for delivery on a promise after Newcastle had asserted the authority of the Lord Chamberlain's office: a request to Newcastle that the Lord Chamberlain cause Drury Lane to produce Gildon's play.[47]

Newcastle was, of course, disposed to agree with Dennis and Gildon that something had to be done about the theater, but his meditations were less clouded with considerations of art, enlightenment, and such matters that interested authors. He had in mind control. On 25 January he signed the warrant he had sought from the King. "For the Effectual Prevention of any future Misbehaviour, In Obedience to his Majestys Commands, I Doe, by vertue of My Office of Chamberlain of his Majesties Household, Hereby Discharge You the said Managers and Comedians at the said Theatre in Drury Lane in Covent Garden, from farther Acting. . . ." [48] Two days later Cibber, Wilks, and Booth received new licenses. Steele was thus effec-

---

[46] Loftis, p. 168. *Battle* is ascribed to Gildon by John Robert Moore in "Gildon's Attack on Steele and Defoe in *The Battle of the Authors,*" *PMLA,* LXVI (1951), 534–38.

[47] This interesting document, BM, Add. MSS., 32, 686, fo. 352, has not been noted previously to my knowledge. It is a letter from Lord Chancellor Macclesfield to Newcastle dated 16 October 1723. An excerpt reads: "Mr Lloyd who brings this is poor Gildon's assistant & amanuensis, & comes to me from him to beg your Grace immediately to fixe [?] his Play on ye House, & to order it to begin on Tuesday ye 11th of Dec[r], [that] so his third day may fall upon Thursday. He hopes at least [that] it may be acted before the middle of December & so as [that] the third day may not fall upon a Wednesday or Saturday, w[ch] are ye usuall Opera days. And I hope y[r] Grace will be so good as to let them know you expect [that] they perform it to ye best advantage. . . ."

[48] PRO, LC 5/157/281.

tively excluded from Drury Lane, though he continued to try his case in *The Theatre*. If the controversy had been decided by popular vote of his readers perhaps Steele would have won. Dr. Thomas Rundle observed to a correspondent, "I am sorry I could not get for you a whole set of *Theatres;* the very best are wanting. The demand for them was so great, that even his fiercest enemies bought them up, and enjoyed the author, while they persecute the man." [49] Political controversies were not settled by popular vote in eighteenth-century England, however, and power had spoken. It would speak again when Walpole returned to office.

It is worth noting that Steele, throughout the dispute, kept up the fight. As his enemies asserted, he brought it on himself. He could, and by precedent should, have rolled over at the Chamberlain's command. He did not. Although hemmed in by the best lawyers Newcastle's money could buy, instead of surrendering and begging a pardon he continued to maintain that he had a case which should be tried by due process. He had said the same when he was expelled from his seat in Commons for sedition in 1714. Steele disliked arbitrary authority and bullying. His statements were no doubt self-serving. How could they be otherwise? Who would plead his case if he did not do so himself? "But as great as my Sufferings have been," he wrote in the last *Theatre,* "I find there are, even among impartial Readers, those who think I have treated a great Man with too much Freedom and Familiarity, in the State of our Case; but I hope Gentlemen will consider, that only to omit Ceremony and Complaisance, is a very gentle Return for Violence and Oppression. . . ."

For rhetorical purposes Steele did not, certainly, understate his difficulties, and the chronicle of woes recited during the theater controversy has obscured recognition of the fact that this was one of the most productive periods of his life. If his

<hr>

[49] *Letters of the late Thomas Rundle, LL.D., Lord Bishop of Derry, in Ireland, to Mrs. Barbara Sandys* . . . (Glocester, 1789), II, 11–12.

gout twinged now and then, it did not prevent him from writing a good periodical or taking an active part in debates in the House. Most importantly, he had at last managed to finish the new comedy. In the final number of *The Theatre* he promised to see to its publication "forthwith." This was the play that would be called *The Conscious Lovers,* and it would be neither published nor produced for two more years.[50] There was no reason to rush it into print, Steele may have reflected, while the tide of politics was running against him; once back in the governor's box at Drury Lane he could demand a production that would benefit the deserving author.

He was busy in Parliament as well during these days, ignoring the scowls of the leadership. Ireland was much on his mind and he was able to speak for the old homeland on a number of occasions. John Dennis had remarked sarcastically several times in *The Characters and Conduct of Sir John Edgar* on the resemblance of Steele's life and writings to things Irish. "Indeed," Steele replied temperately in *Theatre* No. 11, "he [Steele] has more Pretension to a Likeness in other Circumstances than this named, for he was born in *Dublin.*" The Irish were in fact better represented in the British Parliament than has been generally recognized, and Steele was able to add his considerable talents to those of the Irish lobby.[51] During the debate on 11 February he objected to classifying Irish cloth as a foreign manufacture and, by implication, Ireland as a foreign nation. "[A]t least," he said, "let us allow it to be a Sister or daughter Kingdom. . . ." He had, he contended, birthright knowledge of such matters: "I was begot in Dublin by a Welsh Gentleman upon a Scots Lady of Quality."[52] The measure under debate, having to do with restrictions on the importation

---

[50] See *The Conscious Lovers,* ed. Shirley Strum Kenny (Lincoln, Neb., 1968), p. xiii.

[51] See Francis G. James, "The Irish Lobby in the Early Eighteenth Century," *English Historical Review,* LXXXI (1966), 543–57.

[52] BM, Add. MSS., 47, 029, pp. 23–24. The statement raises interesting problems for the biographer.

of manufactured cloth, involved many interests : the Spitalfields silk weavers, who had rioted during the autumn of 1719 against the threat of Manchester-made cotton fabrics; Irish linen manufacturers; Scottish woolen producers; importers of foreign-made cloth. Steele wrote a tract under the pseudonym Rebecca Woolpack, entitled *The Spinster: In Defence of the Woollen Manufactures,* in which he pointed out the dangers of imported luxuries by describing the apparel of a fashionable lady : "According to this Rule, Foreigners sell this Lady to the Value of a thousand Pounds, where the English sell her to the Value of five. . . ." [53] An unfavorable balance of trade ensues, as a later age would put it. He voted in favor of a bill that answered the objections of the Irish linen manufacturers and on 4 March spoke in a losing cause against a bill that removed appellate jurisdiction from the Irish House of Lords. Perceval provides a brief but interesting glimpse of Steele during debate in the Commons : Grey Neville opened for the government, complaining of a pamphlet written in opposition to the bill. It showed, he contended, that the Irish were "in a fair disposition to shake off their Dependency." He cited the Irish tax on the pay of English officers as further evidence of their intractability. Steele, opening for the opposition, "answer'd what he said by Shewing, that whoever went about to create a misunderstanding between the two Nations might properly be call'd Enemies & disaffected persons to his Maj[esty's] Govern-[men]t. . . . [T]hat as to the taxe laid [on] the Officers, he really thought it an argument not of their hate but love towards them, for thereby they Shew'd they wish'd in Ireland for more of their Company. . . . He urged Several things from the general topicks of Liberty and the growing Power of the L[ords] of Great Britain & moved to reject the Bill." Steele's ironic defense of the tax on English officers would have evoked

---

[53] *Tracts,* p. 553.

snorts of laughter in Dublin if not in Westminster; he had developed a good debating style, relaxed and humorous. He was serious about the issue, however; it was the calculated nature of the affront to Ireland which galled him and others, not for the last time.[54] Irish antagonism notwithstanding, the bill was carried, 140 to 88.

The government was harassing the opposition where it could. Steele complained in *The Theatre* No. 28 that his adversaries were descending to the "poorest and meanest Examinations" of his private affairs. If the investigators had found anything substantial, he would probably have been expelled once more as an example to dissidents.[55] The only apparent result of the examinations was a debt of one hundred pounds found to be owed to the Crown, which he proposed to repay even if it entailed going to Wales to raise the cash from his estate.[56] He could not afford to let his opponents find an opening.

Great issues were stirring in the spring of 1720. Steele was alert to them and, as it transpired, although seeming to lose again, he was in the end on the winning side. His conduct in the South Sea crisis was admirable, and there were not many other men in public life of whom that can be said. He announced his opposition to the government's proposals early, buttressed his arguments in writing and in debate with careful study, maintained his side of the case in good weather and in bad, and finally, after the bubble had burst, counseled forgiveness instead of vengeance. If Steele ever reached the high ground of states-

[54] BM, Add. MSS., 47, 029, pp. 43–44. Cf. other letters there from correspondents in Dublin, including Archbishop William King.

[55] Vanbrugh wrote to Jacob Tonson (the elder) on 18 February that "it wou'd not be impossible to see him very soon expel'd the House." Washington, Folger Shakespeare Library, MS. C.c.1 (53).

[56] A reasonable conjecture is that the £100 represented the standard £50 travel allowance to Scotland for the years 1718 and 1719, during which period he had not been to Edinburgh. His stipend had been checked for the last two quarters of 1719, it will be recalled, a judgment, Steele admitted, delivered "by right Justice" (*Corr.,* p. 151).

manship, it was during the troubles of the South Sea crisis. If only, one is forced to reflect, he had been able to bring to his own affairs the discipline and knowledge which he brought to those of the country in this troubled time. But "Sir *Richard,*" as Cibber put it well, "though no Man alive can write better of Oeconomy than himself, yet, perhaps, he is above the Drudgery of practising it. . . ." [57] At any rate, his was a moderating voice during a time when few such were to be heard.

Never in a long career of tilting with windmills did Richard Steele seem so misguided as in the spring of 1720. As if it were not enough to have opposed the minister to whose patronage he owed his seat in Parliament, to have turned against the ministry that possessed the confidence of the King (and of the King's mistresses), to have asserted the independence of his patent in the theater until means had been found to remove him from control. In the spring of 1720, as if all these deeds had not been sufficiently provocative, Steele opposed the measures by which the South Sea Company was to be enabled to relieve the British of their national debt, measures that many were sure would bring unexampled prosperity to the nation and rich gains to the individual. "There never was a more projecting year than this," the Earl of Egmont exclaimed happily in April, "but above all that great one the South Sea is to be admired, w[hich] maugre the difficulties cast in the way by the Bank, and Enemies of the Gover[nment] is now fixed on So Solid a foundation that it cannot possibly fail of answering the Parliament's intentions of paying off [the debt] . . . & this without any manner of force or hardship on the Annuitants, by the prodigious rise of the Stock which is now at 350 p cent. . . ." [58] Patriotism, sound economics, and enlightened self-interest appeared to be marching hand in hand on the road to Utopia.

[57] Colley Cibber, *An Apology,* ed. B. R. S. Fone (Ann Arbor, 1968), p. 289.
[58] BM, Add. MSS., 47, 029, p. 58.

The plan proposed by the South Sea Company (which was of course not yet trading in the South Sea) and accepted by the ministry, envisioned the company's assuming the national debt, on the analogy of John Law's scheme in France, then at the pinnacle of success. The directors of the Bank of England, who saw a monstrous financial holding company in the process of being created, one large enough to swallow the Bank whole, offered an alternative plan of managing the debt. Theirs was an attractive scheme, but the South Sea directors, if not so skillful in finance as the bankers, were more skillful in politics. They were busily about the work of building parliamentary support by purchasing members' votes with outright grants of stock in the company or with offers of stock at bargain prices. Steele's colleagues on the Scottish board, Haldane and Munro, each received about three thousand pounds' worth.[59]

There can be little doubt that it was this widespread bribery which aroused Steele to full opposition. Secrets were seldom kept in the eighteenth century, least of all in Parliament. The proposal was easily carried in Commons on the first of February, after strenuous opposition from its opponents. That day Steele published *The Crisis of Property*. His objection to the transaction, as set forth in that pamphlet, stemmed from the fact that it represented a breach of faith on the part of Parliament to turn the annuities of the public debt over to a private company. These annuities had been issued to citizens who in time of war "lent their Country Money, because they lov'd their Country. . . ." Steele objects throughout to the injustice of the proceedings, using the term injustice so frequently that a knowing reader might conclude he was impugning the honesty of the bill's sponsors—as he certainly was: "After this Declaration, who cou'd be confident that their Money is as safe with such Dealers, as in their own Pockets? And when it is otherwise,

[59] John Carswell, *The South Sea Bubble* (London, 1960), pp. 123, 125.

there is an end of Credit." [60] He was even more forthright in *The Theatre,* where he wrote on 8 March (No. 20) : "The Skill of Stock-Jobbing is nothing else, but to act boldly when others are in fear; to be cautious when others are bold. If this should be done by those who may get the Secret of publick Affairs, they would not be so honest as Highway-Men; they would be Setters [i.e., decoys] and Highway-Men too; with this further Advantage above the Gentlemen of the Road, that they would have nothing to deter them but Guilt, as to the rest they would act with Safety and Impunity." This amounts, of course, to a direct charge of malfeasance, delivered in the public press by one in a position to know whereof he spoke. It represents, as far as I know, the first public charge of official misconduct. It is not surprising, then, that there was talk of Steele's expulsion.[61]

Two weeks later Steele published *A Nation a Family,* in which he proposed a plan for converting the debt to self-liquidating loans. As has recently been pointed out, he was thus the first advocate of a principle that was eventually put into effect during the Napoleonic Wars. When he came to settle his own debts he adopted a self-liquidating plan, in the "Indenture Quadripartite." [62]

But he was swimming against the tide. Further essays in *The Theatre,* although widely read, did precisely nothing to stem the hysterical passion for quick profits.[63] Egmont reported in June that "Party fewds Seem to be laid aside, . . . no Side haveing leasure to talk or think of any thing but the funds & of Schemes for encreasing their Fortunes by them." [64] By then the shares had soared, from 129 in February to 1,000. Sir Robert

---

[60] *Tracts,* pp. 565, 568.
[61] See note 55 above.
[62] P. G. M. Dickson, *The Financial Revolution in England* (New York, 1967), p. 21.
[63] *A Nation a Family,* published on 26 or 27 February (*Tracts,* pp. 573–89, 650), and *Theatre,* Nos. 22, 23, 24, 25, 27.
[64] BM, Add. MSS., 47, 029, p. 67.

Walpole himself, who had criticized the plan during the debate on 1 February, was having a cautious flutter in the South Sea. The Duchess of Marlborough, it is true, had persuaded her husband to unload his stock even though his son-in-law Sunderland was deeply involved, but not many mortals shared Sarah's unrelentingly astringent view of life.[65]

Steele, it should be said, though he knew the South Sea project to be dishonest, had not turned his back on projecting as such. By no means. He was floating his own scheme that summer of 1720, the Fish Pool, or, more formally, the Company for Importing Live Fish. The device itself had received the flattery of imitation: in the autumn of 1719 one Joseph Avery, "Mathematician and Shipwright," had applied for letters patent for a vessel "for bringing Fish alive expressly different from the Well Boats, S' Richard Steel's Vessell or any other Ever Invented."[66] Dozens of other projects were formed in the spring and summer of 1720, encouraged in their growth by the greatest bubble of them all. Two million pounds was to be raised at Coopers Coffee House in Cornhill "for preventing & Suppressing Thieves and Robbers, both by Sea and Land," and another twelve hundred thousand pounds was sought from investors "to be employed in undertaking and furnishing of Funeralls," though the latter scheme, it was reported in April, 1720, had raised only five shillings sixpence.[67] Alarmed at the proliferation of stock companies and at the competition for capital which they represented to the South Sea enterprise, the ministry put forward the so-called Bubble Act, passed on 24 June, which provided penalties for companies acting without a charter. The Fish Pool, having been organized under letters patent, was beyond the scope of this measure and Steele con-

[65] J. H. Plumb, *Sir Robert Walpole: The Making of a Statesman* (London, 1956), p. 309; David Green, *Sarah Duchess of Marlborough* (London, 1967), p. 218.
[66] PRO, SP 35/18/92.
[67] PRO, SP 35/21/2.

tinued to distribute "permits," allowing the fortunate holder to purchase one twelve-hundredth of a share in the company. Crusty old Jacob Tonson had a permit and the Duke of Chandos a year earlier had promised to subscribe. Bishop Hoadly was given three permits and even Miss Keck, the children's guardian, was allowed to invest.[68]

As had been his custom for many years, Steele rented lodgings out of the central city that summer of 1720, at Brook Green in Hammersmith. Eugene may have been in school in Hammersmith.[69] The region was becoming fashionable and it provided Steele the variety of both city and country living, which he valued. Perhaps his sister Katherine, still pitifully alive, could join him there with her companion. Steele had her as well as his children in his care. In May, 1720, his eldest daughter, Elizabeth Ousley, was married.

Although according to one eighteenth-century tradition [70] Prue had accepted Steele's illegitimate daughter into her household, it appears more likely, from the absence of reference to her in letters between Steele and his wife, that she was reared by her mother's family, the Tonsons. Steele had once proposed that Richard Savage marry her, Savage told Samuel Johnson, but he had refused. Savage's stories about Steele must be received with skepticism, but there is no reason to doubt that Steele was concerned to find the older Elizabeth a husband.[71] All evidence indicates she was fortunate in the outcome. Jacob Tonson had recently bought an estate in Ledbury, near Hereford, and the bridegroom, William Aynston, was a resident of Almeley, also

[68] Jacob Tonson's permit is in BM, Add. MSS., 28, 275, fo. 107. For Chandos, Hoadly, and Miss Keck, see *Corr.*, pp. 140–41 and 536–37.

[69] See note 1 above.

[70] John Nichols, *The Epistolary Correspondence of Sir Richard Steele* (London, 1809), II, 672n–73n.

[71] Cf. Clarence Tracy, *The Artificial Bastard* (Cambridge, Mass., 1953), pp. 45–46.

not far from Hereford. It appears probable that the match was arranged under Tonson's auspices and that Steele settled five hundred pounds on her as a portion, to be paid in installments.[72] This would have been a respectable dowry for a village housewife in those days of interest at 10 per cent, and Aynston seems to have been of solid stuff, becoming a churchwarden and overseer of the highways.[73] Life with Richard Savage would have been different.

Did Steele attend the wedding at St. Paul's on the fourteenth of May, 1720? I have no doubt that he did, but there is no evidence to prove it. It is not difficult to imagine Steele standing under Wren's great dome, the words of the marriage service echoing in the air, reflecting on those days, nineteen or twenty years earlier, when Elizabeth Tonson conceived and bore their daughter. If Elizabeth was still alive, did she attend? There is no answer.

However much Steele may have disliked leaving the Fish Pool company when it was in process of being formed, it was necessary for him to go to Edinburgh in the summer of 1720. His colleagues addressed a letter to him from Scotland on 9 July entreating him "to repair hither as Soon as possible," coupling this appeal with a polite reminder of the consequences: "by which you will prevent our certifying your absence which otherways in obedience to the Act of Parliament in that behalf wee Shall be under a necessity to do . . . much against our Own Inclination. . . ." [74] That brought him. Steele was not in a position to afford another round with the Treasury; Newcastle

---

[72] This would account for the £500 debt to Tonson recorded in Steele's journal in the autumn of 1720 (*Corr.*, p. 538).

[73] Willard Connely, *Sir Richard Steele* (New York, 1934), pp. 381, 450, citing parish records.

[74] Edinburgh, Scottish R. O., MSS., FEP 1715, General Management No. 9A. An office copy. The original and Steele's reply, if any, have not been located.

had ordered him not to bother him further, and pleading letters to Henry Pelham, Newcastle's brother, had done no good. Steele now had an amanuensis and agent, William Plaxton, in whose care he left his business affairs. The children could be entrusted to Miss Keck. He set off for Edinburgh, arriving there on 1 August 1720.

CHAPTER IX

Drury Lane

STEELE MUST have been well pleased to leave London, fervid in the South Sea summer, and travel through the green English countryside to the cool hills of Scotland. He had said his piece, on the theater and on the South Sea; at the moment he was without further political capital. On his first visit to Edinburgh three years earlier he had been able to spend only a few days; now there was no need to hasten back to London and a number of good reasons to make a virtue of necessity and enjoy the interlude in Scotland.

Before all other considerations was the fact that the Commission still had a great deal of work to get through. Although enabling legislation had reduced the difficulties under which they labored, the sheer volume of business demanded regular attendance on the part of the commissioners. Day after day, six days a week the Commission met at their quarters in Parliament Close, hearing claims, reversing or amending the decrees (some forty of them) passed by the Court of Session, and exercising general supervision over the execution of the Forfeiture Acts.[1] After hours, of course, there was opportunity for

---

[1] The minutes for this session have been lost. See, however, the so-called *Fifth Report: A Further Report Humbly Offer'd by the Commissioners and Trustees of the Forfeited Estates, Who Acted in Scotland. Presented to the Honourable House of Commons; Wednesday the 18th Day of January, 1720 [/21]* (London, 1724).

convivial relaxation. Edinburgh extended Steele a welcome, as it had three years before. He had entrees in plenty. On the cultural side, there was the circle of writers which included Allan Ramsay. Ramsay saw published before the end of the following year the first collected edition of his poems, in which he included a pastoral elegy on the death of Addison, the lament sung by "Richy and Sandy," that is, Richard Steele and Alexander Pope. Pope and Steele returned the compliment by subscribing to the edition, Steele entering his name for two copies.[2] Although there is no direct evidence that he saw Ramsay in 1720, he would have had to use extreme care to avoid him if he had wished to do so, since Ramsay's shop and house were not more than a hundred and fifty yards from the Commission's office in Parliament Close. One can be reasonably certain that everyone of any consequence in Edinburgh social and cultural life arranged an introduction at some time during one of Steele's sojourns in the city. Ramsay's dialect poems may indeed have provided Steele the notion of assembling the beggars of the city for a meal at his expense. "[W]hen the frolic was ended, he declared that, in addition to the pleasures of feeding so many hungry people, he had learned from them humour enough for a comedy. . . ."[3] This was an act of impulsive charity in keeping with Steele's beliefs, evidence of the benevolent heart. His interest in supposed ethnic traits was also of long standing. In *The Theatre* No. 5 he had described the characteristics of the Irish and had warned other nations "to laugh, or weep temperately" because he aimed to extend his investigations.

[2] Allan Ramsay, *The Works of Allan Ramsay,* ed. Burns Martin *et. al.,* Scottish Text Soc., 3d Ser. (Edinburgh, [n.d.–19—]), Vol. I, pp. xxxvi, 106–11.

[3] *London Magazine,* XXIV (February, 1755), 81. The source does not provide a date for the occasion.

At the other end of the cultural scale from the jolly beggars was Steele's landlord William Scott, professor of Greek at the University. He could provide an introduction, if one were needed, to the academic life of the city, as could Steele's former landlord, James Anderson the antiquary. Anderson knew more than any man alive about ancient Scottish legal transactions. A Writer to the Signet, that is, a member of that exclusive group of Scottish attorneys who formed, and still form, the cream of the Edinburgh legal and social world, Anderson could have furnished Steele a great deal of information useful to the Commission.[4] No doubt Steele's leisure hours were well provided for. Nevertheless, he felt keenly the absence of his children. In October, with the Commission still grinding away at the backlog of claims, he wrote to Elizabeth, now eleven:

My Dear Child

I have yours of the 30th of the last month, and from your diligence and Improvement conceive hopes of your being as excellent a person as Your mother; You have great opportunityes of becoming such a one by observing the maximes and Sentiments of Her Bosome Freind Mrs. Keck, who has condescended to take upon Her the care of you and Your Sister, for which You are always to pay Her the same respect as if She were your Mother.

I have Observed that your Sister has for the first time Written the *Initiall* or first letters of Her name, tell Her I am highly delighted to See Her Subscriptions in such Fair letters, and how many fine things those two letters stand for when She Writes them. M.S. is Milk and Sugar, Mirth and Safety, Musick and Songs, Meat and Sause, as well as Molly and Spot, and Mary and Steele.

You See I take pleasure in conversing with You by Prattling any thing to divert You; I hope We shall next month have an

---

[4] For Anderson, see *DNB*. A large quantity of his correspondence is to be found in the National Library of Scotland.

happy Meeting, when I will entertain You with some thing that
may be as good for the Father as the Children, and consequently
please us all.

I am, Madam,

Edinburgh   Y^r Affectionate Father &
Oct^{br} 7th, 1720   Most Humble Servant

RICHARD STEELE

He continued to brood over the fate of his children and the
tangle of his financial affairs. Overseeing the accounts of the
Commission perhaps put him in mind of his own; he prepared
for his own use a balance sheet showing creditors and debtors.
He was beginning to draw in somewhat, though he still most
carelessly neglected to have a lawyer look at the debt to Minshull, which had become a debt to Minshull's creditor Gery and
then had become a debt to Gery's creditor William Wolley [5]—
and which had soaked up untold hundreds of pounds from
Drury Lane, almost 25 per cent of the profits since 1716. Steele
forgot his creditors unless they stirred his memory. Unfortunately, he forgot his debtors too.

While he was in Edinburgh the market broke on the South
Sea Company, share values falling in September from 755 to
180. He returned in November to a Parliament crying for
blood. Those who had accepted stock as bribes found the bribes
shrinking in their pockets. Many others had staked in good
faith, if in poor judgment, whatever they could raise on the
South Sea funds. Vengeance demanded a victim and the directors of the company were the logical sacrifices. Steele was in a
strong moral position, having opposed the original measure—
though as will be seen in a somewhat less strong position than
he might have been because of the mismanagement of the Fish
Pool company. From the beginning of the debates in Parlia-

[5] Loftis, pp. 93–97.

Richard Steele and his family

Steele, Elizabeth, Eugene, and Mary (lower right). From the age of the
children, perhaps done in 1722 or 1723. Four miniatures on ivory, attributed
to Christian Richter. From the originals in the National Portrait Gallery,
with permission.

ment his efforts were concentrated in drawing away some of the criticism from the directors, doing whatever he could to cool the situation.

The situation was indeed overheated. When the King rode up to present a message to the House of Lords in early December, the crowds were so thick and so violent that a detachment of Horse Guards had to be ordered in to clear a passage with the sword. Steele had an innate dislike for the sort of vendetta which the outraged public was calling for, however much he had opposed the policies of the South Sea directors. Moreover, he maintained an affectionate regard for Robert Knight, cashier and treasurer of the South Sea, whom he had consulted about forming the Fish Pool company. Later, after Knight had fled to exile in Paris, Steele continued to correspond with him. Steele's temperate approach accorded with Robert Walpole's efforts to restore confidence, and he seconded Walpole with enthusiasm. Walpole was advocating a scheme to divide part of the South Sea Company's capital between the bank of England and the East India Company. In December 1720 he presented for Parliament's approval the agreement he had worked out in skillful and persistent negotiation among the companies involved. It was, as he saw it, to the nation's advantage if violent tempers were damped down. Such would have been his advice to Steele and Steele would have been disposed to take it.

Steele was still effectively barred from working at Drury Lane, had he been inclined to do so. Most of his energies were taken up with the Fish Pool company, with the Scottish board's business, and with the great South Sea inquiry, which opened in the last month of 1720. There was no sidestepping debate on the South Sea failure, however strenuously Walpole maneuvered to prevent it. Too many had lost money because of their own greed; too many losers called for retribution. Steele tried to strike a lighter note in the chorus of pomposities floating upward from the House floor during the debate of 15 December 1720:

> Mr. Sloper made a Speech and among other things Said, he wou'd not for a million offer a Scheme in favour of South Sea. Sir Wilfred Lawson got up and answer'd him and said he was surprized at that Gentleman's declaration; that for his part he wou'd not only be content to lose all his fortune but a million more. Sr Richard Steel upon that Said he found Millions were still talk'd of as much as when South Sea was at a 1000 and to Shew he was not less zealous than the Member that Spoke last, he declared that in order to attain those desirable Ends he wou'd be content to part with 2 or 3 Millions more than he had.[6]

The House, fingers still tingling from the flames of September, did not wish to be diverted by Irish bulls. At the least, Steele's wit provided laughter when it counted and took the edge off some of the bitterness.

Meanwhile he was faced with a shareholder's revolt in his own company, which like the South Sea was the victim of mismanagement. Sometime before December, 1720, Steele had disposed of his patent for the Fish Pool, presumably by selling his patent rights to a Mr. Dale. Inasmuch as shares in the Fish Pool had been quoted at one hundred and sixty in September, Steele may have made an advantageous transaction. He was at worst protected from further losses, except in the decline of values of any shares he still held. If Dale was William Dale, the "Political Upholsterer" of *Spectator* days, he apparently achieved prosperity in a dramatic degree, for on 10 December 1720 Applebee's *Original Weekly Journal* printed a report that Dale, the upholsterer of Covent Garden, had purchased Bolingbroke's forfeited estate for fifty thousand pounds. Whether the upholsterer was the Fish Pool's Dale and, if so, whether his

---

[6] BM, Add. MSS., 47, 029, p. 85.

fortune was derived from pillaging the company is unknown; what is certain is that newspapers reported nine more Fish Pool vessels under construction on the ways at Deptford in December and printed notices of a special meeting of the shareholders the same month. At the meeting Steele attempted to cool the investors' tempers. "[A]fter clearing himself from any share of the mismanagement," an onlooker reported, "[he] offered to be the *Knight-Errand of the Company,* and to prosecute Mr. D[a]le at his own Charge." [7] Another meeting of the shareholders was agreed upon and set for 3 January 1720/1721. This controversy was proving to be almost as interesting as the South Sea debates, and *The London Journal*'s reporter wrote an account which for its circumstantiality is as good as a scene in Fielding or perhaps Dickens. It also provides important information about Steele's associates in the company. [8]

On Tuesday the 3d Instant, was a general Court of the Proprietors of the Fishpool, at Sir R[ichar]d St[ee]le's Oratory in York Buildings, where several ingenious Gentlemen concerned in that wise Undertaking exerted themselves.

After a Long Deed, made between Sir R[ichar]d St[ee]le and others had been Read, the Knight spoke to the following Effect.

Gentlemen, the Intent and Meaning of this Meeting is to prove (what I hope every Man here is fully convinced of) that I am, *in this particular,* an honest Man, and that Mr. D[a]le is a R[o]gue; and that I will prosecute him my self upon my own Bottom, and therefore I desire as many as will, to joyn with me in that Design.

Upon this, up rose a Person of the Law, who said, Gentlemen, I have been a treble Fool; first, I was a Fool in thinking to get Money by any Project of Sir R. St[ee]le's: Secondly, I was a Fool to think Mr. D[a]le an honest Man: And, Thirdly, I was a greater Fool to part with my Money.

[7] *The London Journal* (Bodleian, Nichols copy), 24 to 31 December 1720.
[8] (Bodleian, Nichols copy), Saturday, 7 January 1720[/21].

When Mr. K[illi]grew [9] interrupting him, went on, I own I never saw the original Deed, between Sir R. St[ee]le and Mr. D[a]le; but to my Knowledge, says he, I saw a true Copy of it, and—

Here he was broke in upon by a Gentleman, who said, he wondred at the Gentleman's Knowledge who spoke last, that he should be so certain of the truth of the Copy, when he had not seen the Original; which Objection Mr. K[illi]grew, in his own Vindication, answered, by assuring the Company, that he was told so.

Next stood up Sir R[ichar]d himself, who said the same as he did before; and would have added more, but that Poet J[ohn]son [10] interrupted him, saying, that he had been very unfortunate in all his Designs; that for several Winters past he had several Plays acted, which brought him in several large Sums of Money, which he feared now was all drowned in the *Fishpool*.

To which Mr. K[illi]grew replied, that he much admired that Gentleman's Plays, tho' he had never read them indeed; but that nevertheless Mr. D[a]le was an honest Man, and that the old Saxon Proverb was very good, *Caveat Emptor.*

Then Mr. Cooper very handsomely and clearly exposed the unjust Practices of Mr. D[a]le upon which Mr. D——y [Durfey?] observed with his usual Warmth, that the Conduct of Mr. D[a]le was worse than that of the South-Sea Directors.

Mr. B——tram of St. Martins Church Court, Coffee-man,[11] said, he thought Mr. K[illi]grew's Words were not much to be regarded, since that very Morning he had given him very broad Intimations of great Preferment, if he would second him in his Motion in favour of Mr. D[a]le; To which Mr. K[illi]grew replied, that as that was Matter of private Conversation in a Corner, and not fit to be published on the House Top, he therefore expected Mr. B——tram would be as mute as a Whiting on

[9] Presumably Charles Killigrew (1655–1725), son of Thomas Killigrew and himself Master of the Revels in 1680 and patentee of Drury Lane in 1682. See *DNB.*
[10] Charles Johnson, the playwright.
[11] Not identified.

that Occasion; adding withal, that he apprehended he could not with any Safety drink Mr. B—tram's Coffee for the future, tho' he owned it to be, to his certain Knowedge, the best Coffee in Town, having several times designed to have tasted it.

This Speech of Mr. K[illi]grew's so nettled Sir R[ichar]d that he could not avoid standing up again, and speaking as followeth: My Neighbour is an honest Man; and as he declared that Mr. D[a]le would not let him read the Deed when he signed it; therefore, to argue in Mr. K[illi]grew's way, It must be presumed that Mr. B—tram to his certain Knowledge, is well acquainted with what he signed. He farther [word illegible], that he would not avow any thing upon his own *certain Knowledge;* but he *believed* that *Caveat Emptor* was no Saxon Saying.

Upon this, up rose a Gentleman of the Peace, and said, that for his Part he had no hand in the Affair, but apprehended that by the *Statute* of King *Canatus the Dane,* the Justices of the Peace were impowered to take Cognizance of all Cheats; and thought that as he was known to be a Proprietor, they ought to have paid him so much Respect, as to have applied to him for a Warrant to apprehend Mr. D[a]le and Mr. H—ley; and that he could assure 'em his Clerk was the most reasonable in his Fees of any in Town: He declared *upon his Honour,* he never went Snacks with his aforesaid Clerk, and aimed at nothing in his present Advice, but proceeding in a legal Manner according to the Statute in that case made and provided.

Mr. K[illi]grew to this reply'd, that tho' he had never seen that Statute, yet he very well knew the Purport of it; however, there was a Gentleman who sat by him, who could give a good Account of the Affair. Upon which the Gentleman referred to, stood up and said, He entirely agreed with his ingenious Friend Mr. K[illi]grew, who, in his Judgment, was the only Person in England fit to talk to the Point. Being ask'd to what Point? he ansered, what Point! what Point! Why, why, why, every Body knows what Point.

Upon this, Poet Johnson sat down with his Hat on, and said he would insert this in his next Play.

The Question then being put, viz. Whether Mr. D[a]le should

be hanged, drawn and quartered; It was agreed in the Affirmative, *Nemine Contradicente,* except Mr. K[illi] grew.

Then another Question being put, whether they should meet
at the Crown Tavern in *Arundel-street,* Mr. C[i]bber objected,
That if they met at a Tavern, the Company would get Fudled,
and Joke; so it was agreed to meet again at Sir R[ichard]
St[ee]le's Oratory aforesaid.

From this account, it is evident that Steele had netted a number
of his associates at Drury Lane in the Fish Pool. The more
investors, the less Steele's personal stake, of course. The Fish
Pool was in troubled waters in early 1721, but Steele himself
appears to have been relatively clear of the project. The legend
of disaster to the contrary notwithstanding, there is no evidence
that Steele came out of the project much the loser and he may
have profited considerably at the expense of Cibber, Poet Johnson, and the other proprietors.

In January, 1721, the interrogation of Robert Knight by the
House of Commons was to take place. Sir Thomas Pengelly,
Newcastle's attorney in the Drury Lane dispute, announced to a
thunderstruck House that Knight had absconded to Holland.
The pent-up fury of Parliament turned against the other directors and against the ministry itself, which was weakened soon
afterwards by the sudden deaths in early February of Stanhope
and young Craggs. Of the major figures in the Stanhope-Sunderland government, only Sunderland remained. It was within
the power of Walpole and his followers to preserve Sunderland
or to see him sacrificed, with the danger if the latter course were
followed of allowing the Tories back in. Decisive power was in
their hands after the death of Stanhope and Craggs.

Steele, who was in Walpole's camp, at once seized advantage
of the altered situation by submitting a petition to the King,
asking that his answer to Newcastle's order revoking his license
be heard in the Privy Council. In a letter of transmittal to
Townshend, Walpole's principal ally, who was then Lord Pres-

ident of the Council, Steele temperately states his motive: concern for his family. A longer letter to Newcastle is more florid and less convincing. He has been ill, which has awakened him "to a Quicker Sense of the Duties of Life." He intends to petition the King to review his order. "I never provok'd your Anger or Resisted your Will in any thing wherein it was in my power to shew my Duty and Respect to you. . . ." [12] This is the variety of statement to which Steele was from time to time given to uttering in letters, neither dignified nor accurate. Worse yet, it was unnecessary. Although it was well to placate nobility, and especially ambitious, insecure young noblemen like Newcastle, there was no reason for Steele to overstate his fidelity now, as the balance of political power was shifting.

Sunderland was worth saving, as Walpole saw it, because he enjoyed the affection of the King and of both of the King's female companions, and because he had a large and loyal following in the House. [13] If he was to be saved, someone in the government would have to be thrown to the wolves, however, and with both Stanhope and Craggs dead, the choice was limited. John Aislabie, Chancellor of the Exchequer, was tapped. Years earlier Steele at his own expense had sent him a handsome set of the collected *Tatlers* on royal paper, as a token of his esteem. [14] Now Aislabie accepted his fate with philosophy, even humor, patiently answering every article of the accusation but allowing himself the observation that "he was to be a sacrifice to a people incens'd by their misfortunes. . . ." Only Steele, Minshull, and a handful of Scots members rose to speak

[12] Undated, but clearly written about February, 1721; see *Corr.*, pp. 159–60. Steele's illness was reported in *The Exchange Evening-Post* (Bodleian, Nichols copy) of 23 January 1721: "Sir Richard Steele Member of Parliament for Borough Bridge lies dangerously ill of a Fever." The issue of the same paper for 25 January, however, reported that "Sir Richard Steele is recovered and hath been abroad."

[13] J. H. Plumb, *Sir Robert Walpole: The Making of a Statesman* (London, 1956), pp. 344–45.

[14] See Tonson's statement of accounts, printed in Aitken, I, 330.

in Aislabie's behalf.[15] He was expelled from the House and
dispatched to the Tower. On 15 March Walpole faced down the
testimony of four witnesses who had individually sworn that
Knight said he had given fifty thousand shares of South Sea
stock to Sunderland, and won Sunderland's acquittal, 233 to
172. Steele spoke up in the debate of 29 March, which considered Knight's papers, criticizing Knight's being forced to give
evidence against himself, but few were in the mood to listen to
this constitutional scruple.[16] With Sunderland safely home, the
rest were fair game. Sunderland's place in the government had
been preserved at the price of greatly strengthening Walpole's
hand. Townshend assumed Stanhope's vacated post as Secretary of State and Walpole himself became Chancellor of the
Exchequer and First Lord of the Treasury on 3 April.

The next day Richard Steele began a detailed journal "for
the perusall and consideration of . . . My Beloved Children."
The first entry is an account of his reading Tillotson's sermons
on Easter, followed by an Easter prayer. The next, dated 9
April, moves from the realm of God to that of Caesar and tells
of his resolution "to pursue very Warmly my being restor'd in
my Government of the Theatre Royall . . . from which I have
been violently dispossessed by the Duke of Newcastle. . . ."[17]
He goes on to reveal in the journal that he had already applied
to Sunderland and Walpole for their good offices and had
addressed a letter to Henry Pelham on 5 April. The letter to
Pelham, a rather disingenuous document, represents Steele as
"wholly Friendless for no one is obliged to one (who will do
nothing but what he thinks just) because His Suffrage never
attends persons or Partyes." Never attends persons or parties.
One wonders what Jonathan Swift would have made of that

[15] BM, Add. MSS., 47, 029, pp. 100–101. See also John Carswell, *The
South Sea Bubble* (London, 1960), pp. 241–42.

[16] [Richard Chandler, ed.], *The History and Proceedings of the House of
Commons of Great Britain. . .* , I (London, 1741), p. 240.

[17] Journal printed in *Corr.*, pp. 540–42. There are only three later entries.

statement. The pose of humility was probably assumed, as has been suggested, to minimize Newcastle's opposition to his reappointment.[18] Steele had already consulted Walpole and Sunderland and knew perfectly well that he was in a fair way of recovering the governorship. On 2 May Newcastle capitulated, ordering the actor-managers to account with Steele for his share of the profits "as he would have been Entitled to by any Agreement between You and him . . . and to Pay him hereafter from time to time his said Share, till further Orders from me, or Determination of that point be made by due course of Law." [19]

Having lost many battles, Steele had won the war.

ii

Steele had suffered a slight fever in January, 1721, but after being reported near death he was up and about in a few days. Illness was still slowing him in March, however, and the long, tempestuous session of Parliament, with frequent divisions and debates lasting into the late night, wearied him. His own mode of treatment, "being much in the Air," probably contributed more to his recovery than did Dr. Woodward's calomel. With Walpole back in the Treasury Steele promptly received payment of the two hundred and fifty pounds he contended had been due him for the quarter January–March, 1720, when he was suffering under Newcastle's displeasure.[20] He saw his children, had a tooth extracted, corrected daughter Elizabeth's prose style: "[R]emember that plainnesse and Simplicity are the Cheif beauties in all Works and performances whatsoever."

---

[18] Loftis, p. 156.

[19] PRO, LC 5/157/416.

[20] Presumably this had been the subject of Steele's petition (see *Corr.,* p. 153) that the Treasury lords had referred to the Attorney and Solicitor Generals on 7 May 1720 for an opinion, the "Lords thinking the principal Matter therein contained to be a point of Law . . ." (PRO, T 27/23/76). For payment, see T 60/11/158.

Although now legally entitled to return to the active managership at Drury Lane, he did not do so. The recourse of the actor-managers, yielding to expediency, in carrying on without him may have provoked his resentment. He had written an epilogue for a performance of *Measure for Measure* at the rival house in Lincoln's Inn Fields, in which he recommended Shakespeare as a corrective to the depraved British taste which preferred Etherege.[21] "Be Men," he counseled Britons, "or hope not Heav'n will long secure ye/ From quicker Pestilence than that round *Drury.*" He would have been in worse temper yet that spring if he had known his fellow managers had since January, 1720, been deducting five pounds a day from Steele's share of the profits and dividing the sum among themselves.[22] From the time of his dispute with Newcastle, Steele's relations with the actor-managers were more formal than they had been earlier, though both Cibber and Wilks were fellow proprietors of the Fish Pool. In September, 1721, accounts were settled in accordance with Newcastle's order, and articles of agreement signed which stipulated the property rights of the managers and provided that no one of them should alienate his share without permission, a provision obviously directed at Steele, whose share was, however, already in part alienated.[23] In December he complained that the actor-managers were denying him payment of money they owed. Cibber's explanation in his *Apology* reveals the managers' point of view:

> Sir *Richard* . . . was often in want of Mony; and while we were in Friendship with him, we often assisted his Occasions: But those Compliances had so unfortunate an Effect, that they

[21] *Verse,* p. 52. The epilogue, with a prologue by Welsted, was printed but not spoken. Perhaps Rich did not wish to become involved in a dispute with the Lord Chamberlain.

[22] Loftis, pp. 214–16, corrects information in Aitken, II, 303, and *Corr.,* p. 171n.

[23] Loftis, pp. 216–17.

only heightened his Importunity, to borrow more, and the more we lent, the less he minded us, or shew'd any Concern for our Welfare. Upon this, Sir, we stopt our Hands, at once, and peremptorily refus'd to advance another Shilling, 'till by the Balance of our Accounts, it became due to him.[24]

Cibber's statement is probably near the truth, with allowances made for some normal sharp practice on the part of the actor-managers. Steele's capacity for touching his friends was without limit. On the other hand, he had in his possession a potentially valuable property, his comedy, still unpublished. He had proposed publishing it a year and a half earlier but then had not done so, realizing no doubt that he would lose some leverage with his fellow managers if he did. Now he was finally in a position again to reap profits both as playwright and manager. It was the existence of *The Conscious Lovers* manuscript that kept the relationship between Steele and the actor-managers tolerably polite. But he spent little time at Drury Lane now.

When he had money he was a notoriously easy mark himself. The antiquary James Anderson, with whom he had become acquainted in Edinburgh, had a wayward son who was determined to seek his fortune at sea and who had sailed before the mast for three years without prospects of bettering himself. Steele greeted the young man when he came to London in the spring of 1721, lent him five pounds, and secured him a midshipman's berth on the East Indiaman *King George*.[25] When he received a polite letter of thanks from young Anderson, Steele sent it along to his father, with a note belittling his own part in the matter, which nevertheless had cost him time and trouble.

Steele could not cease fretting over the future of his children. Eugene had never been a strong boy. He had been operated on

---

[24] *An Apology*, ed. B. R. S. Fone (Ann Arbor, 1968), p. 290.
[25] *Corr.*, pp. 163–64, and National Library of Scotland, Anderson Papers, Vol. I.

in 1717 and he was troubled by persistent kidney stones. During the summer of 1721 Steele sent him to Wales to stay with his cousins,[26] and before he left for Scotland in the autumn he proposed to deposit his will with Benjamin Hoadly, now Bishop of Hereford, naming him executor and guardian. By this time Eugene was old enough to take part in the juvenile theatrical performances of which his father was fond, and Steele, according to the plausible legend that John Nichols records, employed him in one or more sessions at the Censorium.[27] The most immediate means of caring for his children was of course clearing his own estate. This was his purpose in entering an agreement with the actor-managers in September, and it was the motive for his continued activities in the Fish Pool company. In April four new sloops for the company fleet were launched at the Rotherhithe yard, two of them named after Steele's daughters, the *Maria* and the *Elizabeth*. The eponymous *Fish Pool* was at sea, bringing in on one occasion a "cargo of 1500 Rock Cod, alive, and in good Health." [28] Company meetings were held from time to time, at the Fish Pool Office in the Royal Exchange or at his rooms in York Buildings. *The London Journal* for 12 August 1721 reported that the Fish Pool project "has answered the most sanguine Expectations of the Gentlemen concerned in it, who push it on with great Vigour, and have made considerable Improvements since they first set out; their Expences are now pretty well fixed and certain, the Charges of One Voyage, for Men, Provisions, &c. generally amounting to Fifty Pounds and no more." [29] Steele did not let the Fish Pool get in the way of his responsibilities with the Commission for the Forfeited Estates, however. He

---

[26] See Eugene's letter to his sisters in *Corr.,* p. 394.

[27] John Nichols, ed., *The Epistolary Correspondence of Sir Richard Steele* (London, 1809), II, 578. See also Rae Blanchard, "A Prologue and an Epilogue for Nicholas Rowe's *Tamerlane* by Richard Steele," *PMLA,* XLVII (1932), 772–76.

[28] Notice in an unnamed newspaper, quoted in *Corr.,* p. 503.

[29] Copy in Hertfordshire Record Office, Panshanger MSS.

attended a plenary meeting in April at Essex House in the Strand and began thinking about the annual journey to Edinburgh.

The session of Parliament dragged on in the meanwhile, with Steele speaking up from time to time on behalf of one or another of the South Sea directors: Aislabie in April and Sir Theodore Janssen in June.[30] Parliament was at last prorogued in August and Steele set out for Scotland the following month. The work of the Commission had by that time settled to a routine in matters of hearing claims, advertising estates for sale, and amending the sequestration decrees, but major problems persisted for the commissioners' solution. Collecting rents in certain parts of the Highlands proved impossible. The Highlanders would not pay. When a party led by William Ross, the Commission's factor, ventured into one mountain area they were ambushed. Ross's son was killed, and several of his companions wounded. In spite of such problems, however, the end of the Commission's work, if not yet at hand, was in sight.[31] This was consolation for the hard-pressed commissioners. There were also the diversions which Edinburgh offered. These included the presence of Steele's old friend, Dr. J. T. Desaguliers, since 1719 Grand Master of English Masons, who had come to Edinburgh in August for conferences with the Edinburgh Lodge.[32] Desaguliers, who had conducted a series of scientific demonstrations in Steele's Censorium in 1719,[33] was received as a brother by the Master Masons of Edinburgh. The

---

[30] [Chandler], *History and Proceedings*, I, 249; William Coxe, *Memoirs of the Life and Administration of Sir Robert Walpole, Earl of Orford* (London, 1798), II, 215.

[31] The so-called *Sixth Report* contains Ross's account as an appendix and treats the Commission's activities for both 1721 and 1722. Full title: *The Farther Report of the Commissioners and Trustees Appointed to Enquire into the Forfeited Estates in Scotland. Presented to the Honourable House of Commons; Thursday the 7th Day of February, 1722[/23]* (London, 1724).

[32] Duncan Campbell Lee, *Desaguliers of No. 4 and his Service to Freemasonry* (London, 1932), pp. 11, 21.

[33] *The Daily Post*, 23 November 1719 (copy in PRO, SP 35/18/110).

Commission continued meeting in Edinburgh after the opening of Parliament on 19 October, probably not adjourning until early in November.[34]

When Steele returned to London in November he found that Tonson had delivered to his lodgings in York Buildings four handsome volumes in quarto of Addison's collected *Works,* edited by Thomas Tickell. Painful memories of the final quarrel with Addison were stirred in Steele's mind by the appearance of this edition, for which he had taken the trouble of identifying Addison's contributions to *The Tatler*.[35] He received no thanks from Tickell; the edition represented an insult, it was only too obviously a Parthian shot by his old friend. The epistle dedicatory, dated just two weeks before Addison's death, was addressed to, of all possible addressees, young Craggs, now dead of smallpox and remembered by the public principally as having had a somewhat sinister connection with the South Sea Company. Tickell's preface emphasized Addison's classical education and the extent to which this education contributed to the correctness of his writing.

> There is not perhaps any harder task than to tame the natural wildness of wit, and to civilize the fancy. The generality of our old *English* poets abound in forced conceits, and affected phrases; and even those, who are said to come the nearest to exactness, are but too often fond of unnatural beauties, and aim at something better than perfection. If Mr. *Addison*'s example and precepts be the occasion that there now begins to be a great demand for correctness, we may justly attribute it to his being first fashioned by the ancient models, and familarised to propriety of thought and chastity of stile.

Addison and water. There is a starched primness about the tone of Tickell's preface which would set Steele's teeth on edge, even

---

[34] Steele was still in Edinburgh on 26 October (*Corr.,* p. 168).
[35] Discussion based on Steele's statements in his dedication to *The Drummer,* reprinted in *Corr.,* pp. 505–18.

apart from the content, which is concerned to present Addison as all spirit, an ethereal creature who, if he associated with Steele at all (and a reader would scarcely realize the extent of their collaboration), did so only to "tame the natural wildness of wit." Here is the authorized version of Addison and just offstage, by Tickell's implication, hovers the authorized version of Steele: the prim, correct classical scholar and the boozy Irishman. Because the version was partly true, was in fact a caricature, it has been all the more dangerous to Addison's memory, as well as to Steele's. It ignored, most importantly, Addison's fine sense of the ridiculous. When Steele examined the collected *Works* he found that they did not include Addison's comedy, *The Drummer,* for which Steele had supplied free publicity in *Town-Talk* and which he had sold on Addison's behalf to Tonson for fifty guineas.

This raises the interesting question, by whose decision was *The Drummer* excluded? The comedy does not, to be sure, accord well with Tickell's reverential preface, which describes Addison as meditating during his last days on a very different dramatic piece dealing with the death of Socrates. It seems hardly likely, however, that Tickell would have excluded *The Drummer* if Addison had left directions to include it.[36] Perhaps Addison discussed the matter with Tickell and ordered that the work not be included, as being beneath his high standards. Tickell's portrait of Addison was closer to the one Addison himself wanted to leave behind.

But it was not a full portrait, Steele knew. *The Drummer* had comic merit, though its verbal texture was somewhat dense for a stage play. Steele went to Tonson's shop, bought the copyright back, and published a new edition of the play, adver-

---

[36] Rae Blanchard (*Corr.,* p. 517) believes that Tickell did not know the comedy to be Addison's. But would not Tonson have informed him of Steele's transaction, and would not Tickell have ascertained its authorship from Steele, as he did with the *Tatlers?* Smithers (p. 444) believes that Addison perhaps omitted it because "the author of *Cato* did not wish that triumph lessened by the stage failure of another piece."

tising that it was on the same paper and of the same typography as Tickell's edition. Steele addressed a long and thoughtful dedication to William Congreve, appealing his case to the judgment of the best comic dramatist of the age. Addison had dedicated his works to James Craggs, whom he scarcely knew except as a fellow politician; Steele chose Congreve, whom both he and Addison had known as an intimate friend for twenty years and longer. In the dedication Steele objects to the omission of *The Drummer* from the canon of Addison's works and complains that Tickell did not allow him to examine the contents of the *Works* before publication. He especially resents Tickell's insinuation that he, Steele, had not sufficiently acknowledged his debt to Addison in his writings. Steele quotes from his own generous tributes to Addison and adds succinctly:

> What I never did declare was Mr. *Addison's,* I had his direct Injunctions to hide, against the natural Warmth and Passion of my own Temper towards my Friends. Many of the Writings now publish'd as his, I have been very patiently traduced and calumniated for, as they were Pleasantries and oblique Strokes upon certain [of] the wittiest Men of the Age, who will now restore me to their Good-will, in proportion to the abatement of Wit which they thought I employ'd against them.

Worst of all, Steele felt, was the presentation of Addison in Tickell's preface: "[N]o Man, tho' without any Obligation to Mr. *Addison,* would have represented him in his Family and his Friendships or his personal Character, so disadvantageously, as his Secretary . . . has been pleased to describe him. . . ." Addison was "above all Men in that Talent we call *Humour*" and Steele recommends the play "as a Closet piece." He closes the dedication with a request for Congreve's pardon for laying this "nice Affair before a Person who has the acknowledg'd Superiority to all others. . . ."

Steele had chosen his dedicatee, and his words, with care. He was most concerned to set the record straight about one matter : the reason for his having concealed Addison's identity as author of the periodicals on which they had collaborated. One may regret that he did not go into the personal relationships and working methods of the famous partnership, which can now only be inferred from evidence here and there. What became of the notes which must have passed between the two, for example? We know from Steele's statement in the dedication to *The Drummer* that he then possessed a letter from Addison's father Dean Lancelot Addison which conveyed "his Blessing on [this] Friendship." Steele was an assiduous preserver of memoranda and letters, but those having to do with Addison have almost without exception disappeared. Perhaps they will yet turn up.[37] Without them, one can only say that Steele, in the dedication, paid a generous final tribute to his friend and collaborator. The unfortunate public quarrel about the Peerage Bill is forgotten. That Steele was pained by Addison's dedication to young Craggs is certain, but although he blames Tickell for acts of omission and commission his stance with respect to Addison is *de mortuis nil nisi bonum*. The dedication, as Congreve would have understood, was Steele's valedictory to Addison.[38]

Two other men who had figured largely in Richard Steele's life died during the early months of 1722, Sunderland and Marlborough. The Earl of Sunderland, in whose office in the Cockpit Steele had written *The Gazette* many years before, died in April. He had been displeased by Steele's stand on the Peerage Bill in 1719 but he had since overcome his annoyance sufficiently to allow Steele to contest one of the seats in which he had an interest in the new Parliament, Wendover in Buckinghamshire. Sunderland was building, or rebuilding, a parlia-

[37] Only two letters of Addison to Steele and none of Steele to Addison are known to exist; see *Corr.*, p. 39.

[38] The revived *Drummer,* acted at Lincoln's Inn Fields early in 1722, had a successful run of four nights.

mentary interest and Steele was an early recruit. Another was Steele's colleague on the Scottish board, Sir Henry Hoghton.[39] Steele had been behind the successful move for Sunderland's acquittal in the South Sea hearings and Sunderland, struggling with Walpole for supremacy, probably felt that Steele might provide useful support in the Commons. It may be assumed that Newcastle refused to allot one of his seats to Steele; too much had passed between Newcastle and Steele for reconciliation at this late date.

Steele traveled to Wendover in March and went about the business he now knew well, of buying and cajoling the electors. Wendover presented difficulties. By eighteenth-century standards it was a very democratic franchise. The right to vote was granted to every inhabitant capable of boiling his own pot [40] and two seats were contested. The candidate was required to please the voters. Steele was cast in an especially delicate role. The Tories of course hoped to gain ground as a result of the South Sea scandal. The Whig leadership struck back, using the Jacobite theme: the King's speech at the dissolution warned darkly of the "enemies of our happy constitution" who were reviving the "wicked arts of calumny and defamation," i.e., the Tories. In February the House of Commons had been the scene of an ill-tempered investigation into election fraud at Banbury, in which the government had squeaked through by only four votes.[41] Threats of the sort which Newcastle employed in his Yorkshire constituencies would be out of place in Wendover; even promises had to be meted out carefully to the suspicious

[39] Blenheim MSS., DI-34, letter of Hoghton to Sunderland of 6 April 1722: Could win the election on petition "but this my Lord depends Entirely upon your Lordship's Countenance and protection. . . ."

[40] Robert Walcott, *English Politics in the Early Eighteenth Century* (Oxford, 1956), p. 12.

[41] [William] *Cobbett's Parliamentary History of England . . .* , Vol. VII (London, 1811), col. 965.

potwallopers. The other two candidates, furthermore, were Whigs of untainted constitutional principles, one of them indeed being Richard Hampden, the direct descendant and heir of the famous Parliamentarian. The other was Sir Roger Hill, a barrister of sterling Whig fidelity introduced into Parliament by the late Marquess of Wharton, who had voted against Steele's expulsion in 1713.[42] Finally complicating the electoral process were the intrigues of Walpole and Sunderland against the other's candidates. Although Walpole had been instrumental on Steele's behalf in restoring him to the Drury Lane governorship, Steele was now indebted to Sunderland for financial support and felt compelled to assure him of his "most warm and inviolable Zeal" for Sunderland's interests. This election was an occasion for careful treading.

Because of Hampden's name and because his family were large landowners in the area, Steele's true opponent was Sir Roger Hill. Philip, Duke of Wharton, the erratic son of Steele's Junto patron, was undergoing a brief period of Whiggish sympathies.[43] For reasons best known to himself Wharton transferred his family's interest, deriving from his estates in nearby Winchendon, from Hill to Steele. Steele spent two full weeks electioneering in Wendover, trading on his charm and political acumen. He brought a pair of comedians from one of the playhouses to entertain the crowds between speeches, a device so successful that a hostile observer reported the comedians were almost elected instead of Steele.[44] On polling day, 21 March, Steele revived the stratagem which he had used in Stockbridge nine years earlier of offering an apple stuck full of

---

[42] Walcott, *English Politics,* p. 217; *A Collection of White and Black Lists,* 3d ed. (London, 1715), pp. 19, 30.

[43] HMC, *Portland MSS.,* VII, 309–10.

[44] [Mist's] *The Weekly-Journal or Saturday's Post* (Bodleian, Nichols copy), 7 April 1722.

guineas to the elector whose wife was brought to bed of a child nine months from the day.[45] Steele ran on Whig principles but against the South Sea. His supporters raised the cry, *"No pernicious South-Sea Schemes, but Liberty and Property!"* [46] This was a somewhat awkward election slogan, perhaps, but it served Steele's purposes in 1722. He was able to report to Sunderland that he had carried the election by a majority of seventy-one and that he hoped he was "in a method of continuing Member for this place on any Future occasion." He had, that is to say, developed a system of support: men of substance in the village who could be counted on in the future to nudge votes his way in return for his help on whatever measures affected their interests or those of the borough.

On election day Wharton dined with Steele in Wendover and the next morning Steele and "about 50 substantial Townsmen" returned the visit at Wharton's seat. On the Sunday following, David Scurlock, Prue's clergyman cousin, was reported to have preached "an incomparable" election sermon at Elfborough, a mile from Wendover, which drew such a crowd that chairs were set up on the porch for the overflow.[47] David Scurlock's Whiggery had been confined at Tory Oxford but on this happy occasion he was able, like Mark Twain's preacher, to let 'er rip.

Steele's letter detailing his victory to Sunderland may have been the last he wrote to his new patron. Two weeks later Sunderland contracted a sudden pleurisy and, on 8 April, died. Robert Walpole grasped the opportunity of securing his advantage, for as yet he did not have full control of the government. A Jacobite plot was hatching, which would provide great political capital. Walpole embarked straightway on an elaborate program of political divination and interrogation, sniffing and

[45] BM, Add. MSS., 47, 029, p. 219. Percival to Charles Dering, letter of 27 March 1722.
[46] *The Daily Post* (Bodleian, Nichols copy) 7 April 1722.
[47] *Ibid.*

snooping here and there for Jacobites.[48] Deciding, perhaps, to
test Steele's usefulness, he assigned him some such task which
Steele was delayed in executing because of, he reported, another
apoplectic attack. It was not a promising demonstration of
future usefulness to a new patron but, with Sunderland gone,
Steele had no choice.

The Duke of Marlborough died at last, in June, 1722. He
had been in his dotage for years, but his death took away
another of the men whom Steele had followed in his youth.
Marlborough had assisted Steele from time to time, though the
debts were fairly balanced by Steele's many writings in defense
of the Duke's conduct against Tory attacks. Swift's reaction,
hearing the news in Ireland, was a poem that concluded:

> Let pride be taught by this rebuke,
> How very mean a thing's a Duke;
> From all his ill-got honours flung,
> Turn'd to that dirt from whence he sprung.[49]

Viewing the matter differently, Steele, in one of his last reflections on the Duke and his career, had singled out Marlborough's lack of pride as the most striking trait of his character:
"The common Lump of Mankind know no Greatness but in
Show and Appearance; and he who has nothing Ostentatious,
keeps half of his true Merit out of Sight, at least out of Sight of
all but the Wise and the Good, who are a Party too weak for
the Vain, the Loud, and the Unreasonable." [50] It was one of
many topics on which Steele and Swift would never now agree.
Nothing more is heard of Steele's projected biography of Marlborough.

He was drawing in. The return of his illness, brought on by

[48] J. H. Plumb, *Sir Robert Walpole: The King's Minister* (London, 1960),
pp. 41–43.

[49] *The Poems of Jonathan Swift,* ed. Harold Williams, 2d ed. (Oxford,
1958), I, 297.

[50] *Englishman,* p. 301 (19 August 1715).

the strenuous electoral campaign of the spring, prevented his taking much part in debate at the House. "[I] hope by the blessing of Almighty God," he informed his agent in Wales, "to put my Affairs, and keep them so much within my income, as not to put my friends in any future pain or Trouble for me." As the summer of 1722 came on Jacobite fever rose: troops were encamped in Hyde Park, Carteret's postmen opened mail with splendid zeal,[51] and by the end of the summer a handful of plotters and alleged plotters, including Bishop Atterbury and Lord Orrery, were in the Tower. The King was persuaded to give up his usual trip to Hanover. It was a crowded, febrile summer, an excellent time to be out of London. The atmosphere of tension and excitement, however, was reminiscent of the autumn of 1714—good business for theater companies, as the managers of Drury Lane realized. New sets and costumes were ordered for Steele's comedy.

Later in the summer he was able to get away to Wales, breaking his journey to Scotland there. A local tradition has it that he arranged a reading of the new play at Ty-Gwynn ("White House"), his house in Llangunnor, on the hillside just across the River Tovey from Carmarthen. The tradition is probably true; there is corroborating evidence [52] and it was the kind of occasion Steele most enjoyed: a group of friends gathered in the summer sunshine, pleasant conversation, an informal, homespun theatrical, laughter, approbation. Perhaps he had brought his children, who would be playing with Welsh cousins and friends on the hillsides and in the gardens around

[51] With rather too much zeal in at least one case. Lord Cowper endorsed an embarrassed letter of apology from Carteret: "Mr. Carteret ye Post Mr in answer to one I sent him with a Ltr returned wch his officers had put up in my packet, on opening it at ye Post office" (Hertfordshire Record Office, Panshanger MSS.).

[52] *Corr.*, p. 410. Dennis asserted that the play "has trotted as far as *Edinburgh* Northward, and as far as *Wales* Westward" in *A Defence of Sir Fopling Flutter,* in *The Critical Works of John Dennis,* ed. Edward N. Hooker (Baltimore, 1939–1943), II, 241.

the house. The scene is familiar to those who have read John
Dyer's *Grongar Hill:*

> The pleasant seat, the ruin'd tower,
> The naked rock, the shady bower;
> The town and village, dome and farm,
> Each give each a double charm. . . .

It was a good place to stay. Steele would be coming back to
Ty-Gwynn and Carmarthenshire.

In September he was in Edinburgh with his fellows on the
Commission.[53] The English board was winding up its work that
summer, discharging clerks, preparing balance sheets, moving
to less spacious quarters.[54] Although their task was almost
done, a great deal of work remained for the commissioners in
Scotland. Several hundred claims demanded adjudication and
there was still a large amount of forfeited land to dispose of.
Scottish estates were less easily salable than English. Steele had
worked conscientiously at his duties on the Commission since
1719, but the journey to Edinburgh and back was a long one,
and his financial position was better. The income from his
stipend was no longer the pressing necessity it had once been.
Service on the Commission had never been a sinecure, and after
the session in Edinburgh in the autumn of 1722 Steele took
advantage of an opportunity to exchange his place on the Scottish board for one held by Dennis Bond on the English side of
the Commission.[55]

[53] This, not known before, is demonstrated by a certificate dated from
Edinburgh in September and signed by Steele: Scottish Record Office,
Forfeited Estates Papers, 1715, Vol. 19: General Record Kept by the Commissioners, p. 166.
[54] PRO, FEC 2/9.
[55] This appears to have been an internal arrangement of the Commission,
authorized by the statute establishing it. Steele's last act on the Scottish
board for which I have found a record is an order for prosecution signed by
him and his colleagues, dated 25 January 1722/23 in Scottish R.O., F.E.P.
1715, General Management No. 6.

Back in London he found the Jacobite scare was still generating tension. The King's speech at the opening of Parliament spoke of the conspiracy and of little else. At Walpole's insistence the Habeas Corpus Act was suspended and on 26 October the premier duke of England, Norfolk, was committed to the Tower on suspicion of high treason. A bill was introduced to raise money toward the supplies by taxing Roman Catholics. It was a nervous autumn. Now was the time for a good new play, what would today be termed escape entertainment. Steele had one ready.

CHAPTER X

"The Last Blaze
of Sir Richard's Glory"

OVER THE years, Steele and his partners at Drury Lane had
their differences. He had touched one or another of them for
loans, he had led them into a pitched battle with the Lord
Chamberlain, he had promised them a play and then had not
delivered the manuscript. But there was another side to the
story as well. He had brought the great ones to Drury Lane,
and he was still doing so : his literary and political fame acted as
a powerful reinforcement in the defense of the theater against
both politicians and reformers, and as a guarantor of its financial health. In May, 1721, for example, *The Funeral* was acted
"At the Desire of the Two Princes, Brothers to the King of
Delago in Africa." [1] Although one may doubt that the African
princes had journeyed to London solely in hopes of seeing *The
Funeral,* the fact that they selected Steele's play, or that someone suggested that they select it, illustrates the quality of support that his presence as governor and dramatic author was able
to lend Drury Lane. No precise figure can be attached to the
value of this presence but it was certainly considerable. Over
the years, Steele had learned to live with Cibber, Wilks, and
Booth—and they with Steele. The chronicle of their disputes
should be read like that of a couple long married : there was
plenty of noise and recrimination but seldom anything to the
ultimate disadvantage of the relationship. The prospect of a

[1] *Daily Courant* (Bodleian, Nichols copy), 26 May 1721.

successful run of the long-expected comedy was enough to induce them all to sink their differences in the past and work for present profit.

Casting the play gathered professionals who had worked together for decades. The managers themselves took leading roles: Barton Booth as Bevil, Jr., Robert Wilks as Myrtle, and Colley Cibber in another substantial comedy part as Tom. Anne Oldfield, who had played Biddy Tipkin to Wilks's Captain Clerimont in *The Tender Husband* seventeen years earlier, created the long-suffering Indiana. New settings and new costumes had been ordered, and the managers had thoughtfully raised the admission prices to take care of the crowds they expected.

They had gone to some lengths to ensure public curiosity about the new play. Steele himself had mentioned it now and again in his writings over a period of several years.[2] John Dennis, still smarting from the failure of his *Coriolanus* at Drury Lane several years earlier, gave Steele's play unintended assistance in his pamphlet *A Defence of Sir Fopling Flutter,* published a few days before the opening. Alluding to the informal presentations which Steele had arranged in Wales and Edinburgh, Dennis predicted that it had been "read to more Persons than will be at the Representation of it. . . ."[3] By the time of the opening, discussion of the play had risen to the point that, as one writer remarked, "a Man of no very great Curiosity would have ventur'd to squeeze into the Crowd that went to see it the first Night." The usual advertising campaign was undertaken in the London newspapers.[4]

---

[2] Loftis, pp. 183–93.

[3] Reprinted in *The Critical Works of John Dennis,* ed. Edward N. Hooker (Baltimore, 1939–1943), II, 241–50.

[4] Statement in *The Freeholder's Journal* (BM, Burney copy), 14 November 1722. Evidence of the surviving newspapers does not support Hooker's statement (*The Critical Works of John Dennis,* II, 495), repeated by many other scholars, that "no English play had ever received half of the advance

The Conscious Lovers opened at Drury Lane on Wednesday, 7 November. A "greater Concourse of People was never known to be assembled," according to one newspaper's account.[5] Those who were fortunate enough to get into Wren's theater saw Steele watching from a box in the center gallery, accompanied by his young friend Benjamin Victor, who many years later would recall that Steele was pleased with all the portrayals except that of Griffin as Cimberton. The actor-managers no doubt were stirred to heightened performances by the great concourse of people out front who had paid the higher admission price; applause was prolonged and enthusiastic, a famous general was observed shedding tears at Indiana's pathetic dilemma ("I'll warrant he'll fight ne'er the worse for that," Steele commented in the preface to the printed play)—it was a great opening night. The Member of Parliament for Wendover, who had almost lost his artistic identity on the backbenches of Parliament, was once more a renowned literary figure.

Performances of the play continued through Saturday of the first week and into the next. Princess Caroline graced the theater on Friday, 16 November. After eighteen consecutive nights (omitting Sundays) the partners replaced *The Conscious Lovers* with the usual repertory run (*Love for Love, The Recruiting Officer,* and so on). In December it was brought back again for three more performances "at the request" of those importunate "several ladies of quality" who had not been able to get places earlier. How the money rolled in. Steele had three benefits, from which he received more than £300, and he secured of course his share of the profits as paten-

---

publicity which *The Conscious Lovers* enjoyed." Addison and Steele's campaign on behalf of Philips' *The Distress'd Mother,* for example, had been much more extensive. The oft-quoted newspaper advertisement which Dennis asserts was placed by the "Author, or one of his *Zany's*" terming the play "the very best that ever came upon the *English* Stage" was not located by Hooker or Aitken or the present writer. Did it exist?

[5] *Daily Journal,* 8 November 1722, quoted in *London Stage,* II, 694.

tee, without mentioning the £40 and "divers other good Causes and Considerations" Tonson was forced to pay for the copyright of the play.[6] The printed version, appearing on 1 December 1722, carried a dedication to the King that warned against the "Insinuations of Malecontents" and decried rebellion: "Tis to be a Savage to be a Rebel. . . ." These seasonable remarks in a year of Jacobite alarms brought another reward: £500 of His Majesty's bounty.[7] This was political recompense; Robert Walpole employed the King's bounty to reward the faithful and steady the wavering, but the politics of *The Conscious Lovers* are all in the dedication. The audience was drawn from all parties.

What brought them to the theater? The attraction was not, as has often been asserted, to see the first sentimental comedy. A critical controversy about the play sprang into being in the periodical press and this encouraged attendance. The controversy, however, was not over the presentation of the pathetic on stage—London audiences had long been used to tears in the theater [8]—but about the play's derivation from Terence and about the nature of instruction on the stage. To the first charge, that he had adapted the plot from Terence's *Andria,* Steele cheerfully pleaded guilty. He took it for granted that his audience, or the educated members of his audience, would recognize his source and, as in Pope's *Imitations of Horace,* derive added pleasure from the echo of the Latin classic. "I am extremely surpriz'd," he wrote in the preface to the printed version, "to find . . . That what I valued my self so much upon, the Trans-

[6] Agreement with Tonson quoted in Rodney M. Baine, "The Publication of Steele's *Conscious Lovers,*" *Studies in Bibliography,* II (1949–1950), 170.

[7] Warrant on the Sign Manual, not previously located, is PRO, T 52/32/265, printed below in Appendix E. The money order, dated 17 December, is in Order Book T 60/12/25.

[8] See Loftis, pp. 196–201. See also Shirley Strum Kenny's discussion in her edition of *The Conscious Lovers* (Lincoln, Neb., 1968), pp. xvii–xxv. Though my point of view is somewhat different from theirs, I am much indebted to both of these critics.

lation of [Terence], should be imputed to me as a Reproach." [9]
To the other charge, that he had violated classical decorum by
seeking to instruct through a mixture of the comic and the
pathetic, Steele again admits his guilt. Steele has this to say
about the reunion scene of the long-lost Indiana and her father:
"[Anything] that has its Foundation in Happiness and Success, must be allow'd to be the Object of Comedy; and sure it
must be an Improvement of it, to introduce a Joy too exquisite
for Laughter, that can have no Spring but in Delight, which is
the Case of this young Lady." The syntax is broken-backed but
the meaning is tolerably clear: the basis of comedy is happiness
and success. Situations may be presented which are beyond
laughter, that is to say, pathetic situations, if they culminate in
happiness and success. Though attacked on this point by classical critics such as John Dennis, who objected to the mixture of
genres, Steele in his theoretical statement was directing the
attention of his readers to the self-evident: that English drama
had been mixing genres for a long time, quite oblivious of
classical rule or precedent. Shakespeare and Beaumont and
Fletcher had mingled comic and pathetic without a nod to the
critics' gallery, and John Dryden had done so as well, though
Dryden had felt compelled now and again to defend his practice.

A more truly controversial point is Steele's contention that
the end or intention of his play is instruction, in a direct sense.
A play is, or can be, a guide to action: "[F]or the greatest
Effect of a Play in reading [i.e., in reading a play] is to excite
the Reader to go see it; and when he does so, it is then a Play
has the Effect of Example and Precept." This was a theme
which Steele had treated many times in his writings: the educa-
tive aspect of literature. The Horatian *aut prodesse aut delec-
tare* is in the background here—Steele quotes Cicero to add

---

[9] Quotations are from Tonson's so-called Third Edition of 1730. See
Shirley Strum Kenny, "Eighteenth-Century Editions of Steele's *Conscious
Lovers*," *Studies in Bibliography*, XXI (1968), 253–61.

support to his assertion—but the impulse is in the spirit of the Enlightenment rather than of Augustan Rome. Steele in invoking Cicero is employing what Peter Gay has termed the "useful and beloved past" for the improvement of the present and the future.[10] Since a play affects the playgoer more directly than a book affects the reader, the drama, in Steele's view, is to be a prime instrument in the reform of society, but all literature is capable of guiding society along the upward road to a better day. Domestic situations such as those presented in *The Conscious Lovers* are especially suitable for edification, or so Steele had long contended. Years earlier, in *The Spectator* (No. 428), he had called for literature on new topics, for example, the misfortunes of being in need of money:

> When we are come into Domestick Life in this manner, to awaken Caution and Attendance to the main Point, it would not be amiss to give now and then a Touch of Tragedy, and describe that most dreadful of all Humane Conditions, the Case of Bankrupcy; how Plenty, Credit, Chearfulness, full Hopes, and easie Possessions, are in an Instant turned into Penury, faint Aspects, Diffidence, Sorrow, and Misery; how the Man, who with an open Hand the Day before could administer to the Extremities of others, is shunn'd to Day by the Friend of his bosom.

Or, as Diderot was to put the theme more pungently years later: "The worst of it is the constrained posture in which need holds you. The needy man doesn't walk like the rest, he skips, twists, cringes, crawls." [11] Domestic situations, the drama of the commonplace, are better suited for instruction than the sorrows of kings and the ambition of princes. In an amusing instance of life imitating art, Steele, who had known well enough the

---

[10] See *The Enlightenment: An Interpretation* (New York, 1966), pp. 31–71.

[11] *Rameau's Nephew and Other Works,* trans. Jacques Barzun and Ralph Owen (New York, 1956), p. 84.

sorrows of need, followed his own precepts, illustrated the afflictions of domestic poverty in *The Conscious Lovers*—and was rewarded with a shower of money. The example could scarcely have been more apposite.

As is usual in Steele's writings, there are autobiographical echoes here and there in the play. Indiana's name is reminiscent of Steele's Aunt Bellindia, and both names are reminders of the wealth of the Indies which Indiana's father sought in fiction and Steele's grandfather Richard in fact, that quick wealth which could cut through life's problems with such ease. Myrtle's duel returns, of course, to a theme with which Steele had been preoccupied since his own duel with Kelly twenty-two years before. The pathos of Indiana's situation derives from the plight of an unmarried young woman without financial resources in a society which placed great, and increasing, importance on the size of the dowry or portion the bride could bring to a marriage settlement.[12] With two unmarried daughters Steele had reflected on the specific aspects of such a situation.

The play was good theater, with a well-constructed plot, crisp dialogue, and meaty parts for Steele's friends, the actors and actresses he had known since the turn of the century. Anne Oldfield, who had played Rowe's pathetic heroines, could coax tears from the sternest audience. The pert, witty servant Tom was an ideal part for Cibber.

The happy ending of *The Conscious Lovers'* opening night was a result of more than the money it brought Steele. For once in his life, of greater importance perhaps, was the renewal of his literary fame, the revival of his reputation as a writer rather than as a controversial Member of Parliament. Although the play is perhaps in the second rank of his works, among his many interesting but flawed productions, and although he received a stern critical drubbing from several quarters, the play

[12] See H. J. Habakkuk, "Marriage Settlements in the Eighteenth-Century," *Transactions of the Royal Historical Society,* XXXII (1950), 15–30.

was warmly defended by other critics and received that vote of confidence ultimately reassuring to the dramatic author, large and enthusiastic audiences.[13] The applause must have delighted Steele. His best writing days were over; he knew that. Prue, who would have enjoyed the excitement with him, was four years in her grave at the Abbey. He was a hundred years away from those days, only a decade or so earlier by calendar time, when he would write her a note directing her to dress and call for him at the *Gazette* office in the coach to "spend some time together in the fresh Air in free Conference." But three hundred persons at Drury Lane were willing to vote that his literary craft had not entirely deserted him. He was drawing in, but something remained to him from the past.

Not, of course, that Steele was without ways of spending the money which *The Conscious Lovers* was bringing into the playhouse.[14] The Fish Pool had been in difficulties for some months, probably as a result of competition and of Dale's mismanagement. One newspaper reported that standard fishing vessels were able to bring in more fish at the same cost, which, if true, forecast the end of the Fish Pool company.[15] The entire British fishing industry faced stiff competition from the Dutch.[16] No doubt the Fish Pool's catch was fresher, but the freshness was, one infers, not enough to overcome the price disadvantage. Dale's errors had probably drained off capital at a critical time. Steele and his mathematical associate Gillmore

---

[13] In a deposition of 1727, quoted in Loftis, p. 193, Steele stated that the play brought £2,536 3s. 6d., or "more . . . than any play was ever known to do" (Aitken, II, 312).

[14] In addition to his share of the profits and the royal bounty, Steele had three benefit performances from which he received £329 5s. (Loftis, p. 194).

[15] *Applebee's Weekly Journal* for 6 January, quoted in *Corr.,* p. 503.

[16] See the pamphlet of 1720, which affirmed that without state support no private undertaking could "be able to beat the Dutch out of the fishery." Quoted in William R. Scott, *The Constitution and Finance of English, Scottish and Irish Joint-Stock Companies to 1720* (Cambridge, 1912), II, 374–76.

dabbled with another related device called the Navivium for a while in 1722 and 1723, but the Fish Pool itself "went into Brunsden's dock" on 1 November 1722.[17] After that nothing is known.

The Commission for the Forfeited Estates, too, was winding up its business. Steele continued to meet with the Scottish board until Lady Day, 1723, when he exchanged posts with Dennis Bond of the English group. The English Commission had almost no duties to perform, and Steele was saved the punishing journey to Edinburgh but his stipend ceased, as did those of the other English commissioners, with the quarter ending Michaelmas, 1723. The Scottish board, on the other hand, petitioned for a continuation of their stipend and were eventually allowed £7,500 for service after 1724, which was almost purely nominal.[18] The Commission for the Forfeited Estates in Scotland became a sinecure, that is, after Steele had left it.

Parliament was preoccupied with Jacobite plots during the session of 1722–1723. Steele served on a committee, chaired by Walpole, which drew up a humble address to the King expressing the Commons' indignation for "the horrid and detestable Conspiracy" of the Jacobites. Walpole pursued Jacobites everywhere and found some : in May Christopher Layer, one of those involved with Swift's friend Bishop Atterbury, was beheaded. In that month, too, Bishop Atterbury himself was examined by a committee of Parliament that had employed a decipherer to interpret cryptic passages in several of the Bishop's letters.

[17] Memorandum in Steele's hand quoted in Aitken, II, 255n. For Navivium, see *Corr.*, pp. 180–81.

[18] PRO, T 60/12, pp. 28, 88, 176, 256, 262. The order of 15 May 1724 (p. 256), under which Steele was paid for the quarter ending Midsummer, 1723, contains the explanatory comment after the date: "the time to which other the Commrs (especially those acting on the part of England where Sir Richard has been present) are paid. . . ." Scottish Board payments: Scottish R.O., MSS. FEP 1715, Vol. 19: General Record Kept by the Commissioners, p. 65.

When Atterbury asked the expert to explain how he arrived at his results, the man answered "he hoped he should not be obliged to answer that question. It was betraying his art by which he got an honest maintenance. . . ."

Atterbury responded: "[What] are these decypherers? They are a sort of officers unknown to the English nation. Are they the necessary implements and instruments of ministers of state?"[19]

The question was rhetorical and the intended answer "No," but Atterbury's speech, "full of the best and finest oratory" young Dudley Ryder ever heard, was not sufficient to save him from exile in June. Atterbury had, in fact, been found out by an early application of the budding science of cryptanalysis.[20] He could only deny his complicity, attempt to explain away the passages, denounce his accusers, and rely on his oratorical ability to answer the unanswerable.

Atterbury's defenders were quick to rise to his assistance. He was a convinced and able Jacobite but the evidence the government had against him appeared flimsy to the uninitiated, relying as it did on the interpretation of cant names such as "Illington" in intercepted correspondence. Great amounts of time and effort were expended in attempting to prove that references to the dog Harlequin, sent from France by the Earl of Mar to Atterbury, were inserted to convey secret information about the plot. They did, but the dog Harlequin provided an irresistible subject for Tory wits. The whole inquiry was later spoofed for posterity by Swift in *Gulliver's Travels* ("So, for example, if I should say in a letter to a friend, Our brother Tom has just got the piles, a man of skill in this art would discover how the same letters which compose that sentence may be analyzed into the following words: Resist—a plot is brought home—the tour.

[19] Sandon Hall, Harrowby MSS., Document 29, Dudley Ryder's diary entry for 6 May [1723].
[20] Kenneth Ellis, *The Post Office in the Eighteenth Century* (Oxford, 1958), pp. 128–29. For a good popular account, see David Kahn, *The Code-Breakers* (New York, 1967), pp. 170–71.

And this is the anagrammatic method.") and in his poem "Upon the horrid *Plot* discovered by *Harlequin* the B---- of R----'s *French* Dog"

> His Answers were exceeding pretty
> Before the secret wise Committee
> Confess't as plain as he could bark;
> Then with his Fore-foot set his *Mark*.[21]

Philip, Duke of Wharton, after his brief flirtation with Whiggery had become a full-blown Jacobite and was pursuing the government in a new, and effective, periodical, *The True Briton*. Thomas Burnet's friend George Duckett had with Nicholas Amherst started a pro-government periodical in November, 1722, entitled *Pasquin*. In July, 1723, Steele contributed two numbers to *Pasquin*, no doubt at Duckett's request. These two papers are, as it happened, Steele's valedictory to political writing, not his best but by no means without bite. The bench of bishops, Steele maintains, have lost little by Atterbury's departure "except that now he is gone, they could not write so good an Epigram, if it were put upon them to produce one. . . . For it was the peculiar Excellence of that Prelate, to keep alive in himself the kind of Learning we are admired for when Boys, and play it against his Adversaries in his ripe or declining Age; from which he would with great Readiness, no matter what Decency, skip to a Text of Scripture, and enjoy the Advantage of the Bishop, and the Vivacity and Pertness of the School-Boy, at the same time." [22] This is a skillful line of attack, under the circumstances. If Atterbury was merely indulging in literary games in those damning letters, then this was boyish conduct unworthy of his position. But Steele allows the odor of espionage and treason to linger: Atterbury was a

---

[21] *Gulliver's Travels and Other Writings,* ed. Louis A. Landa (Boston, 1960), p. 156; *The Poems of Jonathan Swift,* ed. Harold Williams, 2d ed. (Oxford, 1958), I, 300.
[22] *Tracts,* p. 615.

composer of epigrams, that is to say, messages known only to the initiated, or, secret messages; that is—treasonable messages. The reader is obliged to select the interpretation of Atterbury's conduct which seems the more plausible, from two disagreeable alternatives.

Though there was never a direct confrontation, Steele and Swift were, for the last time, trading blows in a propaganda campaign. Swift in this instance was cast in a defensive role, whereas Steele was on the attack. It is something of a relief that the last exchange of the two combatants dealt with issues worthy of their stature.

In the spring of 1723 Steele's health worsened again, as it had done every spring for the past several years. He was usually able to get rid of the paralysis in his arms and legs by rest and mild exercise but in 1723 his resiliency left him. Sir John Vanbrugh saw him in July and decided to seek the reversion of the Drury Lane patent after Steele's death.[23] Steele would outlive Vanbrugh by three years, but in 1723 that seemed unlikely.

Creditors were still after Steele now and again, restoring the defective memory he had for his debts by hauling him into court. In the Michaelmas term Catherine Yale, widow of Elihu Yale, sued him for £122 10s. Perhaps Steele had sought a loan from Yale before his death. A certain irony adheres to this particular suit, by the widow of Yale University's benefactor against another benefactor, Steele, who had been first on Jeremiah Dummer's list of donors to the library of the infant institution.

One way out of financial difficulties was the theater. Steele in September was said to be at work on a new play.[24] This was a means of protecting his interest at Drury Lane against the acquisitive instincts of the actor-managers. In January, 1720, it

[23] Vanbrugh, *The Complete Works of Sir John Vanbrugh,* ed. Bonamy Dobrée and Geoffrey Webb (London, 1927–1928), IV, 151.
[24] *London Journal* of 14 September 1723, quoted in Aitken, II, 293. Original not located.

will be recalled, Booth, Cibber, and Wilks had begun deducting five pounds a day from Steele's share as their compensation for Steele's absence from his duties at the playhouse. Unknown to him, they were still taxing his earnings in this manner.[25]

His energies, though, were flagging and his painful illness sometimes brought on a querulousness that was out of keeping with his normal disposition. He chided Elizabeth for not dating a letter to him. "I ought not to find faults in so kind and so affectionate an epistle, but exactnesse is an excellent Quality which every one may be mistresse of, and therefore I would not have You want it." The children's guardian, Hannah Keck, had married John Bullock about 1722[26] but was supposedly still keeping an eye on the education of Molly and Elizabeth for the time being. In September Steele set out for Bath, to try the restorative qualities of the famous waters. On the first of October he wrote to the two girls from there:

> This confesses to my Dear Children that I came to this place three Weeks ago with a very Heavy heart, but I hope I am now better, and desire Betty to write to Me and let Me know What she hears from Mrs. Bullock, and the like accounts, For my soul is wrapped up in y^r Welfare and I am Dear Children
>
> > Y^r Most Affectionate Father
> > and Most Humble Ser^{nt}

The clouds were swirling in around him now. About the twentieth of November, poor Eugene's tormented body failed him. Elizabeth sent her father the news. His reply expresses the agony of the helpless:

> My Dear Child
>   I have Your letter with the news of Eugene's Death and y^r reflections thereupon. Do You and y^r Sister stay at home, and do

<hr>

[25] Loftis, pp. 214–15, correcting information in *Corr.*, p. 171.
[26] Rae Blanchard, "Steeleiana: An Eighteenth-century Account Book," *Studies in Philology*, XXXIX (1942), 502–509.

not Go to the Funerall. Lord Grant Me Patience, Pray write to Me constantly.

Y^r Affectionate Father
and Obedient Servant

November 22^d 1723

RICHARD STEELE

Why don't you mention Molly. Is she Dead too?

On 30 November *The Weekly Journal or Saturday's Post* reported: "Sir Richard Steele lyes very ill; his Son, a Youth of extraordinary Parts, dy'd some Days ago." [27]

As the year drew toward its close and Steele regained a bit of strength, he realized that he must direct whatever resources remained to him to ensuring the girls' well-being. Everything else must be sacrificed to that. It would not be easy. Hannah Bullock had a husband to look after now and wished to put the sisters to board with a Mr. and Mrs. Matthew Snow. A new governess had been engaged for them and if she was a good person at least some of Steele's concerns would be lessened. But was she? He must recover enough of his strength to get back to London and arrange matters as well as he could, hoping in the meantime for the best and relying on Elizabeth's steady good sense. He had no choice at all.

My Dr Child

You must pardon me if I write by a Servant's hand (to you) because I have a great deal of business to do to-night and therefore Cannot under my present Infirmity do it in my own Hand. I know nothing of the Gentlewoman with whom you are left but depend very much upon Mrs. Bullock's Conduct and Judgement. You say y° gentlewoman who is your Governess is a very well bred Woman. If she proves so to me I shall honour her as my sister for y° Justice and kindness she shews to you. Pray shew her this letter, and tell her so. You say she never was abroad in

---

[27] BM, Burney copy.

any dependent way before. Pray desire her to write to me, to let me know what terms she is upon, that I may proceed accordingly for her service. I am, my Dear Child, most tenderly affected with the kind and prudent Expressions in y^r Letter but Cannot speak my mind to you till I see you wch I hope will be about ye time ye Parliament meets. I am, dear Betty,

Y^r Most Affectionate Father
and Most Humble Ser^{nt}
RICHARD STEELE

A brief respite from his illness came in January, but when Steele returned to London early in the new year he had made up his mind to retire.

Epilogue

His career was over. He would, it is true, try to finish the play he called *The School of Action*. But his health was no longer good enough to endure long days in the House, committees that met "at five o'clock in the Speaker's chambers," late evenings at the coffeehouse after Drury Lane closed. He could rely on the income from his Welsh properties and on the profits from the theater; this was enough to pay off his debts and to support him and Elizabeth and Molly if he lived simply. That was the problem, living simply.

On the whole, retiring to Wales seemed the best solution. If he could summon the strength anywhere to finish the play, he could do so in Carmarthenshire, where Prue's relations, the Scurlocks, and their connections dwelled. His money would stretch much further in Wales than in London, and he could stop running up debts his children would have to pay off after his death. Keeping the estate unencumbered was the best he could do for the girls.

As a first step, he directed a proposal be drawn up for the payment in full of all his debts. These ran, it was calculated, to something over £4,000, against which the income from the theater would be applied, estimated conservatively at £700 a year. "And likewise," the proposal provided hopefully, "that the said debts may be sooner paid by the accidental advantages of a new

Play, which Sir Richard may produce next Winter."[1] Steele named Prue's cousin David Scurlock his attorney, and in June, 1724, an Indenture Quadripartite, based on the proposal, was entered into by Steele, the actor-managers, eighteen assorted creditors, and Scurlock. The indenture spelled out the debts and set up a timetable for their repayment with interest.[2] There was still £900 due on the £2,000 Steele had borrowed in 1716 by mortgaging his share of the theater profits and on which he must already have paid more than £4,000. Although recovering the full amount of his share from Cibber, Wilks, and Booth required a lengthy lawsuit, most of the money due him eventually was paid, and the agreement apparently ran its course. Widow Yale got her money; William Oliphant, the innkeeper who stabled Steele's coach and horse and who was owed £186 for hay, forage, and other merchandise, got his. George Filkin, the undertaker, received his £33 15s., due no doubt for Eugene's small coffin. Pounds, shillings, and pence, they would all be paid off if he lived long enough. He could do this much for Molly and Elizabeth, and this much he did.

He could not do much more. His political influence was now almost nil. In the spring of 1724 he had petitioned the King for an extension of his theater patent, which expired three years after his death, into perpetuity. This required addressing the Lord Chamberlain, his old patron Newcastle. Even at this late date, Steele could not bring himself to grovel before Newcastle. He blamed his intractability on his illness:

My Lord

I am under Great indisposition and therefore cannot write so much as I would to Apologize to Y[r] Grace for many things that dwell upon my thoughts, but the businesse of this is only to

---

[1] Proposal printed in Aitken, II, 298–99.
[2] Summarized in Aitken, II, 300–302.

acquaint Your Lordship that I am preferring [?] the inclosed petition by my Lord Townshend's favour, and to let Y^r Grace know that there shall be what Clauses you think fitt subject to [?] the honour of Y^r Office

I am, My Lord

Y^r Grace's Most Oblig'd Most
Obedient Humble Servant
RICHARD STEELE

No action was taken on Steele's petition. He was still member for Wendover and would continue to be until 1727,[3] but his days as a working member were over. During the summer of 1724, after entering the Indenture Quadripartite, Steele left London forever. His rooms in York Buildings, where the Censorium had entertained a "Hundred Gentlemen, and as many Ladies, of leading Taste in Politeness, Wit and Learning," were advertised in August as vacant.[4] In February, 1725, someone remembered that he was still alive, and he was given a hundred pounds of the King's bounty.[5] Perhaps rumors reached London that he would have *The School of Action* ready for production and a courtier saw possibilities of wringing political advantage out of another stage success. Perhaps someone even had a moment's twinge of pity, though this appears improbable.

Steele owned property in several parishes around Carmarthen and he chose to reside in Llangunnor at his farm Ty-Gwynn. Here the town of Carmarthen spread before him in a panorama to the west, the castle walls of the ancient fortress, the spire of St. Peter's, the low houses of the town reaching down to the riverside. The parish church of Llangunnor was on a hilltop a few hundred yards to the north. From the churchyard Steele could look up the valley of the River Tovey as far as

[3] That is, until the general election which was required to be held after the death of George I.
[4] *The Daily Post* (BM, Burney copy), 17 August 1724.
[5] PRO, T 29/25/13.

A view of Carmarthen

This is approximately the view of Carmarthen that Steele would have had from his house across the River Tovey. From Samuel and Nathaniel Buck, *Buck's Antiquities* . . . (London, 1774), III, plate 13. The plate was published separately on September 8, 1748.

Grongar Hill, and during his last years he came to know the young poet John Dyer, who was a witness to his will. It was, and is, a peaceful setting and Steele's last years were quiet ones. From time to time he was able to work on his play there, and when he did not feel equal to working he could receive the occasional visitor and watch the life of the farm around him. Now and again his daughters would come to see him and their cousins. The first of a long line of suitors for Elizabeth's hand was a Welshman, Edward Morgan, who in 1724 asked Steele's blessing on the match through an intermediary, Mr. Prichard. Elizabeth was only fifteen but she was accustomed to making up her mind. "I told Mr. Prichard that he who was to have her must win her & Wear her that She was a Girl of Good Sence. . . . [B]ut upon Speaking of the same Subject that Evening and mentioning Your Civility for her to her she told me with a great deal of Calmnesse & Ease [that] she was very Young & very well Contented to waite her time & Choice. . . ." More suitors would follow, but Elizabeth would wait her time, marrying John Trevor (later third Baron Trevor) in 1732.[6]

As the years went on, Steele must have realized that he would not finish even *The School of Action.* He was still well enough in 1727, however, to reply to a lawsuit brought by his colleagues at Drury Lane and to make his will.[7] In the will, Steele, "weak in body but of sound mind and memory," left his daughter Elizabeth Aynston a hundred pounds, and gifts of twenty pounds each to various Scurlock relations. All the rest "I give to my dear dutiful and well beloved daughters Elizabeth and Mary Steele. . . ." Occasionally someone thought of him, mentioning him in a poem, or dedicating a book to him,[8] or

[6] See Appendix F.
[7] See Loftis, pp. 227–30. The will is reprinted in Aitken, II, 321–24.
[8] List of dedications in *Corr.,* pp. 521–22, to which should be added [?], *Arthritifugum Magnum,* advertised in *The Daily Post* (BM, Burney copy) for 6 November 1724. I am indebted to Professor Ronald Paulson for this reference, which I have not seen.

seeking his name as a subscriber to a book. Benjamin Victor,
trying to make his way in London, was in touch with him:

> I was told, he retained his chearful sweetness of temper to the
> last; and would often be carried out in a summer's evening, where
> the country lads and lasses were assembled at their rural sports,—
> and, with his pencil, give an order on his agent, the mercer, for a
> new gown to the best dancer.
>
> In the year 1727, when I was a *levee-hunter,* and making an
> interest with the first Minister, that good old man hearing of it,
> inclosed me an open letter to Sir Robert Walpole, that, I remem-
> ber, began thus—*"If the recommendation of the most obliged
> man, can be of any service to the bearer*—Sir Robert received
> it with his usual politeness.[9]

In July, 1728, the books were finally closed on the mortgaged
share of the theater. His title was clear at last. Of more immediate concern was the life of the farm: "We are here in great
Joy," he wrote Molly that month, "because my Mare has
brought a Foal *a male one* after 11 month's time." It was the
last letter we have of Steele's.

Sometime in August, 1729, it became evident that the end
was at hand. He was moved to a house in Carmarthen and
there he died at ten o'clock on the night of 1 September 1729.
The Craftsman reported his death on 13 September, with the
reminder that he was "well known by his many eminent Writings." Walpole, it later reported, had plans to erect an expensive monument to his memory in Westminster Abbey, but Sir
Robert did not get around to it.[10] Allan Ramsay heard the news
in Edinburgh and began work on a pastoral elegy.[11] Few others

---

[9] Benjamin Victor, *Original Letters, Dramatic Pieces, and Poems* (London, 1776), I, 330.

[10] Issue of 20 September 1729 (not located by this writer), referred to in
Aitken, II, 328.

[11] The manuscript of "Richy & Edi ane Eclogue To the memory of Sr
Richard Steele" is in BM, Egerton MSS., 2023, fo. 59. I am indebted to Dr.
Alexander M. Law for this reference.

remembered. Wearing his periwig, as if dressed for the Mall, Steele's body was laid under the stones of St. Peter's church in Carmarthen.[12] The Censor of Great Britain was gone.

What sort of man had he been, what mark had he left on his world? He was a good companion, a clubman of legendary proportions. The world as he saw it was essentially a club: family, school, army, theater, Parliament. No doubt this perspective had something to do with the fact that he was an orphan and that kinspeople seemed bound to slip away from one. His life confirmed that feeling: from the day in Dublin when he beat on his father's coffin with his rattle, imploring him to come out and play, to the last twilight in Wales, with strangers around his bed as the light failed. The people one loved could not be trusted, because they would die: "Why don't you mention Molly? Is she Dead too?" But a coffeehouse, a committee room, a club sustained one; the faces around the table would not leave, the laughter would not stop. The earliest scene in Oxford and the last in Carmarthen are alike in that respect. Oxford: "[T]he night after I writ my last, Mr. Horne sent for me to the tavern, where he and Mr. Wood, a fellow of that Coll[ege] treated me with Claret and Oysters." Wales: He "would often be carried out in a summer's evening, where the country lads and lasses were assembled at their rural sports, —and, with his pencil, give an order . . . for a new gown to the best dancer."

It is in the context of his need for the club surrounding that one should judge what a critic has termed his instinct to be "so self-abasing; his itch to confess. . . ."[13] His confessions, his desire to make amends, his righting of the balance, are public;

---

[12] Willard Connely quotes the statement of two workers at St. Peter's who had observed Steele's body when the casket was moved during reconstruction in 1876. See Connely's *Sir Richard Steele* (New York, 1934), p. 453. The gravediggers reported Steele had only a half-dozen teeth left when he died, and that his grey hair showed at the temples, under the black wig.

[13] Bonamy Dobrée, *Variety of Ways* (Oxford, 1932), pp. 86–87.

these are amends to the other club members, apologies to his brothers in the lodge. There are few confessions to Prue and very little self-abasement man to man, even to a noble lord whom he has offended. He is indisposed, he tells the Lord Chamberlain, and "therefore cannot write so much as I would to Apologize." Excuses are due the readers of *The Tatler* or of *The Christian Hero,* confessions are made to members of the Commission for the Forfeited Estates, *Apology*'s are addressed to the House of Commons, but in private life Steele goes his own way with scarcely the briefest formal bow to convention.

Not much need be said about Steele's vices, which so disturbed critics in the last century. Dr. Johnson, as usual, strikes the right note: "I mentioned Sir Richard Steele having published his *Christian Hero,* with the avowed purpose of obliging himself to lead a religious life; yet, that his conduct was by no means strictly suitable. JOHNSON. 'Steele, I believe, practised the lighter vices.' " [14] The seven sins called deadly held not much appeal for him; he shared to a certain degree his century's affinity for gluttony, perhaps, though he was scarcely to be termed a slave to his belly. He was not slothful in a conventional sense; in fact he led an extremely busy life, but if carelessness is an aspect of sloth, then this was his besetting sin because he was careless to an exaggerated degree, especially where money was concerned. The other side of this carelessness, the virtue of this defect, was an open-handed generosity, which showed itself again and again: a helping hand for a young poet such as Allan Ramsay or an old friend down on her luck like Mrs. Manley. He would help a talented adventurer, Richard Savage, who would repay the debt by retailing stories after Steele's death that would reflect Steele's generosity of spirit in spite of Savage's intention of discrediting him. He would reply to years of public abuse from John Dennis (much

[14] *Boswell's Life of Johnson,* introd. Chauncey B. Tinker (Oxford, 1948), I, 659.

of it directed at him in the misapprehension that he had written some essays actually written by Addison) by assisting Dennis in getting his play produced at Drury Lane. If he had money, he would give you some; if he had time, he would listen to your story.

Unfortunately, this carelessness extended to his writing. An obvious error in one of his plays, for example, he suffered to go through five editions in his lifetime; in twenty-five years, that is to say, he did not bother even once to glance through the printed version of a play that had cost him a great deal of effort and vexation.[15] Rarely did he revise anything he had written; rarely does one read through anything Steele wrote without thinking of ways it could be improved. "Talking of *The Spectator,* [Dr. Johnson] said, 'It is wonderful that there is such a proportion of bad papers, in the half of that work which was not written by Addison. . . .' " He is essentially correct about *The Spectator;* many of Steele's essays are very good in part but suffer a lapse in plan or execution which is out of keeping with the harmony and polish of *The Spectator* at its best. On the other hand, when he was in the mood he could write very well indeed. One must pick here and choose there: some of *The Lover* essays, some from *The Spectator,* a good collection from *The Tatler* have the energy, humor, and special vision of first-rate literature.

Though his literary lapses stem from carelessness, Steele was, at a deeper level, out of harmony with most of the literary canons of his day. His mark was set principally as a literary innovator. After having made all the allowances for anticipation, influence, and assistance, one returns to the judgment that the essay periodical was effectively his idea. He invented *The Tatler* and the rest followed. He did not invent exemplary drama but his influence and the example of *The Conscious*

---

[15] See *The Tender Husband,* ed. C. Winton (Lincoln, Neb., 1967), p. x.

Lovers gave it a mighty push. He wrote many of the best of the little thumbnail stories, the Inkle and Yarico-style tales, the letter narratives, which constituted part of the creative matrix of fiction.[16] No one would assert that he was the first to come upon that bedrock motif of the sentimental and pathetic, the lady in distress, but no one can deny that he brought it to the attention of an expanding reading public and gave it the cachet of literary approval. After one had read about the misfortunes of Clarinda and Chloe in *The Tatler* it was permissible to read of Clarissa's troubles or those of Lindamire in *The Illegal Lovers* and all the parish knew it. These were works written by persons concerned with religion and morality, so the shivers of delight need not stain one's conscience.

Which is to say that Steele's stance as a defender of religion and morality, as Boswell observed, has always seemed a dubious one. He was, it is true, not hesitant to picture himself in such a role, but as his critics have often pointed out his writings do not square with his precepts. He was a Christian of the radical wing, with strong social views but little sympathy with or concern for the Church visible, with a tendency, in fact, toward suspicion of the ecclesiastical hierarchy. This, perhaps, was an important aspect of his disagreement with Jonathan Swift. Unlike Swift, furthermore, he took a hopeful view of the nature of man and looked forward to a better world here on earth, through amelioration of society's evils. Education would have a major part in this amelioration. These are sentiments that would become worn with use as the eighteenth century moved on; they would be incorporated in the Enlightenment. Most of the specific causes to which Steele committed himself represent attacks on the traditional structure of society: his efforts on behalf of education for women, his strictures on corporal punishment in schools and dueling, his campaign for

[16] Robert S. Day has treated Steele's part in the letter narrative tradition in *Told in Letters* (Ann Arbor, 1966), *passim*.

the charity school movement and for toleration of Dissent. These would become typical Enlightenment causes. His role as defender of religion and morality, then, is only superficially a traditional one; in fact Steele is looking to the future. Religion and morality are joining forces and are admissible insofar as they are socially useful; they are validated, so to say, by their social utility. That way, of course, lies heterodoxy.

His political philosophy, if it can be dignified with such a term, also looked to the left, toward a radical Whiggery. Part of his struggle to become an independent member derived, no doubt, from a desire to rid himself of dependency on the English social structure, simply to be his own man in the most direct sense of the expression. Part, however, sprang from the conviction that the royal authority was only symbolic, that all power resided in the legislature. It followed, therefore, that a Parliament of truly independent members exercising their judgment without reference to patronage or kinship was the best safeguard of the common weal. Modern students of political theory are aware of the many assumptions and rationalizations lurking beneath the surface of this platitude, and the tide of events was running against Steele even as he wrote: Walpole was moving toward effective control of the legislature. By the end of his own career in Parliament, indeed, he had been brought to heel by Walpole, but this is perhaps attributable more to Steele's declining health than to Walpole's power. As late as the election of 1722 Steele, balancing the patronage of so oddly-assorted a pair as Sunderland and the Duke of Wharton, was still trying to clear a place for an independent member in the thicket of party and family groups which dominated political life. The independence he had achieved as a writer he attempted to extend to his life in Parliament. He did not succeed, or succeeded only partially, but it was a bold attempt.

Steele's life was an untidy one, played out in those modes in which he excelled: the comic and the pathetic. He did not respond to tragedy. He was an Irish orphan who became an English knight. He left university without taking a degree. He was a trooper of horse who became a captain of foot. He married a rich widow who died, and at her funeral met the woman who would become his second wife. He loved this second wife and their children intensely and he lost most of them before his own death. He made and squandered fortunes with aristocratic ease, pouring hard money into alchemical furnaces and well fishing vessels and education academies, but at the end he retired to the country, settled his debts, and left his surviving daughters competencies, as if he were a London merchant. He was a founder and director of the academy of painters, though he never laid brush to canvas. He was expelled from one Parliament and elected to three. He wrote three of the most successful stage comedies of the century, he changed the course of literature by inventing the periodical essay. He was the benevolent man, in theory and in practice, but the friendly face he showed to the world overlay a tough and resilient character, as his contemporaries realized. No one could have accomplished what Richard Steele accomplished without extraordinary resources of persistence and determination. As much as any man of his time, perhaps, he owed his success not to family connections or inherited wealth or even luck, but to himself. He bought his independence, and he paid for it.

APPENDIX A

The Commission for the
Forfeited Estates

STEELE'S SERVICE on the Commission for the Forfeited Estates has
been poorly understood, in part because the records of the Commission itself are scattered and in part because the work of the
Commission has not received much attention from historians. There
are brief and somewhat fragmented discussions of his service in
Aitken, II, 94, 153–54, 184, 248–49, 265; and in *Correspondence*,
pp. 126–27n. A. H. Millar's introduction to *A Selection of Scottish
Forfeited Estates Papers 1715; 1745* (Edinburgh, 1909) is judi-
cious but inaccurate in detail and, of course, based only on a selec-
tion of the Scottish manuscripts. There is a lucid introduction,
which relies principally on Millar for Scottish sources, by F. H.
Slingsby in *Calendar of Treasury Books*, Vol. XXX, Part 1:
January–December, 1716 (London, 1958). The records of the
Commission for England and Ireland, indexed as Forfeited Estates
Commission, hereafter FEC, in the Public Record Office of Great
Britain, have recently been calendared by Mr. D. Barlow and are
fairly complete, especially for the years 1720 and earlier. The records in the Scottish Record Office, the Forfeited Estates Papers
1715 (hereafter FEP), were damaged by fire in 1824 and have
serious lacunae, particularly with respect to the correspondence of
the commissioners. The Scottish Commission published six reports
of its transactions, each with a confusing and cumbersome title. For
convenience, these may be referred to as the *First Report* (1717),
Second Report (1718), *Third Report* (1719), *Fourth Report*
(1724), *Fifth Report* (1724), and *Sixth Report* (1724).[1] There

---

[1] *A Report from the Commissioners Appointed to Enquire of the Estates of
certain Traitors, &c. In that Part of Great-Britain called Scotland* (Edin-

are also records having to do with the business of the Commission in the Panshanger Manuscripts at the Hertfordshire Record Office and at the National Library of Scotland. A study of the Commission as a whole that draws on all these sources in Scotland and England would be a valuable contribution to the political and administrative history of the period.

In addition to the material set forth in the text of the present volume, there are a number of references to Steele here and there in those records which demonstrate that the extent of his work on the Commission has been greatly understated. According to the Minute Book (FEC 2/7), Steele attended meetings in 1716 on 27 and 29 June; 3, 7, 10, 11, 12, 14, 18, 19, 20, 23, 31 July; 2, 4, 7 (and a subcommittee meeting at 8 A.M.), 8, 10, 11, 13, 14 August; and, serving as chairman, on 15, 21, 22 August. All these were held at the Speaker's Chambers, Westminster. During the summer of 1717 Steele attended meetings at Essex House in the Strand on 8 June, and on 6, 16, 19, 24, 25 July and 6, 7, 8, 9 August (FEC 2/3). The minutes for the meetings in Scotland in 1717 were not located, nor for those in 1720, 1721, and 1722.

The full text of the letter from the English board mentioned in Chapter VII to which Steele replied is as follows:

---

burgh, 1717) ; *The Report to the Honourable House of Commons, Of such of the Commissioners of Enquiry As have been appointed to Execute the several Trusts and Powers in relation to England. . . . Together with an Additional Report from the Commissioners appointed to Enquire of the Estates of certain Traitors, &c. in that Part of Great Britain called Scotland* (London, 1717[/18]) ; *To the Honourable the House of Commons, a Further Report, Humbly Offered by the Commissioners and Trustees Who acted in Scotland. . . .* (London, 1719) ; *A Further Report Humbly Offer'd by the Commissioners and Trustees of the Forfeited Estates in Scotland. Presented to the Honourable House of Commons; Saturday the 6th Day of February, 1719[/20]* (London, 1724) ; *A Further Report Humbly Offer'd by the Commissioners and Trustees of the Forfeited Estates, Who Acted in Scotland. Presented to the Honourable House of Commons; Wednesday the 18th Day of January, 1720 [/21]* (London, 1724) ; *The Farther Report of the Commissioners and Trustees Appointed to Enquire into the Forfeited Estates in Scotland. Presented to the Honourable House of Commons; Thursday the 7th Day of February, 1722[/23]* (London, 1724).

Sir

Office at Essex House
13th May 1718

Your brethren of England have sate de die in diem since the 25th of March the Commencement of our last Powers, & having already near finished the Claims on Lord Widdrington's Estate are preparing to meet at Preston the 12th of June & before we go shall determine the Claims on Richmond lodge, 'twould be needless to hint to you how desirous a set of People are to find fault, & should they have so just a cause of complaint as the not having a Board at Edinburgh 'twould not be in ye power nor could we expect it from our friends to pardon such an omission. We therefore know you will excuse our reminding you of the necessity of your speedy attendance at Edinburgh in order to discharge the trust repos'd in you by Parliam^t. We are wth true brotherly Respect

TO   Yo^r most hum^{ble} Sev^{ts}

   Patrick Haldane Esqr: Geo: Treby

   Robt Munro Esqr.   Denis Bond

   Sr Henry Hoghton Barr^t.   J. Birch

   Sr Richd Steele Kn^t.   T: Hales

   Arthur Ingram Esqr,   John Eyles [2]

   Rich^d: Grantham Esqr.

This letter further illustrates the fact that the members of the two boards were regarded as interchangeable. In addition to the occasional reports to Parliament, the boards made informal reports to each other, setting forth procedures that had been found to be workable, difficulties that had arisen, and so forth.[3]

The letter of July, 1719, Steele's reply to which is printed in Chapter VIII above, is more to the point than the earlier communication. The full text is as follows:

Sirs

Having received the Enclosed Letter from Scotland and judging the Subject matter of it to be of very great consequence to the Publick, we communicated the same to the Lords of the Treasury.

[2] An office copy is filed in FEC 2/62; original not located.

[3] For example, in PRO, FEC 62/4; and Scottish RO, FEP 1715, Volume 9A.

We are in hopes that you will join wth us in thinking it reasonable
for you forthwith to repair to Edinburgh both in respect of the Publick Service and your own, otherwise this Board will be under a
necessity of sending some of their own Number to make a Board
there, and we are apprehensive that the Commissioners which shall
be then present cannot refuse the Publick the justice to sign a Certificate of your Absence; your immediate answer to this Letter will
be very obliging to

Essex House	Sirs
9⁰ July 1719	Yo[r]. most Affectionate Brethren
Mr. Ingram	& Humble Servants
Mr. Grantham	Denis Bond, T. Hales, Cha: Long,
Sir Rich[d]. Steele	Geo: Gregory, J. Birch [4]
S[r]. Henry Hoghton	

Hoghton's letter of reply to this communication provides a
glimpse of Steele from a colleague's angle of vision.

Gentlemen:

Before I left London Your Bretheren who act in Scotland agreed
to have a Board at Edinburgh on the 15[th] Inst. w[ch] was to be Mr.
Haldane, Mr. Monro, Mr. Ingram & S[r] Rich[d] Steele, the last of whom
promised to begin his Journey Six weeks agoe but I hear is still in
London, w[t] project he's now in pursuite of I know not, but 'tis said
he don't go to'rds Scotland untill Mich[l]mass, as for Mr. Grantham,
(tho' I'm told by a Second Ballott he was ordered to act in Scotland,
he Swears he won't act with us, thô he has had Sev[l]. Letters sent
him, don't answer any, 'tis Surprizing these two of our Body Should
treat the Commission with so much Slight & use us So ill, but whilst
they can make friends to get their Sallarys for doing nothing, I
expect we shant have their assistance, Mr. Haldane & Mr. Monro
have been at Edinburgh for Some time & Mr. Ingram writes from
Yorkshire, he would be w[th] them by y[e] 14[th] [?], I had their allow[n]ce
to Stay here until y[e] 15[th] & as much longer as till they Sent for me
in regard my Wife was so much out of health, having no hopes of
S[r] Richard or Mr. Grantham, they have writt to me to hasten to them
there being a great Clamour both from friends & Enemys against
us, for not having begun business & I must confess not without

[4] Office copy in PRO, FEC 2/63; original not located.

reason, for my part there has not been one day a Board at Edinburgh but I have made one of it, and thô I have been here but five weeks in about twelve months I Should be very ready to go now, did not the Circumstances of my Family make it so inconvenient, as to my private affairs I would postpone them all to attend the business of the Commission, but my Wife being so very bad, I neither can nor ought to leave here, especially to remove to that distance where there's no conveniency of Postage but by way of London and can't have a Return to a Letter in under Twenty Days. Thus Gentlemen having troubled You with the true reason of my not going to Scotland, I hope You will take it into Consideration, and in reguard to the concern I am under for my Wife's health & to the Commission wch must Suffer if a considerable progress is not made this Sumer, I hope You will either lay Your Commands on Sr Richard to go Speedily to Edinburgh or appoint One of Your own Number, as for M^r, Grantham, I fear he's not to be managed now he's gott with his pett Companions at Lincoln, could I have imagin'd I Should have had no better partners I would not have been concerned & if I had thought my Wife would not have recovered before now, I would have resigned wth Mr. Treby, I need Say no more; the Case is so necessitous it pleads for itself, will only add, that there'n none of Yo^r number but were You in my Circumstances, I would readily do for You what I now desire and I am

Gentlemen,

Preston 19th June
1719

Your affectionate Brother,
& very humble Servant
H. Hoghton [5]

[5] Office copy in scribe's hand, PRO, FEC 2/64; original not located. The statement (s.v. de Hoghton) in Burke's *Peerage, Baronetage and Knightage* that Hoghton's wife died on 23 February 1719 is obviously incorrect.

Steele and Freemasonry

"WAS SIR Richard Steele a Freemason?" Rae Blanchard summarizes the evidence on this puzzling question in an article in *Publications of the Modern Language Association of America* (LXIII [1948], 903–17). In the light of Steele's gregarious nature, of the engraving to which she alludes showing Steele in Masonic apron, and of the fact that almost all of his Whig friends were Masons, she concludes that he probably was.

Further circumstantial evidence may be derived from the fact of his association with Dr. John Theophilus Desaguliers. Steele had provided advertisement for Desaguliers' "air-conditioning" device in *Town-Talk* No. 3 (30 December 1715), and the scientist had conducted a series of public experiments at Steele's Censorium rooms in 1719 (see Chapter IX above). Desaguliers, who was probably Master of No. 4 Lodge in London before 1719, became Grand Master in that year.[1] He was instrumental in transforming Freemasonry in the years between 1715 and 1720, according to one historian, not least because he succeeded in inducing prominent persons to join, including Frederick, Prince of Wales.[2] Given their relationship, it seems incredible that he would not have induced Steele to follow his many friends into Freemasonry. When Desaguliers visited Edinburgh in 1721 and was received as a brother by the Master Masons of that city, including many of the Earl of Marchmont's connections, Steele was in Edinburgh himself. The archives of the Grand Lodge of Scotland do not, however,

---

[1] Duncan Campbell Lee, *Desaguliers of No. 4 and His Service to Freemasonry* (London, 1932), p. 12.

[2] *Ibid.*, pp. 11, 14.

reveal any record of Steele.[3] Except for the engraving showing him in Masonic apron, the evidence for Steele's participation in Free-masonry, then, though persuasive, is at present all circumstantial.

[3] Private communication from Dr. A. F. Buchan, Grand Secretary of the Grand Lodge of Scotland, who very kindly caused the records to be searched.

APPENDIX C

Documents Concerning the Revocation of the Drury Lane License

DOCUMENTS BELONGING to Serjeant Thomas Pengelly in the case of the revocation of Steele's patent, which Aitken saw (Aitken, II, 221–29), were at that time (1889) in private hands. They have since been deposited in the Bodleian Library (MS. Eng. letters c. 17). Some of these shed light at various points on the dispute. Lord Chancellor Parker, one of the royal favorites, is revealed to have played a key role in the case by securing the King's acquiescence in the proceedings against Steele.

Folio 24 in the MS. volume, a letter from Parker to Pengelly dated 2 April 1719, conveys Parker's intention "to recommend You to y⁰ King to be his Matyes first Serjeant. . . ."

Folio 23, undated but from internal evidence 24 January 1720 (that is, the day before the issuance of Newcastle's warrant to the company revoking the managers' licenses), is also from Parker to Pengelly. It reveals the extent of the effort being set in motion against Steele:

Thursday night   [January 1720]

Sʳ

   I have sent to my Ld Sunderland & he has wrote me an Answer, I give You his own words, yᵗ, it is not only proper, but even necessary in point of form & Decency yᵗ You should kisse y⁰ King's hand upon this Occasion, & he thinks y⁰ properest time for You to be introduced is, by me as soon as y⁰ King has signed y⁰ Warrant. Therefore if You will go to Morrow to St. James's when I do I will carry You into y⁰ Room at y⁰ Backstaires next y⁰ King's Closet, & go & get y⁰

248

Warrant signed, & then call You in to kisse his Matys Hand, I am w^{t}h great Truth & respect

S^r

Ile send to You to Morrow   Yo^r most obed^t humble
at ye Hall, w^n I am ready to go   Servt Parker C.

Folio 20, Newcastle's letter to Pengelly dated "Fryday Morning" concerning Steele's threat of legal action, was printed in Aitken (II, 229n.), as was Folio 18, a copy of Steele's letter to Newcastle. The original, differing only in punctuation and capitalization, is in BM, Add. MSS., 32,685, printed in *Corr.,* pp. 146–47.

Folio 16 contains the very interesting questions directed by Newcastle to Pengelly (or perhaps arrived at by Pengelly after a conference with Newcastle). They are similar to those directed to Nicholas Lechmere, the Attorney-General, in October, 1718,[1] and are presumably of the same date but contain some important differences:

Whether a patent granted for Erecting & forming a Company of Comedians or Stage players to Act in any part of the Kingdom be not against Law

Whether the Patent granted to Sr Richd Steele for that purpose w.th the powers and Term of Years therein express'd be not ag.st Law & Consequently void

Whether his Majesty may not by the Chamberl.^{n} of his Household make Orders from time to time for the good Goverm.^{t} and Regulation of the Players under Sr Richd Steele, any words or Clauses in his patent to the contrary notw.th Standing

In case of Disobedience to Such Orders, whether the Lord Chamberlain may not by his Majestys Command Silence the S.^{d} Company of players from further Acting, and whether Sr Richd Steele's patent will not thereby be forfeited.

Pengelly evidently retired to meditate on these queries, the results of his meditation being the draft of a series of answers (folio 15), each of them in the affirmative.

---

[1] For the correspondence with Lechmere, see Loftis, pp. 125–27.

Pat[ent] to Er[e]ct a Company of Comedians Void because by
Sev[er]all Acts of Par[liamen]t Declared Unlawful Pastimes [?] &
the p[er]sons acting Vagabonds & Subject to diverse punish[men]ts
& also because Such patent tends to Collect great numbers of people
which at Common Law are unlawfull assemblies & ag[ains]t the
publ[ic] power [?]

Si^r Rich^d St pat[ent] void not only in respect of the priviledge intended to be Granted but in the manner it is granted

The Grant for 3 years after his death is repugnant to the nature &
Kind [?] of the grant which reposes a Trust in S^r R: wch can only
be [*illegible*] by himself

The powers to form a Company to Consist of an Unlimited Number,
to Pe[r]mitt to Act during his own pleasure at all times or without
Impeachm[e]nt of any p[er]son, to have the Sub Govrmnt of Such
Company, & to Impose w[ha]t prices he shall think reasonable and
all powers granted to him also are Inconsistent w[ith] & p[re]judi-
ciall to the royall prerogative and the powers and right of the Officers
of the household especially the Chamberlayne [*lined through*] are an
undue obstruction to the regular [*illegible*] of the [*lined through*]
Commission of the peace and give Incourigem[en]t to [*illegible*] &
oppression.
    Notwithstanding this patent [,] his Majesty by his Chamberlain
may [issue] such Ord[er]s for the Regulation of the players & in
Case of Disobedience may revoke any License formerly Granted to
any of 'em & immediately give Directions to silence 'em and if they
act afterwards they will be lyable to the Correction of the Civile
Magistrate which will be the most effectual method to Determine
their pretensions[?] under the Colour of this patent which seems[?]
of its own nature to amount merely to a License & may be revok'd &
not to pos[ses]se a Durable Interest & propty especially as to that
part of Licensing others to act.
    There May be an Injunction taken upon Acc.^t of Misbehaviour
aleso [*illegible*] committed under Colour of this patent & thereby S^r

R. Steele will be putt out of poss[ess]ion & forced to bring his Monstrans le Droit or to plead to the Injunction. 66ℰ

ℰ6ℰ

The Clause of Non obstant is void & directly I6ℰ

contrary to the Bill of Rights.——————— 06ℰ

1 W & M. c.2. Sect. 12. ℊ8ℰ'W'Z6 [2]

Dalton's Inst. 89.92.322.j. Rolls rep. 109. John Webb's Case 8.Co.49.11.Code.87.5.Mod.142.143.39. Eliz.c.4. Stat. 10.43. Eliz.c.9. Sort. 27.1.James.1.c.7.Sort.1.10.1.Char. 1.c.1.

Notwithstanding this forest of legal learning to the contrary, the final action taken by Newcastle, that of first silencing the company, then of revoking the license rather than the patent, was administrative rather than legal. Newcastle's questions, in the order in which they were presented, represent attacks on the legality of the patent itself, and on the legality of the terms of the patent, turning only in the final two sections to a reaffirmation of the administrative authority of the Lord Chamberlain over the theater. That is what the quarrel boiled down to at last: whether the Lord Chamberlain could exercise administrative direction over the theaters. As already indicated, the theater managers were well aware of the thrust of the Lord Chamberlain's efforts and were prepared to resist in every way they could this intrusion on what they regarded as their own authority. From Newcastle's point of view, however, the problem started with Steele's patent, or rather with Steele himself, and his action began with an attempt to separate Steele from the patent. It is significant that, in spite of Pengelly's opinions, no legal action is known to have been taken against the patent.

Whether Steele would have won the case or not if it had gone to court is of course a matter only of speculation. The question of the legality of such a patent remained unresolved, as John Loftis has shown.[3] Newcastle's lawyers, at any rate, evidently believed that

---

[2] These numbers, in a different hand and reversed on the page, appear to have no connection with Steele's case.

[3] See *Theatre*, p. xxv.

Steele had a case sufficiently strong to justify taking a different tack in moving against him, that is, in the direction of administrative action.

It is also significant that Newcastle (no doubt by design) began immediately to intrude into the details of theater management, to reinforce, as it were, his new or renewed authority. On the second of February, 1720, he issued "orders to the Theatre in Drury Lane" directing the managers "to take care that no benefit Night be Allow'd for the future to any Actor before Mrs. Oldfield and Mrs. Porters benefitt Night and that the prizes [i.e., prices] of the House be never rais'd wth. out my leave first had." [4]

The managers' action in raising the prices in 1722 for the first production of *The Conscious Lovers* may thus be seen as motivated not only by a desire for increased profits but also as a further derogation of the Lord Chamberlain's authority. Since he had forbade it, they would disobey the command deliberately and ostentatiously, using Steele's own play as the occasion.

[4] PRO, LC 5/157.

APPENDIX D

Were Addison and Steele
Homosexuals?

ALMOST AS puzzling as the question of Steele's participation in Freemasonry, and of considerably greater interest to twentieth-century readers, is the statement attributed to Alexander Pope by Joseph Spence in April 1739 : "Addison and Steele [were] a couple of H——s. I am sorry to say so, and there are not twelve people in the world that I would say it to at all." [1] As Spence's editor, Dr. James Osborn, points out, Pope probably said "Hermaphrodites," inasmuch as "homosexual" was introduced by Havelock Ellis in 1897, but his intention is tolerably clear. By modern standards, Steele was at least bisexual, since he certainly fathered four legitimate and two or more illegitimate offspring. It is possible, of course, that he and Addison maintained a homosexual relationship at Charterhouse and afterwards, but I am not aware of any evidence on the subject other than Pope's statement. The practice Steele refers to in the *Plebeian-Old Whig* controversy, is, it may be noted, pederasty rather than homosexual relations between consenting adults. I am content to leave the decision to scholars more competent than I to judge in such matters.

[1] Joseph Spence, *Observations, Anecdotes, and Characters of Books and Men* . . . , ed. James M. Osborn (Oxford, 1966), I, 80 (entry No. 188).

APPENDIX E

Warrant for Steele's Bounty
for *The Conscious Lovers*

	George R
Sr Richd Steele	Our Will & Pleasure is y^t by virtue of Our Genl:
500 $£$ Bounty	Letters of Privy Seal bearing date y^e 29th day of
	Sep^r : 1714 you issue & pay or cause to be issued &
	paid out of any Our Treasure or Revenue in the
	Rec^t. of Our Exch^r : applicable to the use of Our
	Civil Goverm^t. unto Our Trusty & Welbeloved S^r
	Richard Steele Kn^t. or to his Ass.^{e} the Sum of 500 $£$.
	as of Our Free Gift & Royal Bounty without acco :^{t}
	in consideraćon of a Play by him written and dedi-
	cated to Us And for So doing this Shalbe y^e Warr.^{t}
	Given at Our Court at St James's y^e 13th day of
	Dec :^{r} 1722 In y^e 9th year of our Reigne
To the	By his Ma^{ts}. Comand
	Com :^{rs} of Our Treáry A Warrant, on the
	R Walpole. Cha Turner H Pelham
	above Sign Man :^{l},
	Signed R : W. C :T. H :P.
	dated 14 Decr. 1722

Steele's Descendants

THREE OF Steele's children, all daughters, were alive at the time of his death. Mary (Molly) Steele had been under treatment for tuberculosis in 1728 and died of that disease in Clifton, Bristol, on 13 April 1730. Elizabeth Steele, as the heiress of her father's estate, was pursued by a number of suitors in addition to Edward Morgan. Her name was linked with that of a Mr. Lloyd of Pembrokeshire in 1725; Essex McMeyricke of Pembrokeshire in 1730; George Harcourt of Carmarthenshire and James Philipps of Penty Park, Pembrokeshire, in 1731.[1] On 5 June 1732 she was married in St. Paul's Cathedral to John Trevor of the Inner Temple (1695–1764), second son of Sir Thomas Trevor of Bromham, Bedfordshire. His father, created first Lord Trevor of Bromham in 1712, became Lord Privy Seal in 1726 and Lord President of the Council in 1730. John Trevor succeeded his brother Thomas as third Lord Trevor in 1753. A stillborn child was born to the couple in 1733 and a daughter, Diana Maria, in January, 1744. The daughter, who was mentally defective, lived until 1778. Elizabeth Steele Trevor died and was buried at Walcot, Bath, on New Year's Day 1782. Her cousin, the Reverend David Scurlock, the son of Steele's friend, was her heir.[2]

Elizabeth Ousley Aynston, Steele's natural daughter, had one child, Katherine, who married a Mr. Thomas. Both mother and

[1] *Correspondence,* p. 408, and information from his private genealogical collections kindly supplied by Major Francis Jones, County Archivist, Carmarthen.

[2] A good, if little-known, summary article on the Scurlock family is Francis Green, "Scurlock of Carmarthen," *West Wales Historical Records* (Carmarthen, 1923), IX, 135–44.

daughter were on friendly terms with Elizabeth Steele Trevor, who is said to have provided for the education of Mrs. Thomas' two sons.[3] It is through these, the grandsons of his illegitimate daughter, that Steele's descendants, if any, derive. As the name Thomas is one frequently encountered in Wales, the present writer has been unable to trace the genealogy further.

[3] John Nichols, *The Epistolary Correspondence of Sir Richard Steele* (London, 1809), I, x.

APPENDIX G

Steele's Letter to Nottingham

My Lord

When Your Lordship was president of the Council You had the Condescension to interest Your self very much towards my Successe in my Application for a Patent for erecting a Company of Comedians.

As I then gave You assurances of my intention to reform the Stage, I take the liberty to acquaint Your Lordship that in pursuance of that design I have written a Comedy, not only consonant to the rules of Religion and Virtue, in Generall, but also in [*word deleted*] analogy even to the Christian Religion. This attempt will need the need the [*sic*] Support of all who are affectionate to those purposes, and in Gratitude to Your favour in promoting my having an Opportunity to Serve them I presum'd to Signifie this to You, and desire the Support of Your Lordship and Your Freinds in being of the first Audiences when the play shall come on, of which You shall have timely notice from, My Lord,

Yorkbuildings
Jan: 16th—1721/2

Y^r. Lordship's Most Oblig'^{d}
Most Obedient
Humble Serv^{nt}—
RICHARD STEELE [1]

[1] Leicester, County Record Office, Finch MSS., Box 4952.

Index

Academy of Painting (Academy for Painting and Drawing), 16n, 44
Addison, Dean Lancelot, 207
Addison, Joseph:
—life: secretary to Lords Justices, 2–4; relations with Pope, 45, 118, 162; discontent with employment, 72–73; Secretary of State, 105; declining friendship with RS, 105–6, 118, 143–44, 158–63; marriage, 106; death and burial, 163–64
—works: *Cato,* 161, 162; *The Drummer,* 70–71, 82, 83, 205–7; *The Freeholder,* 62, 74, 82; *The Old Whig,* 159–61; revived *Spectator,* 7; collected *Works,* 204–7
—mentioned: 12, 112
Aeneid, 80, 107
Ailesbury, 2nd Earl of (Thomas Bruce), 22
Aislabie, John, 197–98, 203
Aitken, George A., 248
Amherst, *or* Amhurst, Nicholas, 225
Anderson, James, 135, 139, 189, 201
Anderson, James, Jr., 201
Anderson, Patrick, 139n
Anne, Queen: death and burial, 1–3; mentioned, 6, 61
Arbuthnot, Dr. John, 1
Argyll, 2nd Duke of (John Campbell), 74, 99, 125
Atterbury, Bishop Francis, 212, 223–26
Aynston, Katherine (Mrs. Thomas), 255–56
Aynston, William, 184–85

Baillie, George, 125
Baillie, Grizell Hume, 125
Barlow, D., 241
Beaux Stratagem, The, 143, 145n
Benson, William, 103, 113, 136n, 140, 143
Bentley, Dr. Richard, 13

Berkeley, George, Bishop of Cloyne: on the 1715 rebellion, 59, 66, 74; mentioned, 12, 16n, 44, 96
Bevan, Mrs. William (Elizabeth Scurlock), 94, 100, 149
Birch, J., 243, 244
Blackall, Bishop Offspring, 108–9
Blackmore, Sir Richard, 166
Blundel, Surgeon, 1
Bolingbroke, 1st Viscount (Henry St. John): and Swift, 2; impeachment proceedings, 49; with the Pretender, 58–59, 75; mentioned, 21, 35, 37, 147
Bond, Dennis *or* Denis, 213, 243, 244
Booth, Barton, 8, 10, 170–75, 215–16, 227, 231
Boswell, James, 58, 124, 238
Bothmer, Baron Johann G., 3–4, 9
Bovey *or* Boevey, Mrs. Catherine, 16
Buckley, Samuel, 8, 62n
Budgell, Eustace, 106, 163
Bullock, John, 227
Bullock, Mrs., *see* Keck
Burleigh, Ferdinand, 70n
Burlington, Juliana, Countess of, 17
Burnet, Gilbert, Bishop of Sarum, 22
Burnet, Thomas (son of Gilbert), 22n, 35–36, 48
Burnet, Thomas (Master of Charterhouse), 67
Butterfield, Sir Herbert, 14

Cadogan, 1st Earl (William Cadogan), 3, 9, 105, 134
Cairns, Mrs. Alexander, 92
Caroline, Princess of Wales (later Queen), 6, 26, 42, 48, 105, 132–33, 217
Carteret, 1st Viscount (John Carteret), 212
Chandos, 1st Duke of (James Brydges), 139–40, 155, 184
Charterhouse, The, 67–68, 128